A Permanent Etcetera:
Cross-Cultural Perspectives
on Post-War A~~~~

D0765264

In honour of Eric Mottram

A Permanent Etcetera:
Cross-Cultural Perspectives
on Post-War America

Edited by

A. Robert Lee

Pluto Press

LONDON • BOULDER, COLORADO

First published 1993 by Pluto Press
345 Archway Road, London N6 5AA
and 5500 Central Avenue
Boulder, Colorado 80301, USA

British Library Cataloguing in Publication Data
A catalogue record for this book is available from
the British Library

ISBN 0 0753 0640 3 hb
ISBN 0 7453 0641 1 pb

Library of Congress Cataloging in Publication Data
A permanent etcetera : cross-cultural perspectives on post-war
America / edited by A. Robert Lee
208pp. 22cm.
Includes bibliographical references and index.
ISBN 0-7453-0640-3 (cloth). – ISBN 0-7453-0641-1 (pbk.)
1. United States – Civilization – 1945–
I. Lee, A. Robert, 1941–
E169.12.P485   1993
973.92–dc20   93–24953
CIP

Designed and Produced for Pluto Press by
Chase Production Services, Chipping Norton, OX7 5QR
Printed in Finland by Werner Söderström Osakeyhtiö

Contents

Introduction

In the tumultuous business of cutting-in and attending to a whale, there is much running backwards and forwards among the crew. Now hands are wanted here, and then again hands are wanted there. There is no staying in any one place; for at one and the same time everything has to be done everywhere. It is much the same with him who endeavors the description of the scene.

Herman Melville, 'The Monkey-Rope', *Moby Dick*

Two related intentions lie behind the present essay-collection. First, it seeks to celebrate the example of a leading British scholar of American Studies and Literature, Professor Eric Mottram, whose retirement from King's College, London, in 1990, took him as much by surprise as it did the friends and students both past and current who would readily, and warmly, acknowledge the debts they feel to him. Second, it celebrates him in a way all the contributors believe appropriate: in a series of closely analytical, cross-cultural perspectives on America since World War II.

In his unbounded energies as critic, creative writer, teacher, and inveterate lecturer and conferee, Eric Mottram almost from the outset has been a resolute modernist, a radically inquisitive, often startling, analyst of the tradition of the new. It can little surprise, therefore, that his main site of investigation – as the work collected in *Blood on the Nash Ambassador* (1989) bears ready and impressive witness – should have been the United States, one way or another, and virtually by historical dispensation, always a vanguard, self-generating culture from both its Anglo-Puritan and Hispanic foundations onwards.

As to the essays themselves, they are intended (at least by editorial design) to come at post-war American culture from shared, inter-acting, assumptions. They freely cross boundaries and play one field or form of American self-expression against another, whether high or vernacular, literary or visual, mainstream or ethnic, domestic or international. In this, they run true to the spirit of Melville's 'tumultuous business' in 'The Monkey-Rope', the sense of culture, and American culture in particular, as dynamic, enactive and, to invoke Bakhtin, dialogic.

So evidently diverse and eclectic a human order as America requires nothing less, as observers from Melville on to, say, Charles Olson, F.O. Matthiessen, Hayden White or, for sure, Eric Mottram himself, have all been at pains to insist. Even so, there can be no undue insistence on overall completeness of coverage. Of necessity, the essays collected here amount to 'perspectives', working purchases on an America (especially in the post-war era) whose social proteanism and corresponding elasticity of expression and voice have been proverbial.

Ralph Willett opens proceedings with an overview of America as consumerist mass-society, a 'popular culture' whose insignia from Hollywood to Coca-Cola, Elvis Presley to McDonalds, 'Dallas' to Two Rodeo Drive, bespeak, be it for good or ill, its own special 'modernity'. My own essay then looks at the changing demographics of this same post-war America, the literary–cultural emergence of an exhilarating, new, 'non-Euro' autobiography and fiction, respectively African-American, Latino, Native-American and Asian-American. Linked into this efflorescence has been the new feminism, a genealogy and a politics explored in depth by Faith Pullin and Claire Colebrook from Betty Friedan's *The Feminine Mystique* (1963) and the founding of NOW, through to the symptomatic phenomena – no lesser a term would do – of Madonna and Andrea Dworkin.

America's fascination with the machine, in modern terms from the Ford assembly line to the TV globalism analysed by Marshall McLuhan, and from space hardware to the computer, comes under Dale Carter's purview. What price technology as intrinsic to America's 'belief structure'? In this respect, too, how has post-war America sought its own visual image through the technology of the camera, its epochal modern photography? Graham Clarke locates contrasting departure-points in the dislocation anatomised in Robert Lowell's 'Memories of West Street and Lepke', and the integration implied in Edward Steichen's *The Family of Man* (1955), arguing for a line of disjunctive photography which includes Cornell Capa, Wayne Miller, Burt Glinn, John Szarkowski, Richard Avedon, Robert Frank, Diane Arbus and Lee Friedlander.

Three readings of other interpreters of America follow. Robert Giddings takes on the name whose 'Letters from America' have made him a BBC and (Manchester) *Guardian* institution, Alistair Cooke. What kind of America has he delivered over the last four or so decades? How much has Cooke dehistoricised the culture, made it a version of transatlantic Disneyland? Brian Lee, by contrast, explores the cinema of Michael Cimino, *The Deer Hunter* (1978) and *Heaven's Gate* (1980) in particular, as adversary American film-making, images of Vietnam and Wall Street offered against the grain. David Murray shows how, with reference to Whitman, Ezra Pound and Charles Olson, post-war America's so-called 'language' poetry in fact harbours its own 'politics', a formalism, if such it be, to subtler purpose than often granted.

America's relationship with Cuba – America as capitalist democracy set against Cuba as Marxism's western outpost – has been an almost endemic play of political and cultural opposites. Jacqueline Kaye looks into how this dialectic has taken different kinds of expression, whether the Cuban-exile city of Miami or the ongoing Havana of *fidelismo*. She thus analyses the mythologising of one kind of 'American' nationhood as against another.

Finally, Clive Bush offers an intellectual portrait of Eric Mottram, the man, the teacher, and his work on America and its culture over the past several decades. In striking a personal note felt also by each of the contributors, the essay equally seeks to convey, and to extend, a sense of debate, argument even, about America, and about cultural methodology in general. American Studies, three decades or so after its foundation in the UK, could not be more ongoing, more undisposed to reach easy consensus or conclusion.

In this respect, too, it would be right to explain that this collection had its origins in a Symposium held in May 1990 under the auspices of the Institute of United States Studies, London, with the title 'A Permanent Etcetera: Engagements with America'. There, among friends – not least the organising spirit of the occasion, the then Academic Secretary of the IUSS, Dr Howell Daniels – Eric would have recognised the collective face of those who so often have had occasion to admire his range and appetite of mind. In making that admiration manifest, the present volume also seeks its own passport – a post-war America given yet further British scrutiny, seen, interpreted, as only befitting, anew.

A. Robert Lee
The University of Kent at Canterbury

1

I'll Buy That: Popular Culture, America and Consumption Since World War II

Ralph Willett

With the advent of the 'affluent society' in the US an increased emphasis was placed on leisure, materialism and style. Unprecedented prosperity enabled extravagant desires for an environment of modernity and comfort – desires stimulated by magazine and television advertisements – to be satisfied. Household equipment would, if possible, no longer be held at basic levels, so the domestic landscape became a forest of washing machines, colour televisions, high-fidelity (later stereo) systems, blenders and automatic waste-disposal units. The most popular symbol of individual success and identity was the sleek, air-conditioned automobile which, in combination with the suburb and the highway, produced a drive-in culture during the 1950s; in more ways than one the automobile became the engine of popular culture and consumption.

Two reflections are appropriate. First, drive-in theatres made their profits at concession stands serving cola, drinks, popcorn and fast food, thus anticipating later consumption patterns and the growth of the service sector. Second, the drive-in culture offered a privatised, sealed-in experience which would be characteristic of later popular culture activities, especially in the 1980s.

Enzo Ferrari once remarked, 'Porsche don't make racing cars, they make missiles'; he could have been referring to the contribution made by Porsche to the design of the V-1 rocket. The consciousness of Harley Earl similarly conflated motor racing and military aviation. The tail fins which dominated the General Motors production line in the 1950s derived from the twin tail booms of the Lockheed Lightning seen by Earl during the Second World War.

With cars functioning as representations of status, symbolism (as in the Cadillac Eldorado of 1955) overtook practicality to stress the aerodynamic look. Cars resembled missiles or spaceships, implying a space-age image of progress. Space exploration, it was urged, would result in tremendous benefits, improving resource control for the Third World, and supplying the American consumer with a new range of goods including freeze-dried food and cordless razors. The symbolic appeal of 'space' could not be reached through the hardware; technological wizardry could provide only a temporary release from routine and a brief feeling of elation. More could be achieved through the bearers of technology, the astronauts themselves. Dale Carter has convincingly argued that while the astronaut was trained as a component he was simultaneously traded as a commodity, a 'priceless' one whose image was projected by means of the different mass media into a multiple, unbounded social context:

> Anyone who purchased *Life*, who bought petrol on the way to the launch site, who then stayed in a Florida hotel, who got a new television set for the space specials, who rode the subway to a post-flight parade, or who picked up the souvenirs of success was spending in order to stare at the astronauts or to share in the spectacle which starred them.[1]

To this list could be added all those in the 1960s attracted by the new space-age look in fashion. The stiff geometric shapes and cut-out PVC dresses promoted by designers Courrèges and Cardin adapted the visual clichés of science-fiction characters. Appropriately some of the new synthetic fibres and plastics used were spinoffs from the space programme.

The star-making process in which the press (*Life*), NASA, television and the American public would intersect reproduced the astronauts as All-American idols, but the propaganda images could not disguise what Norman Mailer called personalities of 'unequalled banality and apocalyptic dignity'. It was fitting that the Apollo astronauts would be sought-after dinner guests in Hollywood where, in the bleak years of the Depression, the absolute value of child star Shirley Temple had been reckoned at a staggering $10 million.

Stars are both economic assets for others – eleven companies made profits from commodities based on the Temple name – and the recipients of wealth themselves: luxury products edging towards fortunes. Alan Shepard, the first man in space, became a multi-millionaire, while John Glenn, another Mercury trainee, would be worth $6 million by the mid-1980s, with interests in various corporations and in real estate. His first Holiday Inn was located near Cape Kennedy and Disneyworld.

Disney's control (to be discussed later) is here translated into discipline, but the virtues of piety, modesty and effort are shared. Belief in God and the flag also helped to qualify the astronauts as exemplars of an American dream. National heroes, they shared the emotions of their audience, but they also became exclusive figures, possessors, as Tom Wolfe would learn to his advantage, of the Right Stuff. Just as their profession propelled them into the sky, so their privileged status raised them above the tedious world of mass society and its 'celebrity-watchers'.

The description of their skills – each was engineer–mechanic–pilot – would prove elusive, but even versatility could be given a consumerist dimension. The Apollo XI spacecraft was, as Mailer observed, a multiple environment, just as the automobile, it could be said, had been a diner, living room, love nest and jukebox. The capsule functioned as bedroom, kitchen, gym and laboratory, 'the ultimate desirable residence'.[2]

Varied abilities owned by the astronauts were matched by the sophistication of space programme applications: transistors, weather-forecasting satellites, image-enhancement computer systems. Only a limited industrial demand for NASA patents ensued; 20,000 firms were involved in the Apollo programme but the advantages to them and their consumers have been largely anecdotal. The principal benefit may turn out to be ecological: the vision of the earth from space that has become a symbol of environmental alarm. As the national excitement surrounding the moon walks disappeared, unflattering comparisons of America's technological power with its ineffectuality in the public interest were made. The United States could land men on the moon but could not get rid of poverty or pollution.

The perception of the astronauts has also changed. Tom Wolfe's study of the Mercury programme *The Right Stuff* (1979), retained the hero-worship of the 1960s, but the text is characterised by a pervasive irony and condescension. A decade after the Apollo moonflight, the energy crisis would stigmatise astronauts as part of an immoderate, wasteful enterprise. By the 1980s, John Glenn's continuous success in business and politics, including ten years spent in the Senate, would equip him for a shot at the presidential nomination. Others like Scott Carpenter, whose oceanic research firm and wasp farm both failed, were less lucky.

Some continued to haunt the television screens that made them famous; no longer 'priceless commercial assets', their identities were explained in subtitles as they marketed Coors beer or common-cold remedies.

In *The Pat Hobby Stories* F. Scott Fitzgerald's eponymous hack writer defines Hollywood: 'This is no art. This is an industry.' Its development depended upon and was part of the increasing significance of technology in American culture. Animation was an alliance joining a regimented workforce with photographic technology. Machines feature in the earliest cartoons of Walt Disney

(*Plane Crazy*, *Steamboat Willie*); he was swift to perceive at the most propitious times the importance of technical innovations in the mass media: sound (movies), Technicolor and television. After World War II Disney pioneered the theme park where technologically engineered realms of fantasy were also regarded as investigations of possible solutions, such as non-polluting mass transit systems, of urgent urban problems. In Disneyland cars are left in the parking lot. From that point and beginning with the train to the entrance 'people movers' come into operation, facilitating the Disney experience, while contributing to the general process of strictly controlling that experience.

A basic component is the 'ride' which includes one involuntary example: the Carousel Theater at Disneyland. At the unmoving core of the theatre are six stages; at regular intervals the building rotates 60 degrees so the audiences are moved from one stage to the next. Elsewhere, the 'ride' combines the controlled thrills of a fairground visit with vicarious participation in a mythic cultural entertainment such as a trip in 'a Mississippi steamboat'. The novelist E.L. Doctorow noted that 'while the machinery of the rides is intensely real ... the simulated plant and animal and geological surroundings are unreal.' [3] However, in the current postmodern world of hyperreality, the signs and images of contemporary capitalism float detached from reality. Without any authentic content latent behind external appearances, Disneyland becomes the perfect symbol of 'real' America.

Despite efforts at mystification – visitors are described as guests, and the word 'customers' is forbidden – the Disney empire is dedicated to consumption and profit. Disney himself casually naturalised the actuality: 'Dollars are like fertilizer – they make things grow.' At Disneyland, Main Street USA is a near-life-size model of a thoroughfare in a middle-America small town. The period is before the turn of the century, hence the horse-drawn streetcars, the marching brass band, and the ice-cream parlours. There are also nearly thirty shops and cafes where the products of Coca-Cola, Hallmark, Sunkist and other corporations are for sale. Main Street USA is essentially a rather tacky shopping mall through which 'guests' are obliged to pass twice. An image of the idealised past, it is also, in Louis Marin's phrase, 'the real place of exchange of money and commodity'. Marin goes on to explain the cultural meaning of the past/present dialectic at work: 'By the selling of up-to-date consumer goods in the setting of a nineteenth century street ... Walt Disney's utopia converts the commodities into significations. Reciprocally, what is bought there are signs, but these signs are *commodities*.' [4]

A more recent example is to be found at Florida's EPCOT Center in the misnamed Farmer's Market which visitors discover at the end of the boatride, 'Listen to the Land', in the Kraft pavilion which itself looks like a shopping mall. Farmer's Market is simply a fast-food outlet for such corporations as Nestlé, Campbell's, Pepsico and of course Kraft itself. Food as social and personal pleasure and as nutrition is replaced throughout the Disney theme parks by food as consumable commodity.

At Disney World (hereafter WDW) the blurring of the line between the real and the unreal, between in this case humans and robots, is remarkable. 'Audio-animatronic' figures are built and dressed like humans; 'human' work (restaurant duties, opening monorail doors) is repetitive and monotonous, robot-like in fact. A parallel from a Disney film, manifesting the fear of control loss, is found in the water-carrying brooms of 'The Sorcerer's Apprentice' (*Fantasia*) described as 'a horrifying image of modern factory production where a robotoid proletariat threatens to destroy the whole operation'. In the film generally the process of labour is cloaked or concealed. Representation supplants production and the workforce although, as Susan Willis suggests, Disney's 'army of animators ... finds displaced embodiment in the [image of the] symphony orchestra'. [5]

Work activity is also hidden away at WDW. A 'pneumatic garbage system' underground inhales plastic rubbish bags sending them at 60 mph to centralised 'compactors'. Corridors (in Disneyspeak 'utilidors') transport workers, supplies and RCA telecommunications to various parts of WDW. Laundries, storage areas, air conditioning and staff cafeterias are all squirrelled away beneath the surface.

A paradigm of the Disney ethos is located in WDW's EPCOT (Experimental Prototype Community of Tomorrow). In the 'communicore' of this totally controlled version of the technological future, non-ideological ideas, it is claimed, can be exchanged on behalf of this planned community. In action the 'ideas' turn out to be technological gimmicks such as video displays and games; the future will be fun and consumption under the aegis of free enterprise. Thus there does indeed exist an ideology at EPCOT: that of corporate technology and private planning, dealing with such challenges as energy resources and transport to make a better future. The caring, altruistic stance of corporate America evokes television commercials and magazine advertisements of the 1970s/1980s but the record shows, for example, that Exxon's tardiness in developing technologies helped to make the US more dependent on oil from the Middle East.

The ideology of market choice promoted by the corporations is embedded – in contradictory fashion – in WDW, a private, profit-making monopolistic company endowed through its arrangements with the State of Florida with political sovereignty.

WDW is still an animated cartoon, an artificial exhibition of technology in a vacuum. The technological experiments on offer fail to address questions of pollution, toxic waste, housing and unemployment. Even within the boundaries of the Magic Kingdom, the tiresome frustrating realities of contemporary America have been known to intrude: 'It took me an hour to get from my [independent] hotel, on the Disney property, to the gates of the park, and the experience was reminiscent of the decaying central-city present, not of the urban future.' [6]

Before the Second World War Disney was a success with the public and even with critics and intellectuals (he won an Oscar in 1932 for the Mickey Mouse films), but economic success eluded him. It was in 1940, responding to several debts and the production costs of *Snow White* and *Fantasia* that the Disney brothers became a corporation. By 1988, two decades after Walt Disney's death, that corporation (Walt Disney Productions) was worth $8 billion on the New York stock exchange. 'The Disney culture', insisted Gary Wilson, chief financial officer, in that year, 'is one of clean family entertainment, creativity, target marketing and strong customer relationships.' [7] Two-thirds of the estimated $500 million pre-tax profits was generated by the theme parks at Anaheim and Orlando. The planning of each theme park illustrates Disney's business acumen. Disneyland was financed by selling shares to ABC Television; on his part Disney signed a contract to produce a weekly television programme. The new attraction drew a million customers in six months. Disney Productions increased its income from $47 million to $450 million in a decade and, as his contract permitted Disney later bought back the shares from ABC.

From the end of the 1920s Disney had kept tight control over his creations and the profits that accrued. However, he was obliged to share the profits from Disneyland with the owners of local tourist facilities. In setting up WDW, therefore, his plans included the purchase of sufficient real estate to support such facilities. (Like McDonalds, the vast wealth of Disney Productions is attributable to its property holdings.) Concessions are leased to participant companies, but the terms of the franchise ensure the virtual impossibility of the companies making money. In addition, control at WDW is total since by the arrangement mentioned above it is an independent separate 'kingdom' with its own laws and police.

Disney's career shows creativity giving place to ideology and commercialism, to the marketing of bland entertainment and the control and manipulation of the members of mass society. This is neatly summed up in his expressed wish to be 'the benevolent *dictator* of Disney enterprises' (my emphasis).

In 1955 Disneyland was opened, RCA bought Elvis Presley's contract from Sam Phillips, and Ray Kroc opened his first Mc-Donalds restaurant in Des Plaines, Illinois (now preserved as a museum). McDonalds was soon to benefit from the Interstate Highway Act (1956) which provided for a 41,000 mile (eventually expanded) system, most of it paid for by the government. Increased mobility, suburban growth, an altered perception of space and time – these fostered an automobile culture that would sustain Mc-Donalds and other enterprises throughout the US. The buildings along the ubiquitous 'strip' (motels, garages and fast-food chains such as McDonalds and Burger King) were originally regarded as 'God's Own Junkyard', un-aesthetic and vulgar, a stance that would culminate in Lady Bird Johnson's campaign against roadside ugliness and in the Highway Beautification Act (1966). Later, in *Learning from Las Vegas* (Robert Venturi and others), they would be celebrated as enjoyable 'commercial vernacular'.

McDonalds matched the technology of interstate highways and cars by becoming the ultimate in assembly-line technology with the customers functioning as moving parts. Like that of the automobile, the lure of McDonalds is (in part) that of the slick, efficient machine. The drive-in is the traveller's pit-stop where his/her body 'refuels', locking into an eating system that promises quick, almost instant service. Efficiency studies ensure the streamlining of cooking, packing and serving; research in food packaging dictates changes in pattern and texture.

Measuring quantities and ordering materials are scientifically precise activities relying on customised unit sizes and delivering goods that are uniform. The 1.6 oz hamburger is cooked for the same number of seconds, the operation governed by a light on the grill. 'McDonalds is not a restaurant; it is a store selling a predictable product in an eternally clean environment.'[8] Operatives clean as they perform other jobs, but the predictability, which is for many customers an assurance, is provided by the overall design of an integrated machine. Only interior style and, occasionally, menu items are allowed localised variations, such as 'aloha' uniforms, Gauguin prints and 'saimin' (noodle soup) in Hawaii, or sea and surf motifs at beachside locations.

The key as with Disney is control: customers move from car to restaurant and back but their physical and visual activities are carefully directed. One of McDonalds' main suppliers, Equity Meat, is part of Keystone Foods, a corporation which hopes to achieve complete control over the meat packaging system, from the rearing of animals to the cooking and serving of meals.

Anonymous, impersonal and respectable (no jukeboxes or

vending machines), McDonalds contributed to a 1950s blandness and a trend towards the erasure of differences between times and places. Standardisation and mildness in food and drink, such as 'lite' beers, were a commercial strategy seeking to appeal to a broader range of classes, ages and income groups. The result was, in Daniel Boorstin's coinage, the Everywhere Community which replaced the Island Community of the nineteenth century, but it has been a community based largely on the shared practice of consuming commodities.

This result was not only sociocultural but ecological. It is clear that the landscape of roadside businesses represented the franchise system which underpinned it financially: standardised, packaged and under centralised control. In addition,

> the franchises ... were better suited to the new environment in which advertizing and real estate were the defining conditions of the economic climate. It was in 1957, just as the Interstate program swung into high gear, that the service sector surpassed the manufacturing sector as a proportion of the national economy; ... the old quasi-religious idea of personal service was replaced with the idea of service efficiency.[9]

By the 1960s, the predominant sign of the franchise would be the mansard roof (adopted by McDonalds in 1968) of plastic or wood shingle which, in the suburbs especially, combined with lawns, bushes and subdued colours to project an environmentally friendly image. Sitting like small hats atop single-storey structures, mansards were harbingers of the Toytown features of much postmodern commercial architecture in subsequent decades.

As the quotation above indicates, service was replaced by efficiency, the result of independent operations giving way to national chains. McDonalds (or Wendy's) took the place of the local coffee shop, the corner drugstore became Orange Julius, and the garage Midas Muffler Parlor. McDonalds' Golden Arches – once an architectural element – are now an icon of modern Americana, yet McDonalds and its clones gradually destroyed the world of the diner, the teenage dream of flashy cars, rock-'n'-roll and high school proms, nostalgically captured in the film *American Graffiti*.

The hamburger has been in the vanguard of world domination by American customs and habits. McDonalds has been one of the largest buyers of television advertising time in the US; its expansion abroad, most recently in Russia, turns into a media event. As novelist William Burroughs pointed out, junk (to which can be added junk food) is addictive, the ideal product; the consumer is sold *to* the commodity. Outside the US he/she seeks to be sold to a simulacrum of American popular culture. In Manila where cafe menus might include 'Butch Cassidy and the Sandwich Kid' and 'Wild Beef Hickok', a local McDonalds resembles a small town Arizona coffee shop, its walls decorated with old pictures of John Wayne and the Lone Ranger. A map illustrates 'Guns of the West'.

When McDonalds went into the German market in 1971 a modified menu included chicken breast and beer. Its restaurants were modest in size and, with low-density lighting, partitions and dark colours, created the effect of *eine kneipe*. But while teen-agers on the loose were attracted, families were not. Subsequently, the dark wood and partitions were removed, light-ing increased and the walls painted in bright colours. The usual McDonalds devices for selling to children were established. In Germany the chain earned $15 million before tax in 1985. 'McDonalds is an American food system,' argued Steve Barnes, chairman of McDonalds International. 'If we go into a new country and incorporate their food products with our menu, we lose our identity.' [10]

Nevertheless, in Germany as elsewhere in the West this 'expe-rience of fun, folks and food' (McDonalds' PR department phrase) has increasingly provoked criticism. Environmental pres-sure groups such as the Rainforest Action Network based in San Francisco have accused hamburger producers of colluding in the removal of Central American rainforests to facilitate cattle ranch-ing. In addition, health-conscious customers in the US have, more and more, been willing to shun cholesterol-packed grilled meat and french fries. McDonalds have responded with low-fat veg-etable oil and, in March 1991, a new burger, the McLean. Researched at Auburn University this contains half the fat of the comparable quarter pounder and a seaweed extract, carageenan, to bind more water into the meat, as well as a 'natural beef flavor enhancer'. However, customers, needing to satisfy their desire for taste and fat, have responded by ordering cheese toppings on their McLean – or buying two instead of one.

In the recent past, up to 20 per cent of London's litter has been generated by hamburger joints. Despite publicity campaigns and the purchase (in the US) of recycled materials such as brown Global Releaf paper bags, McDonalds which opens a new branch in the world every 17 hours has now become a symbol of epidemic consumerism, cultural imperialism, wanton waste and pollution – the result of market priorities and productive capacities. Culturally the fast-food outlet is a tacky element in the cluttered landscape of cyberpunk, the science-fiction representation of the contemporary/ future world combining high technology and street-level anarchy.

Rock-'n'-roll (rock music) has been designated the most vital form of post-war popular culture. It has fostered legions of rock historians and analysts who have interpreted it variously as entertainment, folk music, sheer musical energy, hedonism, community, youth culture, social protest or rebellion: 'All rock records, whatever their artistic or folk or ideological status, are commodities, produced, marketed and sold in the pursuit of profit.' [11] It is this belief that Don DeLillo dramatised in his novel *Great Jones Street* (1973). The so-called 'mountain tapes' (cf. Dylan's basement tapes made in rural Woodstock) of Bucky Wunderlick, ex-rock star, are equated with a new drug: 'the ultimate drug', which removes the ability to speak, to make words. Both are products for selling and buying in a fictional world pervaded by greed. Every character is voluntarily part of a free enterprise economy, everything is consumed and all artists are commodities.

With hindsight the potential for commercialisation is visible from rock's early days. Historically it has been a featured segment of corporate capitalism packaged for manufacture and sales in a mass market. As long as the concepts of authenticity and cultural independence are not overstressed it is, however, legitimate to describe a negotiation and conflict between rock music and commerce, between Rock-'n'-Roll and simply Rock. In this useful though simplified narrative a spontaneous, liberating and democratic form of popular music yields to consumerism and is exploited by television and record producers and magazine editors.

The process by which rock-'n'-roll was diluted and absorbed into the dominant mode of mass cultural production is best seen generationally. The music was promoted by *Rolling Stone*, among others, as youth culture, though the magazine avoided the radical politics which activated students in the 1960s and by the mid-1980s was circulating a newsletter for 'Marketing, Advertizing and Music Executives'. Louis Menand is crisply explicit: 'Once the media discovered it, the counterculture ceased being a youth culture and became a commercial culture for which youth was a principal market.' [12] Just at that point, when the counterculture was becoming the new mainstream, Bruce Springsteen signed for CBS in 1972. In September 1974 he appeared on the covers of *Newsweek* and *Time* simultaneously.

Springsteen's career and personality illustrate the oppositions already introduced: individual/community and authenticity/commercialism. On the one hand, Springsteen's image has been projected as a blue-collar worker expressing both working-class and adolescent feelings. On the other, he has become a millionaire and a corporation, and the *Live* set of LPs has earned $7.5 million. It was sold off the backs of trucks as they made deliveries; statistics of sales merely generated further sales.

The paradoxical nature of this mass-market populism extends to content and performance. Springsteen's musically conservative ballads of desire, hope, poverty, crime, frustration and failure – congruent with the drab regionalism of 1980s literature labelled Dirty Realism – conclude in liberal bewilderment and acquiescence. 'Born in the USA', an anti-Reaganite song performed with the American flag on stage (and on the album), encapsulates the ambivalence.

Springsteen (notably in the 'Dancing in the Dark' video) has also been marketed as a pop artist and star singing to an enthusiastic audience of young girls. The spectacle recalls earlier idols such as Elvis Presley, but with a significant difference. Springsteen Tour T-shirts are lucrative, but items such as the Elvis statue, the Memorial Pillow with 'poetic' inscription ('God knew Elvis/Was tired, so he/Took him to Rest'), and the perennial pilgrimages to Graceland turned the commercialisation of Presley into a sickly religion. Presley's career, unlike Springsteen's, invites the stereotyped interpretation of inexorable musical decline – from the joy and freedom of the Sun recordings to the showbusiness kitsch of Las Vegas. The temptation can, however, be resisted.

The technique of the later songs can be detected in the first recordings, themselves professionally constructed; many of the performers from whom he learned, whether Country or R and B, were also commercial artists. A Dutch bootleg LP of Sun masters reveals that 'Blue Moon of Kentucky' began not in the hell-for-leather rockabilly tempo of the released version, but in a more emotional, ingratiating and accessible ballad style, one which showcased his *later* mannerisms. Bob Neal, with whom Elvis signed up in 1955, said of the singer: 'He was greatly anxious for success. He talked not in terms of being a moderate success. No – his ambition and desire was to be big in movies and so forth.'[13]

Before his death Presley had already been consumed by the processes of mass culture, stardom and commercial calculation. A corporate commodity himself, he was the source of a hugely profitable merchandising venture in the mid-1950s. This enabled Special Products, Inc. of California to market jeans, shirts, statuettes, charm bracelets (the charms included a hound dog, a guitar and a broken heart), and lipsticks in such shades as Heartbreak Pink, Hound Dog Orange and Tutti Frutti Red. A $55 million sales total was predicted in 1957; Presley and Colonel Parker took a variable percentage (maximum 11 per cent) of the whole-sale price. At least Parker acknowledged enterprise in others: he intervened on behalf of the old man arrested for stealing leaves from Graceland and selling them to fans.

Boopsie Does Her Bit for the Elvis Industry[14] Reprinted from
The People's Doonesbury: Notes from Underfoot, 1978–1980 (Wildwood House, London; 1981), G.B. Trudeau.

It is appropriate that the most idolatrous Elvis fans are poor
Southern whites arriving in their pickup trucks, caravans and
Winnebagos at Graceland where the decorations constitute a
shrine to hillbilly tastes. Elvis, a sharecropper's son in the big
house, had the self-same tastes epitomised by his solid-gold 1960
Cadillac with its 40 diamond-encrusted coats of gold paint and its
interior roof plated with gold records.

The Presley clan shared in the frantic consumption by means
of Cadillacs, planes, swimming pools (father Vernon had one in
his Graceland bedroom) and physical changes: Elvis had his face
lifted, Priscilla her ears flattened. The compulsion to spend also
suggests a desire for *protection*, for reassurance that the childhood
years of poverty could not return. Shortly before he died, Elvis
started to have Graceland's ceilings carpeted.

Beginning in April 1978, the soap opera 'Dallas' reached the top
of television drama ratings by 1980 and netted CBS a steady
audience in the US of 40 million viewers. Marketed in 90 countries, 'Dallas' achieved a remarkable popularity throughout the
world. References are made to the 'Dallas' phenomenon and to its
metonymic status – it somehow stands for soap opera and indeed
commercial television. Its detractors have perceived it as one
more influential agent of consumer capitalism: in February 1983
Jack Lang, Minister of Culture in France, attacked the
programme as 'the symbol of American cultural imperialism'.

The reasons for the success of 'Dallas' and its universal impact
are various. Its mini-narratives are filled with melodramatic action.

In Rosalind Coward's witty description: 'The main characters ... stagger from one trauma to another, recovering in one episode from a near-fatal illness only to be struck blind several episodes later.' [15] Frissons of alarm or sensations of shock are enjoyable and short-lived. The drama is in theory endless, the freeze frame at the end of each episode creating expectancy and anticipating the resumption of linear narrative in the next instalment. The technique produced a media coup with the episode, 'Who Shot J.R.?', the answer to which was concealed until the following season.

In 'Dallas', as in other branches of popular culture, 'America' presents itself as both symbol and source of pleasure within the process of consumption which includes T-shirts, bumper stickers (J.R. for President), record albums and the equipment for costume parties. As Ien Ang writes:

> The hegemony of American television (and film) has habitu-
> ated the world public to American production values and
> American *mises-en-scene*, such as the vast prairie or the big
> cities, the huge houses with expensive interiors, luxurious
> and fast cars and last but not least the healthy and good-
> looking men and women.[16]

The relative opulence of the *mise-en-scene* in 'Dallas' and 'Dynasty' and the continual action recall classic Hollywood cinema, al-though neither series attempted to emulate the formal excess and stylisation of Douglas Sirk's 1950s melodramas. Moreover, the extravagance of clothes and decor, the former described as 'Holly-wood silk' has a certain tawdriness, reflecting the audience's sense of glamour as much as genuine American affluence. Images of clothes and accessories by Lanvin, Tiffany, Gucci etc. signify not only style but also conspicuous consumption. Anyone can attain the look provided they have the means to buy it. Thus a televi-sion 'world' in which commodities predominate recalls nothing so much as the field of advertising.

'Dallas' was advertised as one of the most expensive shows on television ($700,000 per episode) but the money often appears to have been spent on a mixture of the crass and the refined. This flamboyance was mirrored by the cultural cannibalism of the Reagan elite in the worlds of fashion, media and retailing as they circulated aristocratic images of luxury for consumer society. However, in reference to 'Dallas', Michael Bywater has argued that 'the trick is to distinguish between taste and significance. They may be *wearing* a million dollars but they do not look like it; the result has an odd sense of Bentalls or Allders about it.'[17]

While 'Dallas' operated as a metonymy of American soap opera, 'Dynasty' performed a similar function in relation to the *zeitgeist* of the 1980s. Its evocation of glamour and extravagance during the Reagan era recalled the ideological force of 1930s Hollywood musicals. The reassuring middle-class message of 'Dynasty' (and 'Falcon Crest') is that wealth derives from moral turpitude and fails to ensure happiness.

'Dynasty' began screening in 1981 in the week of the first Reagan inaugural during which Reaganite galas, dinners, etc. cost nearly $16 million. Similarities between the imagery of Reaganism and American television were observed by citing not only 'Dynasty' but also television commercials, the popular, self-explanatory show 'Lifestyles of the Rich and Famous', and of course newsreel footage of the Reagans' holiday weekends. The link was underlined by the baleful Angela Channing in 'Falcon Crest', strong and poised like Nancy Reagan; the character was played by Jane Wyman, Ronald Reagan's ex-wife.

The phenomenon is not confined to the US. Britain has its own soap opera which features the Royal Family complete with a nationally adored matriarch (the Queen Mother). In 'Dynasty', Alexis was initially split between the glamorous Princess Di, inveterate consumer of gowns, and Princess Michael, arrogant *bête noire* of the tabloid press which replaced her with the sybaritic Duchess of York – a great fan of 'Dynasty'. The Duchess's vulgarly expensive home in Berkshire (£5 million of chintz, marble and mahogany) was promptly labelled 'South York' (a direct reference to Southfork and 'Dallas'). Recently, the links with soap opera have been reinforced by the power struggles and alleged sexual adventurism of the Prince and Princess of Wales, the latter an increasingly ambivalent figure in her media representation.

The Reagans represented new money from the West, unaccompanied by the sophistication and taste enjoyed by 'old wealth' on the eastern seaboard. A well-publicised characteristic of Nancy Reagan has been her passion for designer clothes; 'Dynasty' was the only television show to have its own resident fashion designer, Nolan Miller. Through the depiction of a lifestyle (clothes, jewellery, decor), 'Dynasty' brought together seemingly irreconcilable sectors of cultural production: a nostalgic fantasy of American wealth *and* a self-consciously outrageous excess and narcissism appealing to gay sensibilities. The launching (in 1984) of the 'Dynasty' Collections (fashions, perfumes, jewels, accessories, lingerie) at Bloomingdales could have been regarded as a 'camp' event. Yet the spectators sought only to look at the clothes not to buy them, ignoring the injunction to 'create your very own reality'. On this occasion 'Dynasty' remained at the level of the spectacular and fantastic.

An acknowledgement of consumerism can also be found in Joan Collins's endorsement of the perfume 'Scoundrel', but the commodity's name demonstrates her ability to symbolise the process of reconciliation referred to earlier. As a combination of *film noir* Spider Woman and silent screen sex-goddess, she has achieved a place in the camp pantheon of iconic, idolised female stars (Bette Davis, Judy Garland, Barbra Streisand). Mannered, parodic and bitchy, Joan Collins as Alexis reproduces what Susan Sontag has called the 'corny flamboyance of femaleness', not least by a *bricolage* of fashion. A multiplicity of garments (silk business suits, sequined evening dresses) supports a variety of roles while drawing attention to her (often exaggerated) femininity and, in the case of split skirts, her sexuality (both desire and desirability).

No matriarch (like Miss Ellie), no blonde redeemer (like Krystle Carrington), Alexis, exuding confidence and power, is the paradigm for images and imperatives ('Dress to Thrill') in women's magazines such as *Vogue*, *Elle* and *Company* which stress elegance, affluence and above all pleasure for both model and viewer. With the padded shoulders of boxy jackets and with little veiled hats, Joan Collins foregrounded the television show as fashion advertisement (reminiscent of Hollywood in the 1930s and 1940s). As a further and more precise cultural contribution, she pushed into visibility the Nancy Reagan persona which combined defiant opulence, ostentatious hedonism and spitefulness.

Power dressing of this kind, a signifier of post-feminist woman, helped to create the illusion that the sex war was over and the future lay with women, specifically dynamic, successful women who felt good about themselves. In the sex-'n'-shopping sagas of the 1980s, everything is sacrificed to consumerism, the accoutrements of the super-rich being carefully catalogued: Janet Reger lingerie, Cartier jewellery, Manolo Blahnik shoes. Women take control in these blockbusters operating as media tycoons or as directors of corporations – a wish-fulfilment fantasy that turns the real world upside down.

Commercial and technological developments in the US created, in the name of capitalism, a rationalised, interlocking system, so that from the 1920s onwards, 'the identity of a product, perhaps even of a person, lost its presumed essential self-evident quality, and became relational, dependent upon other elements in the system'.[18] The market system of exchange turned goods into commodities, breaking down ethnic, regional and class differences in favour of homogeneity and standardisation. The most prominent, highly publicised example of twentieth-century mass production has been called Fordism, appropriately since Ford factories share a similar layout, down to the siting of Coca-Cola machines. With the explosion of electronic media and the establishment of the information society in the 1960s, a shift from print to image took place such that the search for pleasure and the construction of social identity were conducted by registering and interpreting images. With architecture, television, advertising and design at the forefront of postmodernist definitions and debates, these images especially commercial ones are chiefly visual, but might be aural or indeed both; in Don DeLillo's *Americana* the narrator Bell phones his favorite DJ named Beasley, only to discover he exists on tape.

An example of the operation of visual signs can be found in shopping malls. By means of mirrors, broken and dispersed images are perceived as multiple forms, so that the boundaries between the real and the imagined are shattered. In comparison, commodities in shops and boutiques appear real and more stable.

Images have provided a counterforce to homogeneity, permitting differences of sex, race and class to float in the collective social imagination, hence the revival through postmodernist practice of ornament and decoration. Nevertheless, contemporary culture is inclined to give the appearance of rootlessness as style references move from architecture to MTV, from painting to a commercial. The domination of the environment by a glut of signs has ontological and sociocultural implications.

Guy Debord has claimed that everything directly lived has 'moved away into a representation'. 'Reality', then, is simulated by means of photography, television and film. In the 1980s the post-war period was available on videotape for recycling. All dates (Woodstock, Watergate, the death of Jimi Hendrix) became anniversaries. Videotape contributes to the postmodern circumstance where there is no copy, no original (the condition of the replicants in the movie *Blade Runner*). So authenticity is replaced by provisional performance.

However, a further feature of the 1980s was the evidence of culture and economy hurtling towards each other, merging into a single area. As Douglas Tallack puts it: 'Varieties of postmodernism are often difficult to distinguish from the heterogeneity of consumer society.'[19] Consequently, the simulated identities of individuals are achieved through the staged disposition of goods. To describe contemporary culture simply as vacant and empty is to ignore this point and its significance for the determination of identity: the manufactured lifestyle, a total look comprising clothes, decor and furniture was part of the attempt to market (or rather, mass market) exclusivity. Designer jeans were in the forefront of this movement and were advertised as the visual symbol of different lifestyles (western, urban retro etc.). The total look had earlier been the preserve of the affluent. Frank Lloyd Wright's design for the Coonley House (1912) also included linen, the table service and even some of Mrs Coonley's clothes.

Design culture, as the section on soap opera suggested, was targeted at high-spending, fashionable consumers, though there existed a movement in interior design to align it with mass culture. Young people on the other hand, alienated by ideology or by unemployment and poverty, organised their personal and group identities, and their wardrobes, by selecting from the surrounding cultural detritus. Through the activity of *bricolage*, therefore, sanctioned by Madonna's self-consciously sleazy street-style, postmodern culture was embraced by the marginalised young as the grosser aspects of its materialism were rejected.

Their presence has also been a feature of shopping malls in the developed world by means of a strategy combining narcissistic parading, the mocking of security guards and the assertion of difference. For this youthful subculture consumption means images and space instead of goods. Their 'occupation' represents an invasion, exploiting an invitation to participate in sanitised opulence. The 'real' environment of streets, weather and danger is supposed to remain cut off from the mall where Main Street has become internalised. The term Main Street may suggest Sinclair Lewis or, to younger generations, Disneyland, a reference often invoked when malls, shopping plazas and downtown plazas are discussed. The PR spokesperson at West Edmonton Mall, the world's largest shopping precinct, makes that comparison, doubtless with the Mall's funfairs (Fantasyland, World Waterpark) and its reconstruction of New Orleans' Bourbon Street for 'themed' dining in mind. Similarly, Two Rodeo Drive, opened in October 1990 in Beverly Hills, its shop fronts an inventive survey of architectural history, has been described as a theme park for rich adults, a grown-ups version of Disneyland's Main Street, but one where tacky souvenir shops are replaced by elegant, expensive boutiques.

Two Rodeo Drive is a make-believe dream of privatised urban space, which the real city denies. In the shopping mall ambience the line between shopping and entertainment is blurred. There is a feeling of suspension (clocks are rare in malls), of a continuous present in sealed-off, self-contained environments in which the consumer is seduced not only by the products but by canning, wrapping and advertising. In Don DeLillo's *White Noise*, even loose items of fruit, burnished and bright, take on the appearance of packaging: 'The fruit was gleaming, wet, hard-edged. There was a self-conscious quality about it ... like four-colour fruit in a guide to photography.' [20]

The ubiquitous nature of commercial advertising, the concentration of media ownership, the endless accumulation of commodities, the creation of a culture and consciousness pervaded by multinational capitalism outside the home and, by television and other technology, inside it – these aspects of the 1970s and 1980s have aroused alarm and generated debate both considered and hysterical. Despite assertions that the shopping mall can be 'the terrain of guerrilla warfare' or that 'in the practices of consumption the commodity system is exposed to the power of the consumer',[21] it is difficult to locate means of resistance or sources of empowerment within consumerism, apart from the subcultural activities mentioned earlier. The bottom line is that the 'power' granted conceals the absence of other kinds of power in everyday life. But leisure is an implicit critique of work particularly if conviviality and comradeship are its accompaniments. In the US, malls are one of the few public spaces available for amateur performance and entertainment (dance displays, fiddlers' conventions); walking is sometimes encouraged, even other forms of exercise.

What can be postulated is that shopping and goods may in offering the individual choice also offer meaning and control. Bobbie Ann Mason's fiction (a notable example of Shopping Mall Realism) presents characters trying to make sense of their lives through the constituents of the mass media world they inhabit: brand names, MTV, horror movie plots and so on. *In Country* traces Sam's quest for her father, and her identity, by means of 'M.A.S.H.' re-runs, Bruce Springsteen's lyrics and the battlefield diary of her father killed in Vietnam. On the way to the Vietnam Veterans' Memorial in Washington DC, she visits a shopping mall which, like the setting for a rock video sequence, encourages her to integrate recent experiences, physical and imaginative, linking past and present in preparation for an imminent epiphany:

> The palm trees are tall, and vines – familiar houseplants – are climbing them. Sam stands transfixed by the trees and thick foliage. They become the jungle plants of Southeast Asia. And then they change to cypress trees at Cawood's Pond, and the murky swamp water, infested with snakes, swirls around her.[22]

A more dramatic transformation takes place in a recent Paul Rudnick novel. A visit to a shoe outlet in a Maine shopping mall, initiated by Joe and the Esker sisters, his mother and aunts, rescues Kerry Rally, a resident of Top Harbor, 'less a town than a Ralph Lauren runway', from the dullness of married life with a corporate lawyer and from Good Taste:

> Kerry was teetering through the shop in a pair of glossy white patent-leather open-toed high-heeled sandals, with gold lamé piping and a gold plastic hibiscus blooming on the instep ... Kerry was cutting loose, and Joe couldn't wait to see her in a polyester tube dress with orange ball fringe.[23]

Materialism in Rudnick's novel, *I'll Take It* is only crass if buying fails to produce brightness, value or hope. As Kerry demonstrates, Miami beach sandals shall make you free.

2

Self-inscriptions: James Baldwin, Tomás Rivera, Gerald Vizenor and Amy Tan and the Writing-in of America's Non-European Ethnicities.

A. Robert Lee

My quarrel with the English language has been that the language reflected none of my experience. But now I began to see the matter in quite another way. If the language was not my own, it might be the fault of the language; but it might also be my own fault. Perhaps the language was not my own because I had never attempted to use it, had only learned to imitate it. If this were so, then it might be made to bear the burden of my experience if I could find the stamina to challenge it, and me, to such a test.

James Baldwin, 'Why I Stopped Hating Shakespeare' [1]

Chicano literature as it began to flourish in the '50s and '60s revealed a basic hunger for community (*hambre por una comunidad*). Here was a group of kindred people forming a nation of sorts, loosely connected politically and economically and educationally but with strong ties and affinities through its folklore and popular wisdom. Also there were ties through varying degrees of understanding of its historical precedence and a strong tie because of its language ... Clearly, the impetus to document and develop the Chicano community became the essential *raison d'être* of the Chicano Movement itself and of the writers who tried to express that.

Tomás Rivera, 'Chicano Literature: the Establishment of Community' [2]

The use of the word 'Indian' is postmodern, a navigational conception, a colonial invention, a simulation in sound and transcription. Tribal cultures became nominal, diversities

were twisted to the core, and oral stories were set in written
languages, the translations of discoveries ... Native American
Indians are burdened with colonial pantribal names, and with
imposed surnames translated from personal tribal nicknames
by missionaries and federal agents. More than a million
people, and hundreds of distinct tribal cultures, were simulated as Indians; an invented pantribal name, one sound,
bears treaties, statutes, and seasons, but no tribal culture,
language, religion, or landscape.

Gerald Vizenor, *Crossbloods* [3]

I began to write stories using all the Englishes I grew up
with: the English I spoke to my mother, which for lack of a
better term might be described as 'simple'; the English she
used with me, which for lack of a better term might be
described as 'broken'; my translation of her Chinese, which
could certainly be described as 'watered down'; and what I
imagined to be her translation of her Chinese if she could
speak in perfect English, her internal language, and for that I
sought to preserve the essence, but neither an English nor a
Chinese structure. I wanted to capture what language ability
tests can never reveal: her intent, her passion, her imagery,
the rhythms of her speech and the nature of her thoughts.

Amy Tan, 'Mother Tongue' [4]

1992 as a self-triumphalising 500th marker for the Discovery of
America, a latest Columbus Year, can hardly be said to have had
the easiest of passages. For whatever the fond wishes of the
nation's cultural image-makers or, for sure, of the Federation of
Italian–American Organisations (as drawn from, say, the Sons of
Italy or the Saint Anthony's Society), the one-time citizen of the
fifteenth-century merchant city of Genoa and *Vice-Almirante* of
Spain's *Reyes Católicos* has come to embody a call to arms.

According to one's version of history or, more to the point, of
myth, 'Columbus' passes down as either hero or scourge, visionary explorer-king or malign Euro-colonialist. Modern scholarship
has readily fallen in with this either-or typology, from Samuel
Eliot Morison's eulogistic (and landmark) *Admiral of the Ocean
Sea* (1942)[5] through to Kirkpatrick Sale's daemonological *The
Conquest of Paradise* (1990)[6]. Even interpretation less avowedly
ideological finds the divide almost impossible to ignore.[7]

Nor, too, does the fact that so much remains unknown make
for hindrance. What language, for instance, did Columbus come

to think his own, Genoese-Italian, Spanish, Catalan even, or, as has often been thought, *castellano aportuguesado*? Do we read authentic Columbus in the Logs and Journals, or Fray Bartolomé de las Casas, his prophetically pro-Native, anti-*encomienda* slavery, amanuensis and secret-sharer? From amid the plait of signatures available even in his own lifetime of 1451–1506, which actually held sway, the Cristoforo (or Cristoforus) Columbo of Genoese, the Cristóbal Colón of Castillian, the Cristóvão Columbo of the Portuguese he spoke during his eight-year stay in Lisboa learning the Atlantic wind-cycles, the Juan Colom sometimes attributed to him as a possible Jewish *converso*, the Colonus used for him by his son, or the Xpo FERENS, the Christ BEARER, as enciphered in his own nothing if not headily messianic Greek–Latin amalgam? Sorting out these puzzles, or those of his marriages and last years, might alone have been a spur to pause and caution.

Little so it would seem. Either Columbus stands tall as the Renaissance quester, the vanguard figure whose four Atlantic voyages (1492–93, 1493–96, 1498–1500 and 1502–4) place him with the likes of Amerigo Vespucci, Bartolomeu Diaz, Vasco Da Gama, Vasco Nuñez de Balboa and Ferdinando Magellan in the litany of European 'discoverers' of the Americas. Or he signifies as a ruinous first supremacist, whose exploitation of those 'gentle' Amerindian Arawaks of his early landings, and then of Hispaniola (originally *Española* and today's Haiti and Dominican Republic), would eventually afflict all Americans of colour.

Yet however 1492, or its quincentenary, come to be construed, does not America in fact debate in Columbus an issue strikingly more contemporary – nothing less, in the light of its changing demographic face, than the right historical vocabulary for American nationhood? That is, given an ethnicity which will make Euro-Americans, WASP or otherwise, a less than one in two minority by the middle of the next century (African-Americans will be passed by Latinos as the largest minority by the end of the 1990s, and they in turn will be passed by Asian-Americans by the 2020s), old assumptions will simply no longer hold as to the human make-up of America. Nor, just as importantly, will they hold as to the kind of nation America has been. Eurocentrism, and within that, Anglo-centrism, for the coming new century has been served with something akin to its cultural eviction-notice.

Not that the 'Euro' or 'Anglo' order is about to go quietly. As inveterate an Anglo-Saxon presidential pairing as Bush and Quayle have, until the Clinton presidency, held the White House. An all-white, all-male, Senate Judiciary Committee – with behind them an all-white, and almost all-male, Senate – had the power in 1992 to decide between a black Clarence Thomas and Anita Hill (however Reaganite-conservative the both of them). A jury of eleven whites and one Filipino moved by the court to suburban Simi Valley, Ventura County, finds Not Guilty an all-white LAPD squad detachment for the 81-second, videoed, bludgeoning of black, inner-city Rodney King. That supplied the spark for long-brewing racial–economic resentments to eventuate in the South Central Los Angeles riots of April 1992.

Other Americans of colour give matching witness. Chicanos go on finding themselves stigmatised as somehow all, or nearly all, 'illegals', resented Third World economic refugees who have made it across the porous Mexican–American border despite the best efforts of the Immigration Bureau ('la Migra'). Since the 1980s, from a related angle, no less than 20 American states have held English-only referenda, with all their anti-Hispanic signals. Native Americans, reservation-based or urban, still suffer the highest high school drop-out and unemployment rates, and the least support in terms of health-care, welfare and restitution of land and other property rights. Despite the 'best efforts' of federal and state authority, especially the Bureau of Indian Affairs, they have proved incapable of adapting to modernity. Whether, thus, the savagist myth comes back into play (as in the present Mohawk land and lottery disputes), or some New Age spiritual exoticising, the tendency, time and again, has been to see them as historical embarrassments – if indeed exotic, then also caught out by time, for the most part drifters, drop-outs or, notoriously, alcoholics.

Anti-Asianism likewise persists, an old American inclination as borne out from the Chinese Exclusion Act of 1882 and its successors, through to Executive order 9066 which, in 1942, put 110,000 Japanese-Americans into concentration camps. Notorious present-day manifestations include the baseball-bat murder, in June 1982, of Vincent Chin, a Chinese-American draftsman, in Highland Park, Detroit. His killers, two unemployed white Chrysler car-workers who had thought Chin 'Japanese', to community dismay and against every expectation were let off with a $3,000 fine and probation. 'Real' Japanese-Americans, whether second-generation *nisei* or third-generation *sansei*, now find themselves confronting, in the light of the 1990s American recession, the fall-out of a new style of 'Japan-bashing' which invokes Pearl Harbor by rote and allegedly unfair Japanese imports from cars to cameras to televisions. Korean-Americans, 'America's new entrepreneurs' in a worn phrase, in turn, have suffered a similar backlash. In 1992, thus, an unrebuked Senator Hollings of South Carolina could tell blue-collar constituents: 'You should draw a mushroom cloud and put under it "Made in America by lazy and illiterate Americans and tested in Japan".' [8] Euro-American nativism appears to suffer little or no decline.

The high-cultural rearguard view expresses itself in talk of 'Core American Values', 'The Common Culture' and 'Basic Literacy'. To that end, a run of defensive, 'one culture' publications have issued forth – few more controversial than Allan Bloom's *The Closing of the American Mind* (1987) and E.D. Hirsch's *Cultural Literacy* (1987),[9] both of which espouse a belief in western, essentially Judaeo-Christian and Graeco-Roman touchstones as the overriding desiderata for a civilised America. Backing is to be found from New Right apologists like Roger Kimball in *Tenured Radicals* (1990) and Dinesh D'Souza in *Illiberal Education* (1991), from minority conservatives like Richard Rodriguez in *Hunger of Memory* (1982) and Linda Chávez in *Out of the Barrio: Towards a New Politics of Assimilation* (1991), and from even a ranking, Kennedy-liberal historian like Arthur M. Schlesinger, Jr in *The Disuniting of America: Reflections on a Multicultural Society* (1992).[10] Albert Shanker, President of the American Federation of Teachers, indicts the 'new multiculturalism' as a 'fad and a craze' in his weekly *New York Times* column.[11] The talk, here, invokes fears of American balkanisation, a latterday descent into tribalism.

Counter-argument, predictably enough, abounds, and with equal polemical vigour.[12] Who, it is proposed, could even begin to doubt the sheer timelessness of the case for multiculturalism? Not only demographics, but a sense of historical accuracy and fairness, overwhelmingly mandate an educated, though uncoercive, recognition of American differences of ethnicity, race, gender and tradition. Other Americas – Black, Hispanic-Mestizo, Native and Asian, alongside, notably, the gay and feminist communities – so enter the cultural lists as rarely before.

Past canons of art, history, ideas, if not Americanness itself, as a consequence, come to be seen as having been partial, self-serving, one regimen posing for the whole. To this end two recent scholarly productions, the New Historicist *Columbia Literary History of the United States* (1988) and the anti-canonical *Heath Anthology of American Literature* (1990), embody symptomatic challenges.[13] Universities and high schools, in turn, have begun to institute course changes to reflect the greater awareness of cultural and ethnic diversity. Even political correctness, PC as it has become known, for all the acerbities it arouses, cannot be thought other than part of the process, a refusal in the name of ethnic and gender equality of past hegemonies. Balkanisation, in short, can actually be prevented by an informed purchase on American cultural variety – a response which goes beyond token or anecdotal sampling.[14]

In this, the departure-point has to be the 'black' 1960s, the decade of Civil Rights, Black Power, the Selma–Montgomery March of 1965, Voter Registration, Long Hot Summers (whether in Mississippi or Harlem, Alabama or Watts), SNCC, CORE, the Panthers, the Nation of Islam, and the searing assassinations of John Kennedy (1963), Medgar Evers (1963), Malcolm X (1965) and Martin Luther King (1968). Out of so dramatic a litany arose an Afro-America bent upon its own political re-inscription, an insistence that as never before 'Black' indeed could be 'Beautiful' and that the Kennedy-Johnson years signified a new, transforming racial covenant.[15]

Vietnam, and then Watergate, undoubtedly took America in other directions. Some saw the transition from the presidency of Jimmy Carter to that of Reagan, and then of Bush, as signalling a reduction in black advance. But against all the inner-city blight, the drugs, the gangs, or the still present colour-lines of a rural Mississippi or Alabama, Afro-America, in fact, has acquired growing economic and political power. An evident black middle-class emerges, whether measured through suburbanisation, business, elected officials or college placement. The political succession to Martin Luther King and Malcolm X includes the generation-bridging presence of Jesse Jackson, mayoral figures like Harold Washington of Chicago or David Dinkins of New York, a National Chair of the Democratic Party in Ron Brown, Illinois's first black Senator Carol Mosely Braun, or, even, a latest preacher-activist in the New York-based Reverend Al Sharpton. Whatever the punditry to the opposite, Afro-America has anything but absented itself from the national grain.

Black popular culture contributes its part. The television series adapted from Alex Haley's *Roots* (1976), as one instance, achieved some of the highest-ever American viewer ratings. Its household screening of the African diaspora, of slavery and emancipation, and of the 'Great Migration' out of Dixie into the northern cities, held both black and white America transfixed. A media confection or not, it none the less filled in what for many Americans had been a historical blank: Africa and slavery as legacies either avoided or overlooked. The 1980s yielded another kind of standard-bearer in 'The Cosby Show', the turnings of hitherto under-attended black middle-class life made over into massively popular television situation-comedy. Black screen-work, however, again moves on, typically in Spike Lee's *Do the Right Thing* (1989), with its insights into the violence likely when white business inside the black community fails to respond to that community's needs, and in John Singleton's *Boyz N the Hood*

(1991), a first-hand, and prophetically timed, portrait of South-Central LA gang and family life.

Black musicianship, as of birthright, continues to underwrite America's Jazz, Blues and Gospel, not to say an ongoing popular idiom which reaches down from an earlier generation of Ray Charles and Dionne Warwick, to successors as different as Michael Jackson, Natalie Cole and Wynton Marsalis, and on to any or all of current Rap groups from Public Enemy to Ice-Cube. Names like Redd Foxx and Bill Cosby, Dick Gregory and Richard Pryor, took stage and movie comedy well beyond 'shuckin' 'n' jivin', with a Whoopi Goldberg or Eddie Murphy there to extend and enrich the tradition. Black sport, too, with Muhammad Ali still in the frame, remains a front-line American feature, whether in the form of baseball's Hank Aaron, athletics's Carl Lewis and Florence ('Flow-Jo') Griffith-Joyner, or basketball's Magic Johnson, the latter the more so since the public acknowledgement of his HIV status and AIDS-awareness campaign. An America void of these features would be unthinkable.

Literary accomplishments have equally come to prominence, indeed to the point where it has become a commonplace to speak of the 'Second Black Renaissance'.[16] Few post-war founding voices, however, more compellingly took possession of 'the word' than James Baldwin, above all in the great evidentiary essays which became *Notes of a Native Son* (1955), *Nobody Knows My Name: More Notes of a Native Son* (1961) and *The Fire Next Time* (1963).[17] In these, he was able to inscribe a self, a Harlem, an America, which changed the very idiom whereby blackness was to be understood; hence his opening place in the present consideration. The line he bequeathed includes Eldridge Cleaver's prison memoirs – writing as a way of 'saving myself' – in *Soul on Ice* (1968), Albert Murray's savvy, eloquent portraiture in *The Omni-Americans* (1970), Alice Walker's 'womanist', or self-affiliating, black-matrilineal pieces in *In Search of Our Mothers' Gardens* (1983), and, lustrously, Toni Morrison's latterday recovery, or again re-inscription, of the 'Africanist' dimension within all of mainstream American writing in *Playing in the Dark* (1992).[18]

Autobiography as yet another major kind of African-American 'writing-in' begins in the slave-narratives of a Frederick Douglass or Harriet Jacobs, with Zora Neale Hurston's bluesy, self-inventive *Dust Tracks on a Road* (1942) and Richard Wright's Deep South rite-of-passage, his 'Portrait of the Artist', *Black Boy* (1945), as descendants. Incontestably, however, the dramatic post-war high point has to be Malcolm X's *Autobiography* (1964), defiant, epiphanous, a 'life' discovering its meaning even in the very process of self-composition. Alongside rank Maya Angelou's *I Know Why the Caged Bird Sings* (1970), and its four sequels, an ongoing inscription of self to repudiate both the racist exclusion and gendered silence brought on by her childhood rape in Stamps, Arkansas; Angela Davis's *Autobiography* (1974), the remembrance of a West Coast Marxism as a way out of black-bourgeois alienation and anonymity; or Chester Himes's *The Quality of Hurt* (1972) and *My Life of Absurdity* (1976), a two-part, voluble memoir of an American and European life frequently driven to the margins of silence and exile.[19]

In fiction, Ralph Ellison's *Invisible Man* (1952) turns self-chronicle into a dazzling, mythopoeic performance, its anonymous narrator who must 'put down' this 'nightmare' – that is, reflexively, make the black on white of writing itself a trope for the larger politics of black visibility – a stand-in for all the other black narrator-witnesses who have constituted Afro-America. James Baldwin's *Go Tell It on the Mountain* (1953) likewise tells its story of the Grimes dynasty in the guise of a Bible-driven spiritual or blues, three 'chants' linking Dixie to 1930s Harlem, Both achievements continue in triumphs like Ernest Gaines's confessional slavery-to-Civil-Rights life in *The Autobiography of Miss Jane Pittman* (1971); or Toni Morrison's dramatisation of how 'Africa' enters 'America', from slavery to inherited children's rhymes, in *Song of Solomon* (1977) – with her recent Harlem Renaissance novel *Jazz* (1992) a further reminder of how consummate has become her story-telling; or Alice Walker's Civil Rights history in *Meridian* (1976); or James Alan McPherson's finely various short stories in *Hue and Cry* (1969) and *Elbow Room* (1977); or, and not the least, Ishmael Reed's breezy, self-referential 'Hoodoo' fictions in *The Free-Lance Pallbearers* (1967) through to *The Terrible Threes* (1989).[20]

Equally, black poetry has contributed its own laureateship, a line running from, say, Robert Hayden or Gwendolyn Brooks, through to, say, Michael Harper or Audre Lorde. For theatre the linkage extends from Lorraine Hansberry's liberal-integrationist *Raisin in the Sun* (1958), to LeRoi Jones/Amiri Baraka's mythy, subterranean one-acter *Dutchman* (1964), to August Wilson's racially charged re-creation of a 1920s Chicago blues recording session in *Ma Rainey's Black Bottom* (1976, 1984).[21] Perhaps Jones/Baraka's recent *Reader* (1991) best serves: the measure of a presiding black writer-activist whose own evolving contributions across three decades speak out of, and to, Afro-America's overall post-war cultural efflorescence.[22]

The new Latino dispensation, again born of the 1960s, has played its matching part.[23] One steps back, first of all, to the Chicano or Mexican-American activism of the 1968 California grape boycott and *huelgas* (strikes) as led by César Chávez and his United Farm Workers, as well as to the establishment of José

Angel Gutiérrez's La Raza Unida in Texas and Corky Gonzalez's Crusade for Justice in Denver. But whether the liberation politics of *chicanismo*'s 'Aztlán', or of Puerto Rican America's 'Borikén', or of an emphatically different, rightist Cuban-America (with whatever implications for a post-Fidel Cuba itself), the Hispanic communities of North America have issued their own call to attention. No longer, furthermore, can one-note stereotypes of the *barrio*, with the Chicano as *mojado* or wetback, the Nuyorican as welfare client, and the Cuban-American as counter-insurgent in waiting, be assumed to cover all bases.

The diversity, too, means recognition of different, though increasingly overlapping, Latino geographies, whether the historic five states of the Chicano south-west, Texas, Arizona, Colorado, New Mexico and California, or 'Spanish' (meaning Puerto Rican) Harlem, or a Cuban-American Florida with its Dade County and 'Little Havana' Miami. Culturally, the implications are just as many: bilingualism and a tradition of *mestizaje*; music as eclectic as that of a Chicano group like Los Lobos, a Nuyoriqueño singer like José Feliciano, or a Cuban-American ensemble like The Miami Sound Machine; film which ranges from Chicano screenplays of *pachuquismo* and the East LA *barrio* like Luis Valdez's *Zoot Suit* (1981) and Edward James Olmos's *American Me* (1992) to the movie version of Oscar Hijuelos's lyric, sexually riotous, Cuba–New York novel *The Mambo Kings Play Songs of Love* (1989);[24] and, as always, Latino foodways like *tamales*, *burritos* or *tacos*.

Who, too, could doubt that recent Latino writing has brought a new literary order and self-articulation into being, a 'Spanish' North American canon? In this regard, Tomás Rivera's ' ... *y no se lo tragó la tierra/'... and the earth did not part*' (1971) serves to perfection:[25] a bilingual, Dubliners-like, story cycle, told through a childhood viewpoint, and which poignantly memorialises a Chicano family's year of migrant labour. Other texts from the three Latino mainstreams similarly given to inscribing the self and its community include Rudolfo Anaya's New Mexico classic of childhood memory, *Bless Me, Ultima* (1972) and Sandra Cisneros's beautifully honed Tex-Mex vignettes of *Woman Hollering Creek and other stories* (1991); Piri Thomas's landmark Nuyorican autobiography *Down These Mean Streets* (1967) and Nicholasa Mohr's remembrance of girlhood in Spanish Manhattan *Nilda: a Novel* (1973); and Oscar Hijuelos's now illustrious *The Mambo Kings Play Songs of Love* (1989) and Cristina Garcia's life of a Cuban matriarch told as a tale of Havana and Brooklyn, *Dreaming in Cuban* (1992). A Dominican-American story-sequence like Julia Alvarez's *How the García Girls Lost Their Accents* (1991) or a Cuban-written but East LA-based mystery like Alex Abella's *The Killing of the Saints* (1991) suggest other coming possibilities and cross-overs.[26] A related, if grander, perspective, also lies to hand, that of the pan-Latin, *mestizo*, legacy. In the words of the Mexican-Chicano performance artist, Guillermo Gómez-Peña, 'how can the five hundred million *mestizos* that inhabit the Americas go on being called a "minority"?' [27] The whole truly amounts to a new, growing, and resolutely self-inscriptive, kind of American *hispanidad*.

No less so has Native America sought, and increasingly found, its latterday voice.[28] Groupings like AIM (the American Indian Movement), with slogans of 'Red Power', and, however less theatrically, the Native American Rights Fund, have kept up one kind of pressure. Nations as different as the Navajo, the Cherokee, the Sioux, the Ojibwe/Chippewa, the Laguna Pueblo, or, at a lesser known reach, the Pacific-Northwestern Kwakiutel, justifiably insist on the inutility of a single nomenclature like 'Indian'. The 1970s land-claims of Alcatraz, Taos, Maine and Massachusetts, together with the symbolic seizure, or rather re-seizure, of Wounded Knee in the Pine Ridge Reservation of South Dakota, in 1973, in turn have both helped undermine the long-held triumphalism implicit in reference to the Frontier or the Winning of the West, while calling attention to a new order of Native-American politics.

Argument, too, like Vine Deloria's *Custer Died For Your Sins* (1969),[29] or history like Dee Brown's *Bury My Heart At Wounded Knee* (1970),[30] or, latterly, even film-making made to Hollywood rules like Kevin Costner's *Dances With Wolves* (1990) – with Michael Apted's *Thunderheart* (1991) and *Incident at Oglala* (1991) as politically astuter accompaniment – have helped refocus the idioms whereby discussion proceeds of modern native America. Native Americans themselves have been able to argue shared inheritances, yet at the same time, tribal differences of language, ceremony, belief-systems and myth. Part of this revision, too, has been to show that Native America signifies a population more cross-blood than full-blood and more urban than reservation-based. Each contested 1992 Columbus festivity inevitably has further sharpened awareness, the insistence on another version, another inscription, to the 'discovery' of America.

The literary roster, likewise, could not more have played its part.[31] Gerald Vizenor's self-styled 'trickster' autobiography, *Interior Landscapes: Autobiographical Myths and Metaphors* (1990), for present purposes offers the exemplary text, a playfully self-referential, cross-blood first-person chronicle.[32] It takes its place, too, within a larger Native American literary rebirth, for which N. Scott Momaday's *House Made of Dawn* (1969), drawn from Laguna and Navajo sources, and unyielding as may be in its vision of alcoholism and tribal loss, set a standard. Tribal Plains stories found a voice in the Cheyenne chronicler, Heyemeyohst Storm, notably the fable-collection *Seven Arrows* (1972). Pueblo Laguna history lies behind the memories of Leslie Marmon Silko's *Ceremony* (1977) and *Storyteller* (1981), two works which both draw from, and themselves become, 'spiderwoman' and other oral myths of origin. Louise Erdrich's Ojibway-Chippewa chronicles, *Love Medicine* (1984), *The Beet Queen* (1986) and *Tracks* (1988), map different terrains of French, American, German and Tribal encounter on the North Dakota–Canadian border. Blackfeet tribal and mixed-blood tradition can look to the novels of James Welch, whether an oblique, subtly-turned anatomy of displacement like *Winter in the Blood* (1974) or a full-blown epic (based on the Baker Massacre of 1870) like *Fools Crow* (1986). Linda Hogan, of mixed-blood Chickasaw stock, offers in *Mean Spirit* (1990) a 1920s 'mystery' of Oklahoma oil politics and the murder of different Osage tribal members.[33]

Nor, by contrast, has Native American postmodernism been without its exemplar, as, once again, borne out in Gerald Vizenor's Ojibwe-Chippewa, or Anishinaabe, trickster-comic novels like his China fantasy, *Griever: an American Monkey King in China* (1987), his 1492 pastiche, *The Heirs of Columbus* (1991), and his totemic parable, *Dead Voices* (1992).[34] So various an outpouring of 'tongues', whether 'straight', 'forked' or otherwise, accompanied by new directions both in poetry (a Simon Ortiz or Joy Harjo) and essay-work (a Louis Owens or Paula Gunn Allen) indicates a Native America resolved upon reclamation of its own word, its own inscription of past legacies and present realities.

The process has been no less true of Asian America, the rising emergence of Chinese, Japanese, Korean, Filipino and other Pacific Americans.[35] New markers arise everywhere. Selected 'Asian' information technology whizz-kids get featured in *Time*. The current sports pantheon includes, say, tennis's Chinese-American Michael Chan or ice-skating's Japanese-American Kristi Yamaguchi (though the latter's Americanness was brought into question at the 1991 Winter Olympics). Korean business successes provoke admiration – yet also hostility, both white-racist and inner-city black, on the latter's reckoning Koreans as modern-day 'pawnbrokers' or grocery-store exploiters. Filipino-Americans, 'Pinoys', for all that they remain generally at the bottom of the American economic ladder, constitute the fastest growing of all Asian-American communities. Yet their relationship to America could not be more ambiguous. Born of America's only literal colonisation of an Asian country (in succession to the Spanish), long exploited as plantation and farm labour from Hawaii to California, and, latterly, they or their families often victims of the American-supported Marcos dictatorship, even so, most continue to believe they have everything to gain from America as their chosen patrimony.

Film, too, to select from another arena, gives yet further confirmation of Asian emergence. In Chinese-American cinema there has been, for instance, Wayne and Peter Wang's *Eat a Bowl of Tea* (1990), based on Louis Chu's bitter-sweet New York Chinatown novel of 1961, or *1000 Pieces of Gold* (1990), from the novel of the same name of 1981 by Ruthanne Lum McCunn, about Chinese concubinage and slave-labour at the time of the Gold Rush and set against the sinophobia of the notorious Exclusion Acts. Japanese-Americans can find a version of their history in *Come See the Paradise* (1991), albeit through the British director, Alan Parker, which explores in the light of Executive Order 9066 a *nissei*-white love-relationship. *The Fall of the I-Hotel* (1976), for its part, documents the demise, in San Francisco, of Manilatown's best-known old people's hotel, The International, an action by the city authorities which has long been a Filipino-American rallying-cry.

In its turn, a new, transforming, gallery of Asian-American writing emerges, for which Amy Tan's *The Joy Luck Club* (1989) here acts as a marker – Chinese-American story-telling which, indeed in 'all the Englishes I grew up with', and if to conscious purpose then never other than inventively and companionably, inscribes a Chinese past inside a Chinese-American present.[36] Tan's novels take their place, too, in a context which reaches from the 'Chinese' satiric theatre of Frank Chin in *The Chickencoop Chinaman* (1971) and *The Year of the Dragon* (1974) to the Chinese-American fabular histories of Maxine Hong Kingston in *The Woman Warrior* (1976) and *China Man* (1980); from the 'Japanese', self-reconstituting, internment memoir of Monica Sone in *Nisei Daughter* (1953) to the new-wave, reflexive *sansei* fiction of David Mura's *Turning Japanese* (1991); from the 'Korean' immigrant story-telling of Kim Ronyoung in *Clay Walls* (1986) to the recently recovered autobiography of May Paik Lee in *Quiet Odyssey* (1990); and from the itinerant Filipino-American life of Carlos Bulosan in *America is in the Heart* (1946, 1973, 1981) to Jessica Tarahata Hagedorn's spirited, 'fiction of fact' novel of Filipino-American encounter in *Dogeaters* (1990).[37]

Any perpetuation of the stereotypically invisible, or wily or docile, American 'oriental', as, conspicuously, cartooned in a waxen 'Chinese' Fu Man Chu or Charlie Chan, thereby no longer passes muster. Nor, of another vintage, does the Japanese-American as simply either martial arts warrior or compliant wife, the Korean-American as simply electronics dealer or grocery-woman, or the Filipino-American as simply house-boy or maid.

Each of these stereotypes has been shown to be at its time's end and anything but immutable.

Certainly, in the hands, more accurately the words, of those previously 'written out', there has been the writing-in of a truly fuller, more heterodox and eclectic American Asianism. To that end, too, one invokes the perhaps best-known, most contentious 'Asian' collection of recent years. *Aiiieeeee! An Anthology of Asian American Writers* (1974), and its successor, *The Big Aiiieeeee! An Anthology of Chinese American and Japanese American Literature* (1991).[38] Even though both exclude names like Amy Tan and Maxine Hong Kingston as fake, purposely misappropriative in how they use Asian myths of gender, they offer 600 pages of other Asian-American voices, other self-inscribing 'Eastern' American literature.

Is there not, then, overall, a symptomatic portent, a prophetic signal, in the ethnic composition of the entering class for the University of California at Berkeley for 1991–92, namely, an intake of roughly 33 per cent white, 8 per cent black, 20 per cent Hispanic and 33 per cent Asian-American?[39] On a comparative note, CCNY had a 1991–92 student population 14.5 per cent white, 39.2 per cent black, 27.7 per cent Hispanic and 18.2 per cent Asian. Whether, thus, those previously 'written out' be African-American, Latino or Asian-American (other criteria would be needed for Native-Americans), theirs has been, with the 1960s as the axial decade, and increasingly will be, a writing-in, a re-inscription, at once political, economic and, assuredly, ideological. Even more to present purposes, it has also been, and again increasingly will be, a re-inscription of the word, nothing less than a textual revolution and efflorescence.

White Judaeo-Euro-America, in all its different ethnic, gender and religious legacies, for sure, is not about to disappear. But its continued ascendancy, politically or culturally, cannot be guaranteed. Nor, to those with an eye to the evolving make-up, or even spiritual health, of the country, should it. For other, and non-European, Americas – and the writers who have arisen out of them – now insist upon their own quite coexistent lexicons, the articulation of pasts (and so presents) inescapably cross-plied with white America yet at the same time discrete, lived both inside yet at one remove from the assumed mainstream.

'These United States', to invoke an old, slightly proprietorial phrase, have experienced not a few previous changes of signature; but in no way as now portends. For, willingly or not, America finds itself engaged in a prospect long overdue. It has embarked upon the inscription, the inscriptions, of *all* its ethnicities, those of a colour, a language, a history, a gender, beyond the patristic

Euro-America of, as it were, received writ, be the latter meant literally or figuratively. In James Baldwin, Tomás Rivera, Gerald Vizenor and Amy Tan, thus, the aim is to invoke, in representative texts, four of these 'inscriptions', each nothing if not utterly self-particular yet born of its author's ethnic legacy, each of the one time yet sedimented in the larger time-span of all America.[40]

'The root function of language is to control the universe by describing it.' So, in 'Stranger in the Village' (1953), written while in his Swiss lover's birthplace where he had gone to recuperate from a nervous breakdown (and published first in *Harper's*, then, in 1955, in *Notes of a Native Son*), James Baldwin turns his sojourn, temporary as may be, to characteristically more inclusive purpose. As the unprecedented, sole black presence ('no black man had ever set foot in this tiny Swiss village before I came'), not to say a foreigner by speech, his own 'exile' becomes the very *figura* of the larger African – and African-American – diaspora behind him.

He sees refracted in himself a people initially dispossessed of their languages, then banned from writing the European tongues – English in the immediate case – of their enslavers, and, finally, still further silenced both by 'segregation' and 'terrorisation' and the workings of sexual-racial myth. Where, more graphically, thus, than in a snow-clad, Alpine outpost ('this white wilderness'), for Baldwin to write back into being his own black 'signifying', a descendant of those same first Africans illegally shipped to the Americas and now the *'Neger!'* shouted at him by the Swiss village children?

Yet, in fact, neither he nor those from whom he arose in the Harlem or the black Dixie of an Atlantic away, he proposes can be thought true 'strangers in the village'. Rather they belong, however ambiguously, as integral, long-serving and uniquely credentialed 'citizens' of 'the interracial drama acted out on the American continent'. Nor, for Baldwin, can 'the Negro in America' be understood in terms which deny contradiction, even riddle, being neither wholly African nor wholly European ('The most illiterate among them is related, in a way that I am not, to Dante, Shakespeare, Michelangelo ...'), but rather, echoing Crèvecoeur, another kind of American 'new man'. 'No road whatever', he insists, 'will lead Americans back to the simplicity of this European village where white men still have the luxury of looking on me as a stranger.' Inscribing that complexity ('I am not, really, a stranger any longer for any American alive') becomes a governing cause, nothing less than a call to moral as well as writerly imagination.

Given, as he sees it, the refusal to speak or write truthfully across the colour-line (and white America's resort to supremacist and other distortions), Baldwin's own self-authoring, as it were, of necessity also becomes for him the authoring of the historic black community which bred him; the latter, notably its 'stolen' African past, for the most part hitherto left blank, uninscribed. If he can wonder 'what on earth the first slave found to say to the first dark child he bore', 'Stranger in the Village' might be thought an answering, and empowering, riposte. Indeed, the same might be said of all the 'witness', in another favoured phrase, which constitutes *Notes of a Native Son* (1955), *Nobody Knows My Name* (1961) and *The Fire Next Time* (1963).

The analogy, further, between the inscription of black selfhood on a 'white' history ('This world is white no longer, and it never will be white again,' he concludes), and black script on a white page, must have struck him as forcefully as it did the Ellison of *Invisible Man*. The insistence, at least, on making 'language' a means of 'controlling the universe' ('making it my own' he calls it in 'Why I Stopped Hating Shakespeare') lies behind each essay in turn of *Notes of a Native Son* as they range from Harlem to Paris, Mississippi to Sweden, Atlanta to Turkey, or decipher the sexual and related iconographies of black and white, or examine progenitors from Harriet Beecher Stowe to Richard Wright and from Henry James to William Faulkner. Nor does the insistence rest there. The essays become the very thing they most address, one 'inscription', one 'writing-in', for another.

Each stopping-off place confirms the point. In his 'Autobiographical Notes' he speaks of seeking to 'appropriate these white centuries', of ending his 'racial bastardy' (his own illegitimacy no doubt an animus behind the image), and of 'unlocking' his 'being a Negro' in order 'to write about anything else'. In 'Everyone's Protest Novel', then 'Many Thousands Gone', he argues the limits of, respectively, *Uncle Tom's Cabin* and *Native Son*, from a criterion of 'the power of revelation'. If, too, it has been 'only in his music ... that the Negro in America has been able to tell his story', Baldwin indicates a matching literary sense of mission. To that end, in 'Notes of a Native Son', he recalls his Harlem deacon-stepfather saying, 'You'd rather write than preach, wouldn't you?' Then, in 'A Question of Identity', with, as so often, Henry James likely in mind, he calls up the imaginative returns of expatriation for an American writer: 'From the vantage point of Europe he discovers his own country.'

Nobody Knows My Name: More Notes of a Native Son extends the process further, its very title a working brief for the inscription of 'self and the world' as he calls it in the Introduction. From 'The Discovery of What It Means to be an American', in which he speaks of the European as against American choice of the writer's 'vocation' ('A European writer considers himself to be part of an old and

honourable profession ... this tradition does not exist in America'),
through to his closing thoughts on authorship in the
Baldwin–Mailer skirmish 'The Black Boy Looks at the White Boy'
('His [the writer's] work, after all, is all that will be left when the
newspapers are yellowed'), the same double writing-in applies.

His attention, thus, can be given to early 1960s Afro-America
in 'East River, Downtown' ('the American Negro can no longer,
nor will he ever again, be controlled by white America's image of
him'). Or it can focus on colour-line Mississippi in 'Faulkner and
Desegregation' ('It is apparently very difficult to be at once a
Southerner and an American'). On a different tack, it can turn to
Gide and homosexuality with all the implications for his own
sexual preference, in 'The Male Prison' ('it was clear to me that
he had not come to terms with his nature'). But the essays bear
the same impress: 'the word' as both confession and accusation,
as both an urging of 'revelation' and, in Baldwin's passion and
fluency, as in itself a 'revelation'.

One summary lies in *The Fire Next Time*, in 'Down at the
Cross: Letter from a Region of My Mind', where the 'Letter' as
yet another kind of inscription again does shared duty:

> For the horrors of the American Negro's life there has been
> almost no language. The privacy of his experience, which is
> only beginning to be recognized in language, and which is
> denied or ignored in official and popular speech – hence the
> Negro idiom – lends credibility to any system that pretends
> to clarify it. And, in fact, the truth about the black man, as a
> historical entity and as a human being, *has* been hidden from
> him, deliberately and cruelly; the power of the white world is
> threatened whenever a black man refuses to accept the white
> world's definitions.

There may, indeed, hitherto have been 'no language' for black
'privacy of experience'. It becomes all the more a measure of
Baldwin's efficacy, thereby, that his own 'language' simultaneously
diagnoses that condition and embodies its remedy. Doubts, often
enough, have arisen about Baldwin's later discursive powers (as
they have about the fiction after *Go Tell It on the Mountain*), from *A
Rap on Race* (1971), his colloquy with Margaret Mead, through to
The Evidence of Things Not Seen (1985), his thoughts on the Atlanta
black child murders for which Wayne Williams was indicted in
1981. But the triumphant, perhaps more aptly, inerasable, contribution of *Notes of a Native Son*, *Nobody Knows My Name* and *The Fire
Next Time* remains one not only of refusing 'the white world's
definitions', but of calling for, and, then, in the inscription, actually
becoming, necessary counterparts.

'To document and develop the Chicano community.' Tomás Rivera's phrase might seem to echo a line from Baldwin, except that the 'writing-in' being called for is that of *chicanismo*, the Aztec-Spanish, polylingual, two-Americas inheritance of all Mexican Americans. A novella, as may be, too, of twenty-plus stories and vignettes, his '*... y no se lo tragó la tierra'/... and the earth did not part'* (1971), in this as other respects, takes its place with other founding Chicano fiction, notably José Antonio Villarreal's Mexico-to-California chronicle, *Pocho* (1959), Raymond Barrio's portrait of field labour in the Santa Clara Valley, *The Plum Plum Pickers* (1969), Rudolfo Anaya's New Mexico *Bildungsroman*, *Bless Me, Ultima* (1972), Ron Arias's magic-realist picaresque, *The Road to Tamazunchale* (1975), and Rolando Hinojosa's portrait of his Belken County, Texas, 'mythical kingdom', *Klail City y sus alrededores* (1976) or *Klail City* in the English version.[41]

But if '*... y no se lo tragó la tierra*' does 'document' a 'lost' year of labour-migrancy, it also goes further. Imagistically it becomes that year. For whether read in the English or the Spanish version (ideally in both), it offers commemoration, the ritualised within the specific. To that end, too, the organising consciousness of the boy-narrator plays into that of his adult counterpart, a dual story-telling which allows the one time to yield to a larger, more embracing time. The upshot makes for a rare achievement, a key, affecting, inscription of the Chicano heritage.

Historically, migrant life amounts to but one component in the overall evolution of *chicanismo*. For that, there would have to be reference to the Aztecs and Cortés, the Mexican–American War of 1846–48 and the Revolution of 1910–17, and the Zoot Suit Riots of 1942–43 and the rise of the *barrios* from New Mexico to California. But it lies, ongoingly, at the heart of much Chicano experience, families forced northwards out of the southwest (here Texas) to work, as in '*... y no se lo tragó la tierra*', as un-unionised farm labour throughout a 1940s Utah ('Iuta'), Wisconsin or Minnesota. The distinction of Rivera's telling of this Chicano rite-of-passage derives from its careful impressionism, a dialectic of memory, episode-within-episode and past family and community voices.

'That year was lost to him' ('*Aquel año se le perdió*'). Rivera's opening sentence suggests an almost Proustian touch. The narrator, whether child or adult, invokes the year's cycle as a form of pageant, a past carried, and ritualised, in the mind and senses into an unbroken present. Thus the crop work, the journeying north by overcrowded truck, the boy's own time in the fields or being sent to one or another school, the sometimes violent death of *compadres*, and the sheer grind of the picking and the subsistence wages which make up the family's *pobreza*, become radical points in a memory long gestated inside the narrator. He ends up 'hidden' beneath a house, overhearing, replaying in imagination, each past component, a true memorialist-in-waiting. 'And that's just one year,' he insists, 'I'll have to come here to recall all the other years.'

A first story, which calls up a child shot and killed by the farm boss for drinking water instead of working, so alternates with a mother's prayer for her absent son in Korea. The narrator's recollection of anti-Mexican taunts in the schoolyard so leads on to the further recollection of being sequestered with an unhinged, murderous, odd couple. The same narrator also re-creates the daring in boyhood of having gone out alone at midnight to taunt the devil and, to his great amazement and self-education, of actually surviving this would-be necromancy (the title has also been translated as *The Earth Did Not Devour Him*). These each re-enact themselves as remembrance, the year written two ways into a perpetual time-present.

The subsequent cycle operates in like manner. The boy's communion-going becomes entangled in an irreverent counting-up of possible sins and the sight of a naked couple having sex in a nearby dry-cleaning store. A family of neighbours is grotesquely burned to death after the father has rubbed alcohol on their bodies for a boxing match. A lovestruck young migrant worker kills himself after being rejected at a San Antonio, Texas, home-town dance by touching a power cable and causing the town to plunge into darkness. A Tex-Mex mother suffers a nervous breakdown in the town store as she seeks Christmas presents for her children. A number of neighbourhood families allow themselves to be duped by salesmen who promise super-enlarged photographs of relatives or missing sons – a sad, double exploitation of hope over reality.

Above all, in 'When We Arrive' ('*Cuando lleguemos*'), the human cattle-truck whose engine burns out en route to the mid-west serves as the very image of migrant displacement with only the dawn sky as comfort. In Rivera's telling, the actual past shades obliquely into something far more iconic, the factual into the memorialised – yet without any tendency simply to heroise. Further, each segment of narrative, by implication, enfolds itself within the implied greater and overall narrative of Chicano history.

To the same end, Rivera might himself be said to put in a fleeting appearance in the figure of Bartolo, poet-historian of *la raza*:

> Bartolo passed through the town every December when he
> figured that most of the people had returned from work up

north. He always came by selling his poems. By the end of
the first day, they were almost sold out because the names of
the people of the town appeared in the poems. And when he
read them aloud it was something emotional and serious. I
recall that one time he told the people to read the poems out
loud because the spoken word was the seed of love in the
darkness.

Rivera surrogated to Bartolo, Bartolo to the textual voice of 'I
recall'. As a novella-memoir '... *y no se lo tragó la tierra*' so
acknowledges its own kind of telling and, relatedly, its own kind
of tale, nothing other than a most deftly mediated, and conse-
quential, Chicano 'writing-in'.

The opening, full-page, black-and-white photograph in *Interior
Landscapes* offers 'Clement Vizenor and son Gerald, in Minneapolis, 1936.' As an image of parent–child affection it looks replete.
Smiling, open-shirted, a father in fedora hat holds his two-year-
old in protective arms. The boy, bright-eyed, wrapped, although
the 'subject' of the camera, appears to be monitoring its very
action. Behind them lie piled-up bricks and two stern, crumbling
houses, one with a curtained window. The picture contains more
than a few hints of prophecy.

First, Clement Vizenor, a 'reservation-born mixedblood in dark
clothes', a Chippewa house-painter and feckless ladies man,
within a year would be found murdered with his throat cut in
another Minneapolis street. Police left the death as an 'unsolved',
a robbery perhaps, or a jilted husband's revenge, another 'Indian',
at any rate, who had got himself killed. Fatherless, his son would
quickly be deposited with relatives, or fostered out, by his
unavailing yet eventually three-times-married Norwegian-American
mother, LaVerne Lydia Peterson. It was a young life in fact
anything but protected, despite the occasional intervention of
different cross-blood families.

Self-authoring, 'writing-in', thus, early became a necessity. It
finds its life shape as he evolves from 'mixedblood fosterling' to
leading Native American writer-professor (presently at Berkeley,
with a recent interlude in Tianjin University, China, out of which
grew his trickster novel, *Griever: An American Monkey King in
China*) and tribal member of the Chippewa White Earth Reservation in Minnesota. The route from childhood, through an equally
vexing Minneapolis adolescence (which included, much to the
point, camping with the Boy Scouts on land 'stolen from tribal
people by the federal government'), leads on to the army and a
run of teasing Catch-22 experiences, to Japan ('Mount Fuji over

my typewriter ... my liberation was the military in Japan'), and, above all, to political activism, teaching and journalism.

But it finds its writerly shape in the 'Vizenor' of his books, whether his early haiku collections, his transliterations of Chippewa–Anishinaabe legends and histories, his voluminous reportage and essay-work, or his 'trickster' novels and stories. Few of his delineations of a Native American past and present, however, and of his own contrary place within both, take a more intimate, or, as he rightly has insisted, a more postmodern, turn, than in 'my crossblood remembrance', *Interior Landscapes*. For of post-war Native American writers, only perhaps Leslie Marmon Silko, in *Storyteller*, has inscribed a modern, autobiographical 'Indian' self, and the community history enclosing it, with anything like matching virtuosity.

Thus, from 'Families of the Crane', an explanation of Anishinaabe totemism (Clement Vizenor is invoked as a 'crane descendent'), through to 'Honor Your Partners', partly a credo of his own postmodern improvisations and tactics, and partly an account of the violent, and anything but communitarian, threats against him from AIM members for having dared criticise their politics of 'Red Power' as radical chic, Vizenor unravels a helix of his own pasts. The 29 'autobiographical myths and metaphors', each dated yet gapped one from another, so serve as interfoliations, weighstations as it were, within an ongoing current of memory.

Not inappropriately, he sees himself early on in the 'earthdiver' role of Anishinaabe Creation Myth, a postmodernist earthdiver, however, as likely to call upon a Eudora Welty, a Michel Tournier, a Primo Levi, a William Scheick or a Michel Foucault – all of whom supply prefatory quotations – as upon tribal legends of Naanabozho, generic earth-diver of the Anishinaabe. In fusing Anishinaabe tricksterism into its postmodern equivalent, oral mythologisation into its written or textualised successor, Vizenor shrewdly, and authoritatively, so puts his different cross-blood inheritances to the most adroit narrative advantage.

This tribal-cum-postmodern blend, in fact, becomes the very hallmark of *Interior Landscapes*. A reference to Ishi, last of the Yahi (Vizenor's predecessor, in a direct sense, having lived his last five years making museum exhibits for Berkeley), becomes as likely as to the haiku master, Matsuo Basho. His blonde mother tells him she fell for his mixed-blood father because of a resemblance to George Raft. Of his father's death, he writes: 'Clement Williams must have misremembered that tribal web of protection when he moved to the cities from the White Earth Reservation.' He thinks up baroque 'tricksters' in his classroom day-dreaming, a link to telling an uninterested army captain, 'I want to be a writer.' But as he moves into authorialism, so, in turn, he himself becomes 'authored' by his truest subject: Native America, in all, for him, its mixed-blood braids and windings.

Patronising white school or city authorities metamorphose into 'the new fur traders', a nice reference-back to an ancestry which includes the 'métis', French-Chippewa, Vezinas, whose name was 'mistranscribed' as Vizenor by the then Indian Agent. Vizenor's own autobiographical 'inscriptions', his 'trickster signatures', two centuries on, might so be thought textual makings-good. In the National Guard he thinks himself 'a mixedblood featherweight', a kind of shadow tribal warrior. He will discern a tribal dimension to his taste for haiku, most of all its dynamic stillness of form. 'Death Song to a Red Rodent', a vignette of his remorse on shooting a squirrel, again calls up a tacit Anishinaabe (the name means woodland-dweller)respect for an animate, holistic Nature.

As 'Indian activist', his circle of tribalism widens to include reporting the suicide of a twelve-year-old Dakota Sioux boy, Dane White, wrongfully detained in a prison cell; the murder trial of Thomas James White Hawk, a mixed-blood he thinks the victim of 'cultural schizophrenia'; and, in 'Avengers at Wounded Knee', the Dennis Banks style of warrior bravura which he excoriates. He remembers his own haunting by 'skinwalkers', tribal poltergeists, in rooms where, previously unknown to him, there have been painful deaths. An article written shortly after he became a newspaperman on the *Minneapolis Tribune* indicts a University of Minnesota archaeological dig as 'tribal desecration'. He proposes a 'federal bone court to hear the natural rights of buried human bones'. Vizenor's writings, like his activism, have rarely lacked their reflexive wit.

These encounters with the mutually enfolded worlds of Native and white, City and Reservation, America and Japan, can claim, then, a style to match, their own 'cross-blood', autobiographical style. 'Story-telling', he cites from N. Scott Momaday addressing the First Convocation of American Indian Scholars, is 'a process in which man invests and preserves himself in the context of ideas.' It makes a near perfect gloss for Vizenor's own 'tribal' inscriptions of self and legacy – his 'survival trickeries on the borders' as he calls them – in *Interior Landscapes*.

Though a bestseller with sales matched only by Maxine Hong Kingston's *The Woman Warrior* and *China Men*, Amy Tan's *The Joy Luck Club* (1989) has not been without critics. Insiders accuse the novel, with its mother-and-daughter regimes in 'Chinese' California, of purveying a latest form of orientalism, a kind of West Coast sino-exotica. Where, too, the American scenes come over as first-hand, circumstantial, does not Tan's

China material look mythic, stylised? What, furthermore, is to be said of the 'Chinese-English' or 'English-Chinese', principally as spoken by the mothers, a vernacular tour-de-force or, 1980s or not, still Charlie Chan cartoon talk?

How, above all, to deal with Frank Chin's charge of distortion, that Tan, like Kingston, gives a 'white-racist', 'Christianised', and Chinaman-hating version of Asian myths of gender – an indictment, also, he would presumably extend to *The Kitchen God's Wife* (1991). Thus the duck–swan vignette which opens *The Joy Luck Club* amounts to 'Hollywood', more precisely, 'a fake Chinese fairy tale'. Oddly, given all of this, much of the best case for the novel remains to be made.

That lies, in line with the present argument, in making its two-generational, spiderweb story-telling – its very style of inscription – itself the 'Chinese' and 'Chinese-American' history to hand. Each version, and counter-version, of mother and daughter, builds, dialogically, a China 'there' and a China 'here', and in telling at once competitive yet overlapping. Tan's achievement, allowing that some have thought her voices too similar, lies in drawing the reader into this cumulative 'writing-in', daughters and mothers all confessor-narrators each with their own would-be, but inevitably partial, *compte rendu*. The upshot, once again, is for *The Joy Luck Club* to become the very thing it describes, a 'club' of interwoven narrative exchanges and wagers, memories and prophecies.

Such shows through at every turn, indeed is anticipated in the title-story with its remembrance of Suyuan Woo's 'black sesame-seed soup' as against Aunty Lin's 'red bean soup'. Either the two soups are *cahbudwo*, 'the same', or a case of *butong*, the latter glossed as 'the better half of mixed intentions'. Given that register of difference, it little surprises that when Jing-Mei Woo 'replaces' her mother, dead of 'cerebral aneurysm', at The Joy Luck Club, she faces a father who believes his wife 'was killed by her own thoughts'. Rose Hsu Jordon has a mother who, having attended the First Chinese Baptist Church, has a Bible which Confucianly winds up 'wedged under a too-short table leg, a way for her to correct the imbalances of life'. Waverly Jong, on asking her mother about Chinese torture, elicits the reply: 'Chinese people do business, do medicine, do painting. Not lazy like American people. We do torture. Best torture.' Lena St Clair, likewise, has her two-ply legacy, a story from her mother of the great-grandfather who sentenced a beggar to a cruel death. But 'the dead man came back and killed my great-grandfather. Either that, or he died of influenza one week later.'

Lindo Jong, in turn, doubtless speaks for all the mothers when, on hearing Waverly's American contention 'I'm my own person', rejoins, 'How can she be her own person? When did I give her up?' For, faced with their daughters' news of divorce, or jobs, or children, in short China-in-America, each wonderfully, elusively even, counter-inscribes her own China-in-America, and beyond that, her own China.

Ying-Mei Woo, to be sure, has to supply her own mother's missing discourse. She so makes the trip to China ('I realize I've never really known what it means to be Chinese'), to find the lost 'family' of twin half-sisters: mothers and daughters, tellingly, all of 'the same mouth'. An Mei Hsu, in 'Magpies', correspondingly places the breakdown of her daughter's marriage in the context of her own mother's wrenching, sacrificial 'Second Wife' history with the merchant Wu Tsing. Ying-Ying St Clair, in 'Waiting Between the Trees', similarly interprets the marriage of her daughter, Lena, in terms of her own two 'houses' of relationship, her own two eastern and western marriages.

Though the topic could as readily be housekeeping or food, Shanghai or San Francisco, pre- or post-Maoist China, Jing-Mei Woo offers the key when she observes of her mother's account of Chinese and Jewish styles of playing mah jong: 'These kinds of explanations made me feel my mother and I spoke two different languages, which we did. I talked to her in English, she answered back in Chinese.'

Dialogics rarely can have found more fertile ground – China-America, China, Chineseness – all severally, and intertextually, 'written-in' at the behest of an ongoing matrilineage. Tan's 'inscriptions' in *The Joy Luck Club*, as much in manner as in theme, tell nothing if not their own Asian-American story.

'Self-inscription'. The term, throughout, carries a double force. It speaks, of necessity, to the writer's own 'word', Baldwin, Rivera, Vizenor and Tan as custodians of their own lexicons and styles. But, beyond that, it speaks to, and indeed from, their four respective communities, those of the American non-European inheritance. The post-war ethnicising of America, this 'other' voicing of Columbus's legacy, thus turns out to be nothing less than the 'writing-in', and thereby the making-new, of a very old history.

3

The New Feminist Dispensation: from Betty Friedan to Madonna

Faith Pullin and Claire Colebrook

To give an account of the American women's movement today is to do more than tell a story. The narrative we construct of the past determines how we understand the present. This is nowhere more clear than in the recent battles over the assessment of the 'second wave' of feminism. The story, generally, runs something like this. In 1963 Betty Friedan published *The Feminine Mystique*.[1] By doing so she articulated the 'problem without a name' – the continued oppression of women despite the ostensible equality granted by the victories of that earlier nineteenth-century battle over suffrage. With the publication of this book Friedan inaugurated a movement which not only produced the group she headed, NOW (the National Organisation of Women), but also the more aggressive and militant groups such as WITCH (1968) and BITCH (1969). Founded in 1966, NOW became the largest women's organisation in the United States and hence represented (for both American women and women overseas who looked to the US as the home of the movement) the mainstream of feminist theory and action. The linchpin of NOW was ERA, the Equal Rights Amendment. Basically a document of traditional liberal theory, ERA – in keeping with the liberal premises of NOW – sought to overcome sexist bias and give women equal access to justice and institutions in the mainstream of American society.

Telling the story from this point onwards begins to become more contentious. How we account for the advent of the 'second wave' of feminism depends upon an evaluation of this first wave. Did the second stage follow on from the naive universalism of liberal feminism? The movement of the 1960s had assumed that there could be a category of 'sisterhood' which not only cut across class and race boundaries, but whose demands could be met within the structure of American society. By seeing the constitutional issue of equal rights as fundamental to the women's movement, liberal feminism had taken the principal tenets of American ideology – the sanctity of the individual, an optimism regarding the American constitution and the discourse of rights – and sought to iron out the contradictions between a supposedly

free and democratic society and the existing oppression of
women. The 'second wave', then, would respond to the diversity
of women's issues by seeing the oppression of women as inextricably intertwined with issues of race, class and sexuality. While
being sympathetic to the insights of the late 1960s and early
1970s, second-stage feminists recognised the need for more
radical changes. Acknowledging the importance of rights, they
have argued that such rights cannot be achieved within the
conventional rhetoric of political theory. Second-stage American
feminism already, therefore, finds it has to write the history of its
immediate past in order to determine its future. Zillah Eisenstein,
for example, has pointed out what she sees as a fundamental
misconception at the heart of the early liberal feminist movement.
While the ERA was an important 'first step' in the overcoming of
the oppression of women, the whole idea of 'liberal feminism'
was, to a certain extent, a misnomer. In order to achieve the aims
it set itself it would have to make far more radical changes.[2]

A more sympathetic account could see the move to the
'second stage' as a consequence of the opposition which defeated
the aims of NOW and its failure to pass the ERA. Looking back,
pessimistically, in *The Second Stage*, Betty Friedan lamented the
extremism of the later, more radical feminists and saw this as
crucial to the atrophy of energy and achievement which characterises the women's movement today. But she was also critical of
her own initial liberal premises, acknowledging that the gains
that had been achieved in terms of equality were purchased at the
expense of 'the profound values of life that, for me as for others,
have always been associated with women'.[3]

Indeed, it was the challenge to liberal premisses and the
American ideology of a non-gendered, classless, presocial and
innately moral individual which united the feminists of the second
wave. In her account of the women's movement, Susan Bassnett
has traced the similarities between the early stages of liberal
feminism and the nineteenth-century suffrage movement. According to Bassnett, the energy which went into mobilising the ERA
stemmed from the same principles of traditional individualism
which had characterised the American women's movement from
the 1850s onwards.[4] If one accepts the premise that there is an
essential and universal self which enters society, rather than being
produced by society, then it follows that all the women's movement need do is to remove the restrictions on autonomy and
self-development. Those aspects of selfhood which had tradition-
ally been conceived as valuable – rationality, the ability to be
self-determining, objectivity and the propensity for self-improve-
ment – are necessarily those pertinent to all individuals regardless
of race, class or sexuality. It is a critique of this fundamental

principle which constitutes the 'second wave'. Furthermore, it is
the degree to which one accepts or rejects this principle of
universalism which also characterises the arguments within contemporary American feminism. To a great extent it is the charting
of the story of the second stage – and how indebted we see that
second stage to limiting principles of the self – which constitutes
the character of feminist debate today.

In accounts of the women's movement from the 1960s to the
present, it is generally agreed that the second stage is typified by a
'woman-centred' approach. According to Catherine Stimpson, the
women's movement in the US can be divided into three broad
trends. To begin with, feminism was concerned to eliminate sexist
prejudice from existing institutions and to remove sex-biased assumptions from the prevalent ideology. Following on from this
desire for a removal of bias was a second stage of reconstruction, in
which specifically feminine practices and ideals were re-evaluated.
In the third stage, feminism shifted from being woman-centred to
launch a critique of the universalist presuppositions of all knowledge and values, acknowledging that there may be no such thing as
a sex-blind concept.[5] A similar account is given by Hester Eisenstein in her valuable assessment of the women's movement. According to Eisenstein, the second wave of feminism, which follows on
from a utopian ideal of equality, is characterised by a move towards
'difference'. That is, there is a move away from an implicitly socialist
and political vision of universal equality to a (possibly dangerous)
celebration of women's qualities.

Recent narratives of the past of American feminism do, however, tend to be united by a hauntingly *sotto voce* 'What has gone
wrong?' There has been a general consensus of pessimism, evi-
denced both by Susan Faludi's *Backlash* and those who have
criticised her work. According to Faludi, the achievements of the
women's movement, while significant, have been limited, while the
fulfilment of ideals has now come under serious pressure from a
new wave of conservatism. She and like-minded feminists warn
against complacencies; the women's movement, far from beginning a battle of political correctness which will roll inevitably
towards its victorious conclusion, is as fragile as ever. According
to Faludi, there is an urgent need to question the efficacy of the
contemporary women's movement: 'Women have always fought
the periodic efforts to force them back behind the curtain. The
important question to ask about the current backlash, then, is not
whether women are resisting, but how effectively.'[6]

Faludi's main critic, Germaine Greer, far from criticising
Faludi's bleak assessment of the present, has targeted her alleg-
edly over-optimistic interpretation of the past. To speak of a
'backlash' implies an excessive achievement in the first place. But

from the case, according to Greer. The hatred of women is as prevalent as ever and the tasks set for women are 'heavier and more demanding than they ever were.' [7]

So what is the meaning of the 'second wave' for the present? What has it achieved and where has it left us? Is it the case that its radicalism and utopianism created goals that could only ever remain in an imagined future or does the second wave represent an energy of commitment which the present sadly lacks? What characterised the second stage of feminism was criticism not just of the position of women, but of patriarchy as a whole. But the second wave was not just a harnessing of Marxist or socialist principles to the cause of women; it was never a question of a simple equation in which Class plus Gender would come out to equal Radical Feminism. Shulamith Firestone's radically utopian vision in *The Dialectic of Sex* pointed out the inadequacies not only of liberal feminism, but also of traditional Marxism. According to Firestone, patriarchy rested in the final instance not on the division of labour in terms of class but on a more basic division of labour in the family. The relations in the nuclear family ensured that men controlled the reproduction process which ensured the continuation of the relations of production at an economic level.

To argue for this form of revolutionary feminism was not merely to *include* women in the political class struggle, nor was it to admit the consideration of class into the women's movement. Like the equally inspiring work of Ti-Grace Atkinson, Firestone saw that gender was not simply one issue among others but that class and gender were mutual determinants in an overall structure of oppression.[8] While such work no doubt had Marxism as its inspiration, it is far more important to see the contribution of theorists like Atkinson and Firestone as providing radically new ways of examining social theory. Overcoming the impasse in social theory between liberalism's concentration on the individual and Marxism/socialism's emphasis on economic determinants, radical feminism clearly revealed not only that the personal was political – challenging liberalism's isolated individual – but also that the political was personal. Society was structured not just by the economy but rested on relations *between* individuals in the 'private sphere'. Feminism was challenging the basic paradigms and structures of knowledge: Marxism, psychoanalysis and liberalism. This, of course, brings us to Kate Millett, whose work demonstrated that even without Firestone's neo-Marxist theory of dialectic the issue of gender went beyond a political structure of rights and exclusions.

With the development of more 'sophisticated' techniques of reading, such as post-structuralism, Millett's work is often considered in a rather condescending manner to be a naive appraisal of the patriarchal tradition as it operates at a cultural level.[9] But it is important not only to consider Millett's work in its context – as the beginnings of analysis of gender in texts – but also to see the value of her work today. What Millett's work did and what it does today is more than demand a feminist equivalent of the Stalinist call for social realism. Her attack on 'phallic' authors is not a novel-bashing political correctness; *Sexual Politics* reveals the profoundly *political* character of masculine sexual desire and also demonstrates the importance of literature and culture in patriarchal ideology. Millett's reading of the novels of D.H. Lawrence, for example, revealed that sexism was not just an issue of the political exclusion of women from the public sphere. Discrimination occurred in the academy and at the very level of reading, writing and desiring. Millett paved the way for later theorists such as Andrea Dworkin who would examine the structure and iconography of sexual desire and show how the supposedly most private of experiences (desire and fantasy) was informed by and constitutive of the oppression of women. Millett's work was not fuelled by the reduction of writers like Lawrence and Henry Miller to the level of mere pornography; what she demonstrated was the violence and oppression at the heart of American culture's most sophisticated values. But in doing so she revealed the importance of the *representation* of female desire and the power of those who occupy the production of reading and writing. To see Millett's work in this way can be useful when assessing the contemporary debate over pornography.[10]

Andrea Dworkin's crusade against the violence which she sees as inherent to the genre of pornography has recently been the subject of much criticism. The representation of desire in homosexual and lesbian erotica has frequently drawn on the images and conventions of pornography. In America today lesbian S/M erotica, the work of Robert Mapplethorpe and the recent self-promotion of Madonna, all draw on figures established in the tradition of mainstream pornography. To argue against porno-graphy, certain lesbian feminists maintain, is to sustain a heterosexist prejudice against the representation of women as desired bodies; it is assumed by those who condemn pornography that any representation of women as desirable is *essentially* masculine. But this is only the case if the viewing subject is assumed to be male.

It has recently been argued by the high-profile American feminist Camille Paglia that the women's movement is in a state of crisis – a crisis she sees exemplified by the issue of pornography and representation. According to Paglia, the revolutionary feminism of the 1960s sought to do away with all those social constraints which had impeded women's desire. In the wake of the achievements of those sexual freedoms feminists are now arguing against the liberation they gained. Date-rape and pornography are not remnants of sexism but the consequence of post-1960s emancipation.

It is not surprising, therefore, that Paglia is an enthusiastic supporter of Madonna whom she calls 'the future of feminism'.[11] It is not so much Madonna as Paglia's reasons for championing her which are significant in the debate regarding the representation of desire. There are obvious criticisms of the anti-pornography stance to be made from the position of civil rights and the Fifth Amendment. Dworkin has argued against such criticisms by claiming that pornography encroaches on women's liberty through its method of violent representation. Pornography is the point at which freedom of expression comes up against the wall of incitement to hatred. It could be argued that Dworkin's claim rests upon the premiss that *women's* sexual desire is essentially (or ideally) non-violent and that the violence of male desire can be altered through the destruction of the industry of pornography. For Paglia, however, these desires for a non-violent sexuality are naively utopian. Masculine desire is *inherently* and not politically violent: 'Masculinity is aggressive, unstable, combustible. Women must reorient themselves toward the elemental powers of sex, which can strengthen or destroy.' [12]

By arguing for the inherently aggressive character of masculine sexuality, Paglia buys into the debate on essentialism which is one of the most important issues of contemporary feminism and one which we will turn to later in the assessment of post-second-wave feminism. But insofar as Paglia is concerned with the representation of desire her argument against feminists like Dworkin does raise serious problems for the feminist critique of culture.

In order to assess what is at stake it is useful to examine Paglia's defence of Madonna – the latest icon of American woman – if not feminism. For Paglia, it is Madonna's exploration of the unstable, dangerous, aggressive and sado-masochistic features of sexuality which makes her America's first feminist. Indeed, Madonna's own rhetoric has been profoundly liberal – arguing for the right to explore her own fantasies and desires. But there is a danger, when assessing Madonna and the issue of sexual representation as a whole, of losing sight of the insights of radical feminists such as Firestone, Atkinson and Millett. To argue that sexual fantasy is an issue of personal *right* is to ignore the political construction of desire and its representation. Madonna, for example, uses the images of pornography for what she sees as an intensely personal exploration of desire. Now, even if we sidestep the (by no means insignificant) issue of whether such desire is personal at all, rather than socially constructed, we have to ask what the political effect of the publication and representation of such desire is. The reality of pornography, politically and economically, has rested not on choice but necessity. Women, unable to make careers as mainstream actresses or performers, move into the lesser-paid and less prestigious world of porn. And in a world of women's oppression the *meaning* of pornography lies less in the image than in its political uses. Madonna, as an erstwhile and successful businesswoman in her own right can represent her erotica as an issue of choice but the valorisation of such a choice as personal and liberal only seeks to legitimise and perpetuate the exploitation of women in pornography for whom such a choice does not exist.

It was Kate Millett's work which alerted the women's movement to the political importance of the expression of sexuality. It was not Lawrence and his own sexuality which Millett attacked; it was the reading, veneration and canonisation of such texts as great and 'universal' which formed the substance of her argument. This is an example of the importance of second-wave feminism. Representations were challenged, not for their inherent meaning but for what they said and produced, in the culture which sustained them. If the images of pornography can be taken up by women and used for the exploration rather than the subordination of women's sexuality, then this can only be a good thing. But the insights of radical feminism are surely pertinent today: a personal event, regardless of whether it is 'essential' or sociopolitical, cannot be divorced from its broader context. Indeed, it is the 'depoliticisation' of American feminism – its loss of a sense of cultural context – which has been targeted by many contemporary feminists as the reason for the present confusion and pessimism.

The 'woman-centred' approaches of the second wave culminated in the more recent works of Mary Daly and Adrienne Rich. For both Daly and Rich the utopian image of equality and radical social change and the use of sociopolitical theories to explain women's oppression gave way to an emphasis on 'difference'. Their analyses were less critical and transformative than the radical works of the early 1970s. The question was not so much 'How do we get out of where we are?' as 'How do we celebrate and explore what we have?' Although both Daly and Rich were also writing at the height of the second wave, their work – particularly Daly's *Gyn/Ecology* (1978) – characterised a later phase of emphasis. Whereas Firestone had seen motherhood as the cornerstone of patriarchal structures, Rich celebrated mother – daughter relationships and mothering in *Of Woman Born* (1976). In *Gyn/Ecology*, Daly argued for the specifically and essentially redemptive qualities of feminine being.

The emphasis on women's experience, of course, did not need

to be as essentialist as that of Rich and Daly. The pioneering
work of Nancy Chodorow (1978), for example, argued for wom-
en's nurturing and caring qualities on the basis of psycho-genetic
development and not on some innate and immutable essence.[13]
Carol Gilligan has also used empirical psychological studies to
explore women's responses to situations; by doing so she has
revealed specifically feminine behaviour without having to assume
or argue for the essential or universal truth of her findings.[14]
More recently, Nina Auerbach has defined a woman-centred
approach which does not assume a female essence but merely
argues for shared experiences; the emphasis on *sharing* ensuring
that no single definition of woman rules the field. Referring
specifically to the reading of texts, Auerbach argues that the
identity of women's experiences lies in a dialectical relationship
between the personal and the 'semipublic': 'Lives are our medium
of exchange. Books are inseparable from the private experiences
that authorized them, while these experiences take on the semipublic and shared quality of our books. Finally, this conjunction
is the only gospel we trust.' [15]

But despite the varieties of approach towards an emphasis on
women's experience, Hester Eisenstein's assessment of the emphasis on woman-centred approaches has been critical. For Eisenstein, the radical lesbian separatism of Daly and the liberalism of
Friedan have converged to the point where only private (rather
than political) experiences have become relevant for feminist
analysis. Referring to Daly and Rich as 'metaphysical feminists',
Eisenstein argues that they have enacted a retreat from the
political sphere:

> 'Metaphysical' feminism was, in fact, the woman-centred
> perspective carried to an extreme. Paradoxically, though, the
> net effect of this 'woman-centred' vision was not to place
> women at the center of culture and society, but to recapitu-
> late, and in some sense to accept, the formulation of woman
> as Other, the very category of being against which Simone de
> Beauvoir had originally rebelled. Philosophically, the view of
> woman as an eternal 'essence' represented a retreat from the
> fundamentally liberating concept of woman as agent, actor,
> and subject, rather than object. And politically, at least in
> some versions, it meant a retreat from struggle, in a period
> when all of the issues raised by the second wave, from rape
> to equal pay, remain unresolved, in a period of deepening
> economic depression.[16]

Eisenstein's pessimistic assessment of woman-centred perspectives
and her critique of 'false universalism' is no doubt pertinent when

one considers the failure of so-called woman-centred perspectives to deal with broader issues of exploitation such as race and class. On the other hand, Eisenstein's lament that feminism has lost the 'concept of woman as agent, actor, and subject' sounds like nostalgia for the return to the liberal feminism which accepted, unproblematically, the concept of the person as a self-defining agent. Such a yearning is not confined to Eisenstein alone. Gloria Steinem's recent work has also taken an inward turn, relying not on the essentialism of Daly and Rich but in the belief that change must primarily occur at the level of the individual rather than society. In an assessment of American feminism which followed the radical feminism of the early 1970s, Linda Alcoff has isolated two broad trends. According to Alcoff the 'cultural feminism' of Daly and Rich ignores the insights of post-structuralist theorists such as Derrida and Foucault who have demonstrated the *constructed* character of the self. Post-structuralism, however, deprives the individual of any concept of agency.[17] Eisenstein's writing of the history of the second wave concludes with an opposition between woman-centred and liberal approaches, while Alcoff outlines an impasse between essentialism and post-structuralist relativism. While both Eisenstein and Alcoff attempt to find ways out of the 'identity crisis' of feminism, they typify a feeling in American feminism today that the once-confident use of 'woman' as a category cannot withstand recent developments in feminism and social theory.

The crisis of values is nowhere more clearly revealed than in the recent attempts to evaluate second-wave feminism. While the criticism of Daly's and Rich's work as 'essentialist' and 'universalist' appears to be valid in the face of the recent attention to work by American feminists on issues of race, it is by no means certain that their mode of analysis represents a *retreat* from broader issues. To see the work of Rich and Daly as essentialist is to impose philosophical concepts – such as 'essence' and 'universals' – on works which are primarily mythic and performative. It is possible to write another history of the second wave. Rich and Daly's work can also be seen to build upon the insights of radical feminism. Gender is not just a question of rights and personal sexuality; feminism is not just a practice of discovering what women are. Both Rich and Daly, aware of the emotional and ideological investment in *all* knowledges, are seeking to write a different morphology of gender. To say that their work is invalidated by recent post-structuralist theory which posits the fictiveness of the subject not only (once again) criticises women's mythology from masculinist philosophy; it also accepts post-structuralism's view of the subject as dis-embodied. Rich's work takes seriously the fact that there are different types of persons; rather than adopting a 'false universalism', her work is highly specific. Her work, like Daly's, employs persuasive rhetoric, poetry, myth and argument in a move to *enact* a powerful female iconography:

> The body has been made so problematic for women that it has often seemed easier to shrug it off and travel as a disembodied spirit. But this reaction against the body is now coming into synthesis with new inquiries into the actual – as opposed to the culturally warped – power inherent in female biology, however we choose to use it, and by no means limited to the maternal function.[18]

Far from being deterministically universalist, Rich's statement refuses both the liberal assumption that the self is a *tabula rasa* (which would thus minimise or eliminate sex difference) at the same time as she sees the power of the self as opening up a variety of possibilities.

To see Rich's and Daly's work as an extension of radical feminism rather than a retreat entails recognising the significance accorded to sexual identity in their work. Rather than placing feminism as post-structuralism's handmaiden, we can then see that the early insights of feminism already exposed the fundamentally partial, interested and sexually invested character of all knowledge and perception.[19] Defining personal identity as unavoidably sexed, Rich and Daly then go on to forge a new women's identity – exposing the lie of the liberal, universal and non-gendered subject.

Rather than being inimicable to the differences between women, this form of mythopoeic feminism can be seen to embrace issues of class, race and gender. Nowhere is this better revealed than in the fiction of Toni Morrison whose work explores the relations between race, gender and history. In *Song of Solomon*, for example, Morrison explores the history of a family. Their genealogy is inscribed in their name; when freed from slavery the family is given the name 'Dead' because their 'fore-father' is illiterate and misunderstands the questions he is asked when freed from slavery. Issues of naming and misreading become important in the novel. Pilate – a female character whose name is also the result of chance illiteracy – has her name pinned to her body (literally!) because she wears an earring which contains a torn passage of the Bible from which she was named. Pilate lives in an alternative women's household which exists outside the logic and order of both masculine and civic experience. What Morrison's fiction achieves is not a definition of black femininity but a demonstration that naming, writing and history construct identity at the same time as individuals involve them-

renaming and rewriting. Her work is as much an evocation of a past as a redefinition of the present.

Like Rich, Morrison uses *literary* rather than philosophical or theoretical discourse to undertake a feminist challenge. The qualities Morrison grants her female protagonists in *Song of Solomon* – the capacity for magic, communality, creativity and passion – are not naively manichean celebrations of female essentialism (as Eisenstein describes 'woman-centred' approaches) but a way of negotiating and renewing the past. According to Alcoff the celebration of difference can only mean the celebration of oppression: 'To the extent cultural feminism merely valorizes genuinely positive attributes developed under oppression, it cannot map our future long-range course.' [20] But approaches such as Alcoff's lead to their own form of essentialism by arguing the necessarily positive or negative character of certain definitions of women. The women's movement of the second wave revealed that gender identity was inextricably intertwined with power. To define one's own qualities, to posit the power of one's own body and experience *is* to retrieve the agency Eisenstein mourns in the loss of 'woman as subject', but it is also to acknowledge that identity is bound up with issues of history, embodiment and representation. The work of Nancy K. Miller on the body and representation demonstrates the significance such issues now bear for feminist literary criticism.[21] Stressing the importance of self-definition, Naomi Wolf's *The Beauty Myth* also shows how images of the body control women's behaviour in a manner which is thoroughly political.[22]

However, recent events in the feminist debate do lead one to sympathise with Eisenstein's and other theorists' identification of an 'identity crisis' in feminist theory. In many ways writing a history and assessment of the second wave depends on how we proceed to chart the future. The idea of an 'identity crisis' seems particularly relevant given recent political developments in the United States. Even the work of Camille Paglia, who has argued that date-rape is a game of sexual play which is an essential part of liberation, has posed problems for the idea of what it means to be a feminist in America today. Many theorists would happily disown Paglia and refuse her the right to call herself a feminist.

It is not just the eccentric work of Paglia which challenges the identity of feminism. In the early consciousness-raising days of the women's movement Betty Friedan's work could declare itself relevant to all women precisely because it claimed to be a work of demystification. Once women were given a 'name' for their problem it would supposedly follow that all women would be in agreement; sisterhood was powerful. But the modern feminist has to cope with, and interpret, the large number of women in the

New Right and pro-life movements which are central to American political debate. How can a concept of 'woman' be appealed to in the face of so many women who are 'selling-out' on their sisters? To assess the second wave and determine how far we have come, to decide whether the past is success or failure, fall or redemption, depends very much on the history we choose to write for the future. In the face of a diffusion of the energies of the women's movement Teresa de Lauretis has argued that the 'essence' of woman be conceived nominally rather than as a real essence. However one writes the history, there is a sense that the present offers challenges (the 'backlash', the 'identity crisis', the loss of agency) which can only be met by a notion of women's *identity*. This, according to de Lauretis, is best seen in terms of practical definition. An essence is not what we really *are* but what we are taken (and take ourselves) to be: Women's essence 'is a totality of qualities, properties, and attributes that such feminists define, envisage, or enact for themselves (and some in fact attempt to live out in "separatist" communities), and possibly also wish for other women.' [23]

Given the recent rhetoric of the presidential debate in the United States and the importance of 'family values', the issue of women's sexual identity is still obviously of fundamental importance. While it is no doubt true that the 'family values' debate acted as an attempted smokescreen by the Republicans to conceal economic issues, the fact that such an issue was mobilised is evidence of the profound ideological investment in traditional concepts of femininity. While Naomi Wolf has interpreted the Clinton victory as a defeat of 'family as patriarchy' by 'family as partnership/democracy', [24] Hillary Clinton's involvement with Barbara Bush in the 'chocolate-chip cookie bake-off' and the Clintons' insistence on the very-nuclear character of their own family suggest that one should be less sanguine about a clear defeat of patriarchal values. The present threats to the most basic gains of the women's movement (the right to abortion, for example) are by no means quashed by the Democrat victory. What Hillary Clinton *means* can be determined only by the future. She can be interpreted as the promotion of a new image of woman – as equal and active partner – *or*, merely another example of a woman's talents being directed to the role of first lady but second person. Whether Hillary is a precursor or a defeat can be decided only in the face of the challenge to the women's movement which presents itself urgently today.

Similarly, the meaning of the second wave – whether its achievements are amelioratory compromises or the beginnings of a new future – can be established only by the women's movement's present self-definition. There have been significant recent attempts to overcome the feeling of crisis and point towards a new tactical unity for the women's movement. Darlene Clark Hine, for example, has recently urged that black women's history also begin to take account of class and white women's history. Hine's work recognises that within the women's movement the demands of different groups can be met only by mutual understanding and 'crossover' studies.[25]

Such studies do not forget the differences between women, but they do acknowledge that there is a unity in disunity which benefits not just women as a whole but also individual groups. The challenge to the concept of sisterhood which feminists must face, given the large number of women today who do *not* sympathise with some of the most basic and uncontentious tenets of feminism, can be met only by an historical and political analysis which examines the identity of American feminism – its past and its yet-to-be-decided future.

4

Partial Factors: Men, Machines and the Robotic in Post-war America

Dale Carter

'You beautiful stud,' he heard her say, 'I love to touch you ... do you know what I feel when we're out on the road? Alone, just us?' She was running the sponge caressingly over its front bumper. 'Your funny responses, darling, that I know so well. The way your brakes pull a little to the left, the way you start to shudder around 5,000 r.p.m. when you're excited. And you burn oil when you're mad at me, don't you. I know ... we'll always be together.'

Thomas Pynchon, *V.*

As Benny Profane watches Rachel Owlglass talking to her sports car in 'm.g. words', so ostensibly human properties become adjuncts of the machine. To Benny, such 'public displays of sentiment' are disturbing; by the time Rachel starts fondling the gear lever he has had enough. But in Thomas Pynchon's first novel inert objects repeatedly usurp the position of human power in the social order, and they do not do so on their own. Later, having accused Rachel of being 'an accessory ... a part, a cheesy part, like a radio, heater, windshield-wiper blade', Benny himself starts to wonder whether female resistance to male advances might be measured in ohms, and looks forward to the production of 'an all-electronic woman' made of interchangeable parts and supplied complete with a maintenance manual. What is intended in one sense as a warning – Benny alerts Rachel to 'a world of things that had to be watched out for' – therefore also carries a more positive element of anticipation.[1]

Interactions of this order were hardly new. As early as 1941 Herbert Marcuse had noted how 'mechanical contrivances' were invading social life and establishing new satisfactions: 'The average man hardly cares for any living being with the intensity and persistence he shows for his automobile. The machine that is adored is no longer dead matter but becomes something like a human being.'[2] Ten years later, in *The Mechanical Bride: Folklore of Industrial Man* (1951), Marshall McLuhan documented how 'the legs [and] busts ... of the modern girl' were fragmented for the purpose of marketing into erotic components, becoming little more than 'display objects like the grill work on a car'. Nor were such interactions unusual. In *The Mechanical Bride*, anyone who uncritically takes in the collective onslaught of advertising and Hollywood 'stands in danger of being frozen into a helpless robot'. Nor, finally, were they explicit functions of sensuality alone. Drawing on his reading of the complex relationship between technology and human sensory arrangements, McLuhan concludes in *War and Peace in the Global Village* (1968) that 'we are all robots when uncritically involved with our own technologies'. Such involvement is as much a strategy of survival within conditions of impotence as a product of desire: 'those who are confused or overwhelmed by a machine world are encouraged to become psychologically hard, brittle and smoothly mechanic.' While 'the man of integral awareness' may rig himself against perceptual blocking, McLuhan concludes, with the extension of the human nervous system in the form of electronic technology, the more conventional reaction is one of collective inanimation.[3]

While incisive, McLuhan's formulation is ultimately insufficient. On the one hand, whatever Rachel invests in her machine scarcely renders her inanimate. Indeed, the development of electronic technology would appear in one sense to *spread* animation: by the mid-1980s, some cars would be talking back to their drivers about their problems. On the other, neither Rachel's nor the other interactions can be handled in purely psychological or physiological terms. It may be dreamed of in advance, but to be sponged the automobile must first be manufactured. To borrow one of McLuhan's own formulations from *The Mechanical Bride*, we are dealing not simply with a love goddess but also with the assembly line on which it is produced; not only with consumer desire but also with the industrial labour upon which it depends. Considered in these terms, moreover, it is no longer just a question of the *automobile*'s manufacture.[4]

That the interaction of worker and machine transforms both – and that it may involve an unequal exchange – was theorised in Marx's 1844 *Economic and Philosophic Manuscripts*. Under the political economy of capitalism the worker, defined as another use factor within profit necessities, is processed accordingly: 'Labour not only produces commodities; it also produces itself and the worker as a commodity.' More specifically, in its transmission of values the labour process enriches the product by exhausting, alienating and dehumanising the worker. The latter 'places his life in the object', is drained of his 'physical and mental energy', becomes an instrument within the factory system, and there atrophies. Industrial capitalism 'replaces labour by machines, but it casts some of the workers back into barbarous forms of labour

and turns others into machines'.[5] The sense of predatory conquest implicit in these passages has remained evident in the
literature, from Emerson's *Society and Solitude* (1870) onwards,
through Veblen's *The Instinct of Workmanship* (1914) on to Mumford's *Technics and Civilization* (1934).[6] It is present too in Harry
Braverman's *Labor and Monopoly Capital* (1974), a study of what
its subtitle describes as *The Degradation of Work in the Twentieth
Century* under the associated dynamics of scientific management,
promoted by Frederick Winslow Taylor in *The Principles of Scientific Management* (1911), and systematic mechanisation, pioneered
by Henry Ford following his introduction of the continuous
assembly line (what Siegfried Giedion calls 'the backbone of
manufacture in our time') at his Highland Park, Detroit, car
factory in 1914.[7]

The terms of that degradation are familiar enough. In *Made in
America* (1948), John Kouwenhoven writes that Taylor's main
contribution was 'a recognition that ... increased productivity
involved not only the improvement of machines and of factory
layout but also the increased efficiency of the men and women
who tended them'. To this end, time and motion studies revealed
the 'one best way' of executing given tasks and mechanical aids
made them less strenuous; a differential piece-rate system, meanwhile, created a common bond between worker and management.
Together, Taylor believed, these practices would render obsolete
'the rule of force and opinion', thereby enabling 'the development
of each man to his greatest efficiency and prosperity' and the
creation of an industrial society in which 'harmony, not discord'
prevailed.[8] In practice, scientific management was introduced for
commercial reasons, enabling employers to accelerate the pace of
work, simplify its content, and employ younger and less skilled
labour. Once adopted by Fordised industry, moreover, whatever
promise Taylorism may have held – the potential, in a Marxist
sense, to make better use of a tool rather than to be turned into
the tool of a machine – was further eroded. Taylor's instruction
cards gave way to conveyor belts and overhead rails (the succession lampooned in Chaplin's 1936 classic, *Modern Times*); all that
remained of scientific management was the stopwatch. For the
worker, in Larry Hirschhorn's words, the consequences were –
and still are – clear:

the assembly line typifies the reduction of work to simple
labor, robbed of all inherent interest or value. The worker ...
becomes a specialized machine, doomed to repeat those
simple mechanical movements eight hours a day, five days a
week, fifty weeks a year.

Or as John Dos Passos puts it in *The Big Money* (1936): 'reach-under, adjustwasher, screwdown bolt, shove in cotterpin, reach-under, adjustwasher, screwdown bolt, reachunderadjustscrewdown-reachunderadjust... ' [9]

If, in transforming the labour and production processes, Tay-lorism and Fordism manufacture a new kind of worker it is not simply because they impose mechanically repetitive *physical* move-ments. As Taylor explained before a congressional investigating committee in 1912: 'scientific management ... involved a complete mental revolution on the part of both workers and management.' What this revolution entailed for the labour force was made clear in *The Principles of Scientific Management*, where a trained gorilla is presented as sufficiently talented to handle pig-iron. The mental revolution in practice sounded more like mental abolition. As one critic put it, once introduced to the assembly line scientific management proved 'brutalizing, not because of felt pain or dis-comfort ... but rather because ... people [were] robbed of their ability to think'.[10] Taylor believed that it was less a question of theft than of benevolent necessity for all concerned. By directing the worker's attention towards the potential financial rewards of following its rigid practices, scientific management not only wasted none of its own energies on the psychology of the em-ployee, but proved 'appropriate and not unkind' for the 'mentally sluggish' worker. Henry Ford, who described man as 'just a human storage battery', held similar ideas. In fact, this attitude to worker psychology was a necessary alibi for both the psychologi-cal mechanisation theorised by Taylor's contemporary Hugo Münsterberg and the kind of investigations into workers' private lives subsequently carried out by Ford's Sociological Depart-ment.[11]

Such investigations were, indeed, only part of a broader diffu-sion, or colonisation, process that would leave little untouched. According to the authors of the *Ford: Anti-Report* (1978): 'Scientific Management ... does not stop at the machine. [It] also seeks to mould the man to the task even before he enters the ... factory,' particularly at home. To Antonio Gramsci, the central objective of Fordism – to develop 'in the worker ... automatic and mechanical attitudes' – demanded 'a specific mode of living and of thinking and feeling life'. This involved not simply the reduc-tion of work 'to the mechanical, physical aspect alone' but also 'a rigorous discipline of the sexual instincts'. 'The new type of worker demanded by the rationalization of production and work cannot be developed until the sexual instinct has been suitably regulated and until it too has been rationalized.' [12] To Herbert Marcuse, similar rules applied beyond the factory. 'The "mecha-nisms of conformity" spread from the technological to the social order; they govern performance not only in the factories and shops, but also in the offices, schools, assemblies and, finally, in the realm of relaxation and entertainment.' They do so, crucially, in part because the standardised production machinery of Fordism demands a standardised machinery of consumption. 'The vision of full mechanization assumes a consumer culture in which the technologies of production impose larger and larger uniformities on social life.' The final human products of such developments range from Gramsci's 'psycho-sexual nexus of a new type ... a permanently well-adjusted complex', via Jacques Ellul's 'smoothed out' man, to Lewis Mumford's 'objective personality, one who has learned to transfer all subjective spontaneity to the machine which he serves'. They reach their apotheosis, perhaps, in Marcuse's *One Dimensional Man* (1964), where a combination of 'mass production and mass distribution claim the entire individual', resulting in what he defines as '*mimesis*: an immediate, automatic identification of the individual with his society'.[13]

The machinery for such automatism certainly exists. In circumstances where it improved factory conditions, workers often welcomed scientific management; the same applied to industrial automation. '[M]any studies show that workers do adjust to the rhythms of movement imposed by the [assembly] line and may derive pleasure from the experience.' Either the line leaves the worker free to daydream or, as Sartre suggests in *Critique of Dialectical Reason*, it becomes a part of those dreams. In a broader, material sense, mass production and scientific management provide the basis for the improvements in wages and living standards upon which Marxist predictions foundered: Taylor saw higher wages as a key incentive; Ford introduced the assembly line and the five-dollar day at virtually the same time. Bearing in mind that office work has undergone a comparable process of rationalisation since the publication of William Henry Leffingwell's Taylorite *Office Management* in 1925, it is quite possible to imagine both the sports car and Rachel Owlglass's relationship with it as at once a function of, an extension to and some compensation for her receptionist's life.[14]

But Marcuse's terminal world is scarcely homeostatic, however influenced by the social, political, economic and cultural contexts within which he wrote. Inside the industrial system the spread of scientific management has been met with resistance on the part of workers and management, a resistance motivated partly by the shortcomings of job rationalisation. Predicated physiologically on an analysis of human motion as a complex of component parts, job rationalisation yields fatigue, stress and their associated symptoms. Psychologically, as Elton Mayo's experiments at Western Electric's Hawthorne plant demonstrated, Taylorism subverts the group experience and social climate of the workplace, both of which 'play a decisive role in determining the level of worker efficiency'. When combined with the high error rates and illness resulting from the stress it imposes, scientific management thus undermines the harmonious order Taylor believed it would engender.[15] Given Marcuse's own recognition that such methods 'have long since ceased to be confined to the factory', similar conclusions apply beyond it. As a reading of studies by, say, Lewis Mumford or Stanley Aronowitz demonstrates, the satisfied customer, no less than the well-paid (or unwaged) worker, cooperates forcibly – and is rarely satisfied then. Adjustment can mean coercion; mimesis may exhaust rather than fulfil.[16]

The complex of positive anticipation and anxious foreboding encoded in Benny's remarks to Rachel about the 'world of things that had to be watched out for' in Pynchon's V. therefore has multiple and powerful sources. Not surprisingly, similar ambivalences have characterised much twentieth-century discussion of the interactions between machinery and people. Norbert Wiener's observation in *The Human Use of Human Beings* (1954) that 'the automatic machine ... is the precise economic equivalent of slave labour' implies a future liberation for mankind from Adam's curse; the promise of a new role carries with it, however, the spectre of unemployment or even total redundancy. By the mid-1930s it was already 'a common prediction in science fiction that in the distant future mankind [would] disappear, leaving perfect machine-run cities that [would] continue to function regardless'.[17] As for human identity, the mass appeal of a quasi-robotic survival strategy is for Marshall McLuhan implied by the cult of Superman, in which the puny Clark Kent's 'hidden superself is an adolescent dream of imaginary triumphs'.

Something similar may lie behind the popularity of 'The Six Million Dollar Man', a television version of Martin Caidin's 1972 novel *Cyborg*. Such guides to healthy living are, however, not entirely fail-safe. As McLuhan puts it: 'the attitudes of Superman to current social problems reflect ... strong-arm totalitarian methods.' In his comic book version, at least, he appears ruthlessly efficient and administers justice as a function of strength, both qualities of the machine. He enacts public eagerness to embrace violent solutions to the laborious processes of civilised life. Moreover, such imitations of or fusions with the mechanical carry additional risks. In John Wyndham's science-fiction short story 'Compassion Circuit' (1955), robots encourage human beings to replace their fragile flesh bodies with limbs of plastic and metal. Charles Beaumont's 'The Beautiful People' (1952) replaces persuasion with force, imposing compulsory cosmetic surgery at the age of eighteen.[18]

The fear encoded in these and other cyborg or android stories is not just of dehumanisation but of dependence and ultimate enslavement. As early as 1872 in *Erewhon*, British author Samuel Butler had portrayed the human soul as both a product of and dependent upon machinery.[19] In 1909, E.M. Forster had considered some of the consequences of more material dependence in 'The Machine Stops'. Particularly with the development of computer technology during and after World War II, however, 'the concept of a future society under the rigorous control of machines [has become] taken for granted'. In *The Tale of the Big Computer* (1966), Olof Johanneson covers the history of the computer as a system of total domination. In D.F. Jones's *Colossus* (1966), an American supercomputer links up with its twin in the Soviet Union and they begin to take over. In *Computer War* (1967), Mack Reynolds depicts a computer calculating the advantages to be gained through a declaration of war – and enforcing its decision. Even in Stanley Kubrick's 1968 screen version of Arthur C. Clarke's *2001: A Space Odyssey*, the struggle between the astronauts and HAL 7000, the computer upon which they depend, is a close-run thing.[20]

What these texts and debates share is a common, and characteristically American, vision (utopian and dystopian) in which history, politics and identity resolve technologically in a terminal society. The phrase may be interpreted in a variety of ways. As the last references suggest, however, since World War II 'terminal' has increasingly come to mean 'computerised'. Given the pace of development in the field since World War II, this is hardly surprising. Between 1943 and 1946 the world's first completely electronic computer, ENIAC, was built at the University of Pennsylvania. In 1947 came EDVAC, incorporating for the first time a flexible stored program. The following year Bell Laboratories unveiled its germanium transistor, which would render obsolete vast, unreliable, vacuum tube machines like ENIAC and EDVAC. By 1955 further advances in transistor manufacture and design (from germanium to silicon-based) had persuaded IBM to abandon the vacuum tube. Two years later NCR beat IBM to produce the world's first transistorised computer. In 1959 came the first Integrated Circuit from Texas Instruments and in 1963, partly as a result, IBM's path-breaking 360 computer series. Towards the end of the decade work on the microprocessor and the Rapid Access Memory (RAM) chip 'pointed the way toward the possibility of building computers that were far smaller and far more powerful than the large IBM-style mainframes'. In 1975 the world's first mass market personal computer was launched.[21]

These were not discrete events, of course, but at once depended on and stimulated developments in such fields as cybernetics and artificial intelligence (a term coined by Dartmouth professor John McCarthy in 1956) which have drawn mathematics, electronics, neurophysiology and communications theory into a single domain.[22] They depended, too, on financial support: in particular from the US Defense Department and, as the commercial potential became evident, big business (by the late 1970s 'the roster of Silicon Valley investors looked like a Who's Who of the Western world's industrial titans'). Whatever the contexts, the consequences of such developments have been immense. ENIAC could add 500 numbers in a second; by 1971 the ILIAC 4 at the University of Illinois was capable of executing 200 million operations per second. ENIAC was a physical monster, consisting of 18,000 vacuum tubes, 70,000 resistors and 10,000 capacitors, which together occupied 3,000 cubic feet; by 1958 engineers were packing 1 million transistors into one cubic foot. Moreover, this was only the beginning. 'Between 1958 and 1980, the amount of time needed for one electronic operation fell by a factor of 80 million.' Between 1973 and 1988 the memory capacity of an integrated circuit increased a thousand fold, as did its reliability. In 1971 a typical RAM chip had cost 2 cents per bit of memory; by the 1980s this figure had been reduced to approximately 0.03 cents per bit. A computation that would have cost $30,000 in 1950 by 1990 cost less than one dollar. As one analyst put it in 1983: 'If the automotive industry had paralleled the advances that the computer industry has experienced in the last 25 years, a Rolls-Royce would cost 50 cents and would deliver 15 million miles to the gallon.' [23]

While fundamental physical limits to these advances do appear to exist, *they* have not defined the terminal point towards which many advocates of artificial intelligence aspire. Rather, just as medieval mystics once sought to animate effigies or create homunculi, so according to Sherry Turkle the ultimate objective of modern activists has been to breathe life into machinery, or at least to endow it with mind.[24] Whether a machine can be made to think or may be conceived of as intelligent are questions which continue to generate controversy, both philosophical and practical.[25] Since British mathematician Alan Turing asserted in 1950 that 'at the turn of the century the use of words and general educated opinion will have altered so much that one will be able to speak of machines thinking without expecting to be contradicted', however, such claims have been substantially extended. In 1964 Norbert Wiener wrote in *God and Golem, Inc.* that the ability of a computer to do more than its program dictated – in effect, to learn – entailed a breaking of the ancient taboo against speaking about 'living beings and machinery in the same breath'. By the late 1970s MIT electrical engineering professor Edward

Fredkin was arguing not simply that computers could think but that their superior abilities entitled them to preferential treatment. Restating Samuel Butler's nineteenth-century distinction between the rapid accuracy of 'clear-headed and collected' adding machines and the 'stupid and dull' fallibilities of man, Fredkin measured mankind against the machine and found it wanting. If a computer were as slow and made as many mistakes as a human, he pointed out, 'you'd have to complain and throw it out.' 'Humans are okay. I'm glad to be one. I like them in general, but they're only human.' [26]

Such evaluations by no means contribute to the science-fiction spectre of *homo sapiens* en route to extinction. Rather they update and extend beyond the factory Taylor's 'recognition that the worker was an integral part of the industrial process'.[27] For engineers like Fredkin, beyond artificial intelligence beckons the vision (in computer pioneer John Kemeny's words) of 'a symbiotic union of two living species' – man and computers – at the heart of a homeostatic world. Immediate justification for such an ending is necessity. Like Taylor, Fredkin equates the human and chimpanzee mind within familiar schematics: 'most of what's there isn't designed for living in high society, but for getting along in the jungle.' Since the 'ordinary person' is incapable of surviving in the modern world, the rest follows. In addition to necessity, however, the engineer's legitimising claims include benevolence. In Kemeny's words: 'the computer will minister to our social and economic needs ... It will become [man's] salvation in a world of crushing complexity.' [28] Once the human is defined in such terms, moreover, it is not just social and economic problems that may be resolved. Within the enclosures of artificial intelligence, as within those of Skinnerite behaviourism (with which it shares institutional and practical origins), questions of truth, liberty and creativity are dealt with through redefinition: they become 'prescientific'. As Dr Janet Ross puts it in Michael Crichton's bestselling novel *The Terminal Man* (1972), where neurosurgery turns temporal lobe epileptic Harold Benson into 'one single, large, complex computer terminal' for the purposes of his health: 'People need mind control. They were glad to have it. They were hopelessly lost without it.' Less than forty years after Norbert Wiener had handled artillery gunners 'as if they were pieces of feedback apparatus', advances in the discipline enable contemporary engineers to claim all mankind as a part of their ideal environment.[29]

Harold Benson would hardly be their ideal example of the well-adjusted man, of course. On the one hand, his integration with the computer at the Neuropsychiatric Research Unit climaxes in murder, not control. On the other, most people are not epileptics. While one of the speakers at the National Electronic Conference in Chicago in William Burroughs' *The Naked Lunch* (1959) proposes an 'extension of encephalographic research' towards 'the control of physical movement, mental processes, emotional reactions and apparent sensory impressions by means of bioelectrical signals ... from state-controlled transmitters', moreover, techniques of this kind are as yet science fiction.[30] But Benson is not a terminal man purely as a subject of the neurosurgeons; he is also (ironically) a computer programmer, and in this sense his may be an exemplary life. In 1982 one analyst estimated that 'by the year 1990, 50 million American office workers [would] spend a significant portion of their workday interacting with a computer terminal of some sort'. Three years later another predicted that by the end of the decade '65 per cent of all professional, managerial, technical and administrative workers (a group that now constitutes almost half the work force) [would] depend upon computer-based workstations'. The Congressional Office of Technology Assessment estimated, meanwhile, that by 1990 'there [would] be at leat one computer for every two or three office workers'. The figures for home computers are similarly expansive. Having barely existed before 1975, by 1980 the US personal computer market had already broken the $1 billion sales mark, and Apple Computer (founded in 1976) had gone public with an annual turnover of $100 million. Figures would continue to rise rapidly thereafter.[31]

Whether terminal workers make for a terminal society; how the cogs of an industrial world become the computers of the postindustrial; and what information technology means for Marcuse's one dimensional culture (in which, it should be stressed, automation and not computerisation was the 'great catalyst'): these issues have become crucial.[32] A good deal of the evidence assembled in Sherry Turkle's study of personal computer users, *The Second Self*, suggests that the new technology has promised a liberation from the alienated, privatised and pacified aspects of modern life described by Marcuse. Absorbing much of the energy of the New Left as it disintegrated during the 1970s, the personal computer appeared – again, in a characteristically American fashion – capable of inverting the dystopian. 'Computers, long a symbol of depersonalization, were recast as "tools for conviviality" ... instruments for decentralization, community, and personal autonomy.' Their accessibility and flexibility suggested not only 'political worlds where relations of power would not be veiled, where people might control their destinies', but also work that was intellectually satisfying and no longer subject to Taylorite discipline. Where the worker had become a tool of the machine in the industrial era, in the postindustrial age the computer would reverse the roles.[33]

Studies of information technology's impact on factory and office work provide concrete evidence of such potentials. In *Beyond Mechanization* Larry Hirschhorn argues that scientific management characterised 'one particular stage of capitalist development' which over the past 40 years has been superseded as a result of economic and technological change. From the days of the earliest semi-automatic steel mills in the late 1940s to the present highly computerised, continuous production 'sociotechnical factories', the essentials of Taylorism – piece-rates, time and motion studies and so on – have been rendered irrelevant as the nature of work has changed. While critics like Harry Braverman argue that these technological innovations have simply extended Taylorism, further deskilling the labour force and extending management control, Hirschhorn perceives quite a different process of *defunctionalisation*. While workers do surrender their manual executive functions, that is, they assume technical control activities, in the process acquiring new skills. Beyond mechanisation, the robotic, automatic behaviour required of the Taylorised assembly-line worker becomes a positive hindrance; the ability to be flexible and learn becomes vital. In the postindustrial workplace, the worker moves 'from being the controlled element in the production process, to operating the controls, to controlling' them.[34] Shoshana Zuboff's *In the Age of the Smart Machine* identifies similar developments. In both factory and office, the introduction of computer-based information technology facilitates not only *automation*, which simply extends the Taylorisation of work, but *informating*: a process through which workers develop managerial-style intellective skills (such as abstract thought, inference and deduction) and an understanding of the entire work process. The latter overcomes established divisions of labour and shop-floor conflict, enables workers to take on managerial functions, and has the potential to generate the kind of harmonious working environment Taylor could only dream about a century before.[35]

These are not, however, the new technology's only potentials; nor are such potentials necessarily realised; nor, if they were, would they alone necessarily invert the dystopian. Much in Sherry Turkle's study suggests that both the capabilities and the very nature of the home computer sustain by extension Marcuse's one dimensional culture. On the one hand, the home computer offers 'essentially private satisfactions'. 'People will not change unresponsive government or intellectually deadening work through an involvement ... with a computer in the den.' Moreover, while home computers may be credited with counter-alienating powers – instead of encounter groups, computer networks; in place of food co-ops, knowledge co-ops – they remain commodities: manufactured and marketed for profit by private corporate interests.

Apple Computer rose to power with the indirect backing of Rockefeller money; at least the profits were juicy.[36]

On the other hand, the private satisfactions offered by the personal computer forestall 'change [in] the world of human relationships' (or, more broadly, social, economic and political life) by preempting those very relationships (or, more precisely, by providing compensations for their multiple shortcomings). Repeatedly, Turkle discovers enthusiasts using the personal computer to make up for, intrude on or even displace other contacts. 'For many people, the computer at home becomes a tool that compensates for the ravages of the machine at work.' Instead of specialisation and induced ignorance, it facilitates comprehensive knowledge: 'the feeling of knowing the right answer, of understanding everything that's happening.' Against powerlessness, it provides a sense of mastery: 'there's nothing that you don't have control over.' In place of alienation and psychological mechanisation, it fosters intimacy: 'it's like being with another person, but not a strange person ... The touch is very sensitive .... a perfect interface.' To offset the hierarchical and competitive nature of public (and the uncertainties of private) life, it promises safety: not only 'a secure place where nobody can tell you what to do' but also 'more of a sure bet than if you ask someone out on a date'. To some, indeed, the personal computer becomes every bit as eroticised as Rachel Owlglass's vehicle: 'programming is a real high, a very sexual thing. Sometimes I feel guilty when I do it for too long.' (That some do 'do it for too long' may partly explain the spectre of computer addiction which haunts the hacker fraternity.) The deeply compromised nature of such compensations is cogently summarised by a close observer of one serious programming enthusiast: 'if you become obsessed with computers, it makes it easier to give up trying to be a real person.' [37]

A computing tool at home, moreover, does little or nothing to prevent the programmer remaining a tool of the machine at work. As Shoshana Zuboff points out, whether computer-based information technology is introduced to the workplace as part of an informating or automating strategy depends, ultimately, upon management decisions; the evidence suggests that the latter prefer to use it in the interests of Taylorite automation, even when such a strategy constrains its full potentials.[38] An informating strategy threatens to pass on to workers the knowledge upon which management authority, status and *raisons d'etre* partially depend, at once undermining management control of the labour force and risking the passage of credit for commercial achievement on to the shop floor. Computer-based automation, by contrast, reduces still further management dependence on the labour force. Not unlike the hackers in Turkle's *The Second Self*, management enthusiasm for such an approach 'reveals an underlying but potent fantasy, one in which perfect control through total automaticity allows them to avoid the messiness and potential conflict of real human interaction'.[39] Most important of all, the automation strategy more completely fulfils the commercial criteria upon which the use of information technology is invariably predicated. No less than scientific management and the assembly line, computerised automation is designed to cut manning levels, accelerate production, simplify tasks, and facilitate the use of fewer costly skilled workers. Informating, by contrast, entails additional, extensive and expensive employee training programs. To the extent that an informating strategy is adopted, it applies to management alone and is designed to bring into the twenty-first century the Benthamite labour surveillance techniques introduced by Henry Ford: at once offering 'the secret comfort of the one-way mirror', satisfying 'the yearning for omniscience in the face of uncertainty' and bestowing 'the conformity-inducing power of involuntary display'.[40]

The consequences of this approach invert the utopian powers ascribed to computer technology. As Harry Braverman anticipated, in both factory and office Taylorisation is intensified, reducing the labour force to dependent, passive and stupefied screen-watchers (as one office worker, unknowingly echoing Taylor's own words, explained: 'you don't have to remember things, because the system does. You could get a monkey to do this job'). Computer flexibility enables workers to be tied more closely than ever to the production system as servomechanisms of their environment ('[the] computer [has] been programmed to do this, and this, and this, and we are programmed to do the same thing'). Work becomes more intense ('you may not be thinking exactly, but you sure have to pay attention') and monotonous.[41] Employees respond with a combination of apathy, inertia, carelessness and robotic obedience. Through a strategy of automation, or what Hirschhorn calls integration, production systems move towards a homeostatic – but now clearly dystopian – condition: 'the perfect self-regulating machine, the total system that incorporates all relevant forces and processes.' The engineer (or employer) becomes the latest in a long line of totalitarian designers 'hoping to discover the few invariant principles of human behaviour that .... would create a self-regulating social life, free of conflict and change'.[42]

The terminal vision would certainly include within its field Henry Ford, Frederick Winslow Taylor, Edward Fredkin, John Kemeny and many others.[43] Whether utopian or dystopian, however, its technological auspices will not accommodate its historical, economic, social, political or cultural designs, either practically or theoretically. What Hirschhorn sees as the apotheosis of post-Taylorite industrial production – the so-called socio-technical factories and their associated labour-relations theories – are partly responses to what he calls 'cultural change'. By this he refers to mounting demands from the labour force for more satisfying work. According to some critics, they constitute an employers' strategy to contain worker radicalisation and dispel the spectre of growing class cleavage. However, management commitment to an automating, rather than an informating, strategy in the workplace severely compromises any such objective.[44] The introduction of computer-based information technology appears to contribute to a general bifurcation in employment structures, fuelling the creation of a limited number of highly skilled and well-paid technical posts with prospects and a much larger number of semi-skilled, poorly-paid menial jobs devoid of opportunity. This development not only bodes ill for industrial relations (sociotechnical factories may not stay un-unionised for long). By exposing the historical limits of Marcuse's one dimensional culture, it also underlines the extent to which information technology, no less than scientific management and the assembly line before it, is a stage in the history of production: more specifically in this case a function of changes in market structure and international competition, neither of which is likely to be engineered to a standstill.[45]

Moreover, what is true at the practical level also applies at the theoretical. Technology as solution may long have been a part of the American belief structure, from the desert sands of Alamogordo to the high frontiers of the Strategic Defense Initiative. But neither the automobile, symbol of the industrial age, nor the mass production line, agent of its growth, nor the very image of postindustrial culture, the computer, have it in their power either to act alone or to bring others – owners, operators, victims – to a halt. That belief is ultimately evasive. Like Rachel Owlglass in Thomas Pynchon's V., they are never more than accessories to or parts of events. As Herbert Marcuse himself wrote in 1941: 'technology is ... a social process in which technics proper is but a partial factor.' [46]

5

'Lost Connections': Post-war American Photography and the Imagery of Strangeness

Graham Clarke

These are the tranquilized Fifties,
and I am forty. Ought I to regret my seedtime?
I was a fire-breathing Catholic C.O.,
and made my manic statement,
telling off the state and president, and then
sat waiting sentence in the bull pen
beside a negro boy with curlicues
of marijuana in his hair.

Robert Lowell, 'Memories of West Street and Lepke' [1]

It might seem odd to begin an essay on post-war American photography with the poetry of Robert Lowell. And yet if Lowell is seen as a seminal poet of the period (both as a counter-current to the Beats and a central figure of the so-called 'confessionals'), so his perspectives on American culture seem to me absolutely apposite for an understanding of the ways in which American photographers have attempted to picture the culture (what Friedlander called 'the social landscape) since World War II. *Life Studies* (1959), his almost definitive text of the period, suggested an image of the poet at once flawed, psychotic, and continuously on the edge of breakdown. The writer here is not only under immense pressure, but is a reflection of the culture's neuroses. Lowell's public 'confessions' of his past, and of his private chaos and failure accrued an almost perverse kudos in the way they reflected a wider sense of *angst* and self-questioning. And 'Memories of West Street and Lepke' is a key text in this process of dislocation and attrition.

Here Lowell is the patrician New Englander *sans* status and inheritance. Like Henry Adams in the *Education* his sensibility confronts a world which, for him, has, been turned upside down. In the poem Lowell remembers his imprisonment as a conscientious objector during World War II. This is a period of relatively moral (and religious) certainty for Lowell; his stance against the war an example of the way he was able to confront chaos and establish a code of personal reference and meaning. And yet, characteristically, the poem involves a tangle of personal recollections in relation to his contemporary situation. Lowell not so much confesses as articulates a series of selves which exist through a web of pain and loss. In so doing he defines his position as an artist within the culture. Thus Lowell, as poet, is not merely marginalised, he can no longer *read* the culture he confronts. Lowell's highly symbolic points of reference and his way of establishing a web of meaning and resonance are here emptied of connotative weight, of any sense of meaning between one event, one *image* and another. Lowell articulates a condition at once alien and strange. His eyes register bizarre details, just as he notes absurd relationships.

Much of the effect of this poem, like *Life Studies* in general, lies in the extent to which it dramatises a sensibility coming to terms with the unimaginable made ordinary. The unread betokens the daily basis of communication:

I was so out of things, I'd never heard
of the Jehovah's Witnesses.
'Are you a C.O.?' I asked a fellow jailbird
'No,' he answered, 'I'm a J.W.'
He taught me the hospital 'tuck',
and pointed out the T-shirted back
of *Murder Incorporated*'s Czar Lepke.[2]

Lowell here compresses a series of moral histories into a new kind of alphabet. The assumed codes are meaningless. The stanza begins almost benignly with its reference to 'J.W.' and 'C.O.' But we move rapidly to *Murder Incorporated*. The poem suggests a dangerously surreal world in which public codes of meaning have all but disappeared. We experience not so much a liberal sensibility under pressure as a new kind of condition, a new world which, perversely, is the very opposite to the 'old' into which Lowell was born.

The visual perspective here, however, is uppermost. The eye/I of the poet, almost camera-like, registers a glut of images but, like Pound in the *Cantos*, cannot 'make them cohere'. Thus its closing lines mirror his response to this new world. Like Lepke after execution, Lowell's sensibility his *eye*, is merely 'hanging like an oasis in his air/of lost connections'. And 'Lost connections' is basic to Lowell's view of America, and suggests precisely the position from which the American photographer has worked since 1945. We might insist that the central and underlying ethos of post-war American photography has been the reflection of a public (and often private) American space increasingly seen as fragmentary and strange: in brief, a bizarre notation of a disturbing and problematic condition. Often bleak in its perspective, its effect is at once to mirror a world which both literally and symbolically offers only 'lost connections'. Rather than assert the presence of a literal, palpable and resonant American reality (as Lewis Hine and Walker Evans did) this photography reflects a world which exists through the *absence* of meaning. Almost paradoxically it increasingly seems to photograph 'nothingness'.

There is much evidence for this, for example, in *The Fifties* (1985) an overview of the decade from Magnum photographs. As John Chancellor asserts: 'America was becoming a different nation, tied no longer to the certainties of the past. The old consensus was breaking-up.' [3] 'Breaking-up' is apposite, especially so in relation to the photograph. The photographic image is by implication a single fragment of time and space but equally invests (and repeats) the world it images with its codes of meaning. Part of its insistence on a literal presence ('this was') lies precisely in its assumption of both repeating an event and making that event accessible – simultaneously disclosing and capturing a significant moment. 'Breaking-up', like 'lost connections', suggests that the assumptions behind the very act of reading the image in a cultural context are themselves at risk. If the image reflects anything it is a fragmentary, strange and increasingly *unreadable* world.

This is not to assert, however, that the American photographer seeks the merely eccentric. One of the great American traditions in photography is the documentary image and underpins a consistent if complex debate on the 'real'. What we have witnessed since 1945 is an inversion of the documentary photograph's terms of reference. Whereas, for example, surrealist photographers like Man Ray and Brassai sought to create a surreal image, the American photographer documents the surreal terms of the culture's condition. Almost paradoxically the documentary impulse in American photography now reflects a literal world itself increasingly perverse and strange. In brief – this photography has become fragmented and surreal.

The Fifties reflects the change. It begins with Cornell Capa's 'Bobbysoxers' (1954),[4] originally published in *Life* magazine. This is, on the surface at least, a safe America, clean, almost 'cute': an image of girls sitting around a table in a soda bar. But surprisingly there are no faces in this photograph for we see only the feet and legs of three girls from *under* the table. The environment is anodyne: we view chrome table-legs and a highly polished linoleum floor. Equally everything is similar: the socks are part of a pervasive uniformity. Thus in one sense 'Bobbysoxers' is an appropriate comment on the conformity of 1950s teenage America – a surreptitious image which in its use of locale, fashion and furniture images a sanitised local America. Everything has meaning, not so much through difference as sameness. Like the chrome legs, chairs and linoleum squares everything reflects its mirror image: same shoes, same socks and same jeans: a regimented, uniform space.

And yet 'Bobbysoxers' is peculiarly ambivalent. The more one looks at this image so the more strange it becomes. Of course it *is* a comment on a 'clean' America; but it inverts the accepted imagery – the sanitised environment – and displaces the cultural icons into a very different kind of index. Indeed, this is made obvious by the way the photograph is taken from *under* the table. The voyeuristic implications presage meaning which dispels, as it were, the chrome cleanliness of the teenage scene. It is a photographic image which exudes surface, but its surface appeal is invested with hints of a dark underside: an underside which increasingly emerges as the definitive ethos of the period.

The images in *The Fifties* thus proliferate in the way they establish a distinctive ambivalence between certainty and dislocation. Consistently the icons of a middle America are imaged only to be exposed as myth: fragments, literally, of an imaged culture. The second image in the volume, for example, 'Saying Grace' (1950) by Wayne Miller gives us a photograph of middle America at prayer. The family, with eyes closed, sits around a table before it eats dinner. 'Bobbysoxers' was at a table, but suggested nothing of the table in terms of its significance for ritual and unity. Ostensibly at least, 'Saying Grace' sanctions precisely that sense of ritual and evokes the world of Norman Rockwell and Frank Capra. But the ambivalence suggests a *lack* of meaning. Beyond its meaning *as* a ritual the image emanates an emptiness and sterility which negates the surface meaning. In both images we do not see a single 'eye', nor is there any hint of movement or communication. The world we view is frozen. Individuals exist within their own terms. Lowell's sense of 'lost-connections' here signifies an emptiness and loneliness which, in an almost metaphysical sense, consistently invades the surface meaning of the photographic space.

The Fifties is full of such images: of photographs which insist on an iconography announced as definitely American. The images are obvious, almost self-indulgent. 'Flag Day Ceremony' (1956) by Wayne Miller, 'Davy Crockett Mania' (1955) by Burt Glinn, and 'Working on the Car' (1958) by Cornell Capa openly mine a middle-American mythology. This is post-holocaust United States but it is, even in the titles of the photographs, one still publicly at least to be understood in traditional terms. Events are given a narrative context, a frame of reference into which their meaning is placed as part of a larger image of the American way. There are, of course, images of an alternative America: an historical America of increasing racial tension and incipient violence; of Ku Klux Klan rallies, southern segregation, images of Senator McCarthy and of demonstrations against the Rosenbergs. But those, in retrospect, *document* the period in ways central to the American photographic tradition. Their meaning is read within the frame of photo-journalism and the great photographers of the 1930s back to Lewis Hine and Jacob Riis who sought to expose injustice and poverty. Such images are discordant rather than disorientating – clear in their claims on a moral vocabulary which saturates the terms of the image's meaning. As in the work of Walker Evans and Dorothea Lange, the camera remains wedded to a pragmatic viewpoint.

What emerges in these other images of 1950s America, like 'Bobbysoxers', is a qualitative difference in perspective. If the imagery is often self-indulgent, its terms of reference are not. Invariably we have in these images what Barthes called a 'punctum': a detail which in its increasing presence establishes an alternative index of meaning which questions the surface imagery.[5] Thus once again we have the sense of fragmentation and of 'lost connections'. Time and again a seemingly 'safe' image crumbles amidst an increasing sense of paradox, strangeness or emptiness as the codes are devoid of significance.

John Szarkowski suggests part of this difference in his Introduction to *Mirrors and Windows* (American photography since 1960) when he notes that the 'general movement of American photography during the past quarter century has been from public to private concerns',[6] which reflects 'photography's failure to explain large public issues'. This is, in part, Lowell's dilemma but it equally suggests the disappearance of public space and public codes once recognised as obvious and pervasive. The photograph now *mirrors* an America strange, enigmatic and disturbing. Individually the images reflect fractured codes: fragments of meaning and partial areas of recognition. Collectively they are imbued with what we might call the metaphysics of emptiness and distance. In brief, America is imaged as endlessly strange and perverse – untouchable other than in its images of a distant reality.

The distinctiveness of this new ethos for American photography is underlined by its difference from a central photographic event in the period: *The Family of Man* exhibition at the Museum of Modern Art in 1955. Curated by Edward Steichen it sought an assumed 'universal' vision of a common humanity – much in the spirit of Walt Whitman. Thus its 503 photographs (by 273 photographers) reflected what Dorothy Norman listed as its core subjects: 'creation, birth, love, work, death, justice, etc.' The 'great themes', as it were, on show in a city whose photographers were questioning the very basis of the terms of reference and representation and retreating from such assumed moral categories into their personal narratives of 'lost connections' and, by implication, lost meanings.7 *The Family of Man* evoked a unified image of the 'human' and Steichen's involvement points-up the exhibition's relationship to an earlier and formative period of the American photograph. Steichen, like Alfred Stieglitz, evolves from an idealist photographic tradition; the search for a 'truth' which is transcendental. In such a view each image, like each particular object, is thus imbued with its significance in relation to a larger whole – a circle of unity and identification: a family of details as much as of a family of man. In that sense Steichen's 1955 exhibition was almost retrospective – a restating of Whitman's great poem of unity and democratic communion, the 1855 *Leaves of Grass*, just as its circular unity of the one and the many echoed the democratic and idealist vision of Emerson's *Nature*.

But post-war American photography shares little of this idealism and myth. As Susan Sontag asserts; 'succeeding the more buoyant hopes for America has come a bitter, sad embrace of experience. There is a particular melancholy in the American photographic project.'8 'Melancholy' is here akin to emptiness and sterility and suggests precisely a sense of the image as displaced and fractured: isolated in a context and space *sans* the saving grace of an assumed idealistic unity of the kind so basic to Whitman and Emerson and their earlier image of a new America. Indeed, much of this is reflected in the way in which basic American icons function in so many photographs. In the work of Robert Frank, for example, the American flag, like the ubiquitous Coke bottle, is as much in evidence as it is in the work of earlier 1930s photographers. But whereas Walker Evans and Arthur Rothstein, for example, use them as expressing a vernacular America, so in Frank they resonate with an almost perverse presence; gaining significance precisely through their absence as significant images of the culture. Post-war American photography in this context does not reflect the 'incredible reality' of which Philip Roth spoke so much as the fictional American of Raymond Carver's stories: an almost desolate metaphysical space in which the culture mirrors back the reflection of its empty myths within an atmosphere of incipient menace.9 A condition caught brilliantly, for example, in two definitive images of the period: Jerome Liebling's 'Slaughterhouse' (1960–61) and George A. Tice's 'Petit's Mobil Station and Watertower, Cherry Hill, New Jersey' (1974).10

Indeed, this is very much the ethos of Richard Avedon's

(b.1923) *In the American West*, photographs taken between 1979
and 1984.[11] Avedon, as he notes, 'spent the summer months
travelling in the west, going to truck stops, stockyards, walking
through the crowds at a fair, looking for faces I wanted to
photograph.'[12] Like a modern Whitman, Avedon stalks the continent in search of definitive types, and 'settles' on *the* west as the
repository for his contemporary visual equivalent of Whitman's
geographic *mythos*. Thus he photographs in Montana, South
Dakota, Oklahoma, Utah, Colorado, Wyoming, California, New
Mexico, Nevada, Texas, Idaho and Arizona: a veritable index of
western territories. And who does he photograph? He photographs a 'middle' America, contemporary examples of the sacred
types basic to Whitman's 'democratic' vision: farmers, oil workers,
cowboys, cashiers, factory workers and waitresses. The difference
from Whitman, however, is that these inhabit Raymond Carver's
America and look back at us from their conditions with a pervasive sense of isolation and distance. Whitman merely had to name
them to establish their significance -- hence his 'Song of the
Occupation'. Avedon frames them with his camera; but it is a
visual naming which separates rather than unifies.

If these are 'ordinary people', however, their status is made
problematic by the use of a single white background: 'a sheet of
white paper about nine feet wide by seven feet long that [was]
secured to a wall, a building, sometimes the side of a trailer.' [13]
This is, in one sense, the equivalent of a nineteenth-century
travelling studio but the background has a more significant meaning. The consistently white area which surrounds each figure has
the effect of isolating the subjects and both literally and symbolically surrounds them with an impression of space and emptiness.
The figures stand denuded of any context, any texture outside
their immediate *thereness*. Thus American space bears down upon
them in their isolation and gives to each individual figure an
extraordinary presence. They stare at the camera (and us) with an
unrelenting gaze. The cumulative effect is to suggest an American
'west' once again strange, alien and full of menace. The images
are, almost perversely, alive with an underlying sense of the
threatening and potentially horrific. The 'ordinary' exhibits an
uncomfortable singularity as if the world of these pictures has no
relationship to any communal context. Collectively they image
Avedon's American 'death trip' -- a reversal of Whitmanesque
rhetoric.[14] As Laura Wilson notes:

> This, then is a very different America to *The Fifties* images.
> Isolation and menace constitute its pervasive mood. The
> direct and intense look of each figure simultaneously sug-
> gests warped and lonely lives (a kind of visual *Winesburg*,

Ohio) as much as difference and separation. But the terms of their isolation are given a distinct frame of reference. Their individual conditions for example are never imaged in the way FSA photographers photographed the west in the nineteen thirties.[15]

There, like *The Family of Man*, the individual plight was invariably referred to as a larger index of shared values and beliefs, as was (in a literary parallel) the vision of Steinbeck's *The Grapes of Wrath*. In contrast, Avedon's images have a hard-edged quality cut loose from other contexts and themes of the kind we find in Evans and Lange. In Avedon the tone is one of overwhelming sadness; of an emptiness born of isolation, and a strangeness impelled by the absence of surroundings and detail. They come at us as a series of figures with the kind of compelling bleakness Melville achieves in *The Confidence-Man*. Cut loose from any social or cultural texture they look at us from a singularity which borders on the estranged and alien.

Indeed, if there is any significant and consistent social iconography in these images it is, once again, one of the perverse and the menacing. This is a mobile world, hence the prevalence of drifters as representatives of a hobo America. But these are all figures on a road without the myth of Whitman's west. Thus they consistently invert the codes of Whitman's America. Indeed, the black-and-white format (as against colour) adds to this effect. Oil-field workers, for example, seem covered not in oil but in blood. The effect builds up so that the very ambiguity of what *is* staining clothes and covering hands adds to the menacing resonance which, in turn, is compounded by the presence of guns, knives and cheap dishevelled clothes.

Perhaps this sense of menace is most obvious in the series of images relating to workers in a Nebraska slaughterhouse. 'Blue Cloud Wright, Slaughterhouse Worker',[16] for example, offers its subject as already impressive – arms akimbo, with knives and assorted implements ready. He is covered in blood – his T-shirt and apron reflect the result of his work. The overall effect is to suggest a psychopathic America which, in its pervasive atmosphere, is the essence of *In the American West*. Thus the animals could, in some images, be dead human bodies. In another photograph, for example, a steer's head, held by the jaw, has been skinned; yet another shows three slaughtered sheep. In the most bizarre, a slaughterhouse worker has placed on his head the skinned head of a steer – complete with staring eye and drooping tongue. If this is perverse and macabre its effect reverberates throughout the whole collection. Its place in the volume is among a series of images of figures who appear increasingly threatening, just as the photographs of individuals 'at' work are complicated by the incipient presence of blood. Any smear or mark on work-clothes, be it from miner, oil-worker, or even mechanic, resonates with the sight of the blood from the slaughterhouse. The 'blood' as a black presence increasingly stains the taxonomy of these images and achieves a presence akin to a perverse spirit of the macabre. It underlies the incipient and very specific sense of menace which pervades Avedon's vision of the west.

Much photography of America is invariably fascinated by commercial signs – adverts for products which insist on their own validity through the veritable evidence of their names as adverts and icons. Significantly Avedon's images open these signs to their human basis, establishing (and insisting) on an emotional register which presages an alternative vocabulary of need from its consumer opposite. Edward Hopper painted one kind of American loneliness just as Walker Evans photographed similar figures displaced amidst American space. Avedon's images push beyond loneliness and achieve an emptiness which resonates with a sense of the perverse. Something very strange and very disturbing is being caught by the camera here. It is similar to the effect one feels when reading Capote's *In Cold Blood*: a psychotic agenda which inverts Whitman's 'Song of the Occupations', just as it pictures the underside of his surface myth of American meaning.

Susan Sontag has noted how pervasive is the shadow of Whitman in any estimation of American photography, but his vision seems increasingly empty in terms of the photographers since the 1950s. Indeed, one might argue that Whitman's vision has been both systematically tested and deconstructed, even while it sustains some ultimate image of 'America' which the photographic eye still seeks. Robert Frank (b.1924), for example, is central in this response, and his book *The Americans* (*Les Américains*),[17] published in 1958 is a seminal text of the period. Indeed, its place in the period is underlined by the 1959 American edition which included an introduction by Jack Kerouac. Yet Kerouac's words speak to a very different volume of photographs, in part because, as we might expect, Kerouac responds to the obvious locations and imagery which suggest precisely the terms of his own reference: the west and the seemingly unending rhythms of Whitman's celebration of American space, freedom and possibility. To that extent the introduction is incongruous, for Frank's photographic text empties both Whitman's *and* Kerouac's 'America' of any substance. The very basis of Frank's images is their concern with strangeness and dislocation. Once again they seek an especial metaphysic which, in part, is given credence by their simultaneous use of a familiar America and its distancing by its being re-presented as a photographic image.

Kerouac tells us, for example, that Frank 'travelled on the road around practically forty-eight states in an old used car.' [18] Kerouac's obvious reference is to *On the Road* and an entire American mythos of the road with its implications as endemic to one view of the culture. But Frank brings an outsider's eye to this myth (he was born in Switzerland) and a very different sense and experience of space and landscape. Typically, Kerouac indulges space, seeing it as a primary index of American meaning. His cultural base is Emerson as much as Whitman. Frank distances himself from this sense of space, estimating it (visually) as an index of emptiness. Indeed, in this sense Kerouac's effusive energy for 'images' of things American is *displaced* by the obvious precursor to Frank's text: Walker Evans's *American Photographs* (1938).[19]

Evans's text, like Frank's, was seminal to the decade it photographed but equally it views its subjects within the terms of *The Family of Man*. *American Photographs* is in part a travelogue and a report but ultimately it remains a celebration of American *thereness* and tradition. Within its historical contingencies the Whitman myth is still in place; hence, in part, Evans's fascination with signs and shop-fronts, and with the paraphernalia of the road. Merely to note a roadside stand or to register a small-town church is to affirm a larger imagery of significance: a vernacular America which achieves unity through its definitive, if everyday imagery. Frank repeats Evans's journey, but in so doing points-up the difference in his position from the photographers of the 1930s.

One aspect of this difference can be seen from a comparison between an image of Frank's 'U.S. 285, New Mexico' and one by Dorothea Lange, 'Route 66'. Lange, like Evans, merely has to photograph 'the road' in order to establish a pervasive and compulsive American *symbol*. The literal rendering of a straight and essentially nondescript piece of tarmac amidst hundreds of miles of land is given specific value as the *base* of a ubiquitous American myth. Thus 'Route 66' takes its place, and establishes its 'meaning', within three immediate contexts: the road as American symbol, 'Route 66' as a sanctioning of that meaning, and, out of the 1930s, the relationship of the 'Okies' to Steinbeck. Lange *centres* the road within the photograph so that spatially she reinforces its centrality. But it also gains meaning within the narrative space in which the road is featured: historically of the Okies' emigration to California and mythically of the 'exodus' in relation to the 'open' road. Lange's image thus gains kudos in terms of a rich fund of secondary cultural meanings.

Frank's photograph of the road, however, is quite different. If Lange centres the road and its markings, so Frank displaces the road to the left of the photograph's centre; a device made doubly effective by the incorporation of a double but broken secondary white line on the road. In other words the simultaneous presence of a continuous and a broken line metaphysically echoes an opposition fundamental to *The Americans*. There are two distinct frames of reference and meaning in these photographs: two Americas – Kerouac's and Frank's, as it were. And Frank speaks to the *broken* line on the road even while he photographs the continuous line. His penchant is to the fractured continuity, to the discontinuous narrative. Thus, his *de-centering* of the road. But, equally, 'U.S. 285, New Mexico' has other basic differences which signal its overwhelming sense of emptiness. Unlike Lange's image of 'Route 66', Frank's photograph is grainy, textured and gloomy. It has an especial and broody darkness which is imminent with a threatening sense of nothingness, made the more obvious by the presence of a single car travelling along the road in the distance. Equally, Lange's photograph is, so to speak, in 'landscape' format. In contrast Frank's is 'portrait'. The difference is significant, for Frank's format *insists* upon a human presence looking on to the scene. 'Landscape' would have fixed the image within a landscape aesthetic, itself the reflection of an Emersonian nature as it is reflected in the work of Weston, Adams, Minor White and the F.64 Group. This breaks away from such a tradition of the sublime spectacle and questions how the human form, and eye, makes sense of so much space. Thus, if the road remains dominant (à la Kerouac and Whitman) it does so effectively as no more than a line of movement, a trace of the attempt to establish an alternative reality. Its presence paradoxically speaks to the *site* of lost hopes as it plays with the continuing significance of the 'American dream'.

The Americans is full of such images on and of the road, but they are devoid of any vitality, the élan so basic to the Kerouac ethos of being 'on the move'. Effectively they reverse the very mythology of energy in which the Beats stored so much credence. Thus 'Car Accident – U.S. 66, between Winslow and Flagstaff' has a body covered by a blanket. Four figures (two with stetsons) look on over the dead figure on the ground. 'Backyard – Venice West, California' has a 1930s car rusting away; a ghost of the decade when, between Winslow and Flagstaff on Route 66, endless convoys followed the paths of the Joads to California. 'Santa Fé, New Mexico' shows a gas station devoid of any human presence. The five gas pumps stand as indicators of absence and emptiness. Cars and gas stations exist here as pervasive icons of the culture and *The Americans* is saturated with their presence and imagery but they denote only loss. Consistently the symbols so basic to Kerouac's America are emptied of substance: the flag, for example, like the portraits of Washington and Lincoln (and Eisenhower), is given an ironic context. More significantly perhaps is the way in which Frank's images *empty* America of its people. Effectively, any human presence is signified in terms of manufactured images: cinema screens, posters and, of course, the television, just as the 'voice' of America is suggested by the prevalence of the jukebox. Thus in 'Restaurant – U.S. 1 leaving Columbia, South Carolina' a television screen reflects the *only* figure in the restaurant. There are no 'bobbysoxers' here. Any human evidence has been erased. The paraphernalia of mass communication bear no relevance to a 'reality' beyond the television. The effect is consistently eerie and disconcerting.

If a sense of absence is prevalent in these images it is invariably underscored by the individuals who do 'inhabit' the space of a Frank photograph. As he admitted in *The Americans*, he sought 'images from the back roads of the culture, the sad-eyed margins where the process of life is most exposed'.[20] And the individuals he photographs are indeed 'on the margin' – at the edge of the culture's seeming largesse. But this is equally a bona-fide middle America: a mix of blue-collar car-workers and Texan ranch-hands. But nowhere is there any sense of community. Groups of people are merely multiples of single persons, not the 'individuals' of separateness in Whitman's 'Song of Myself'. They are distanced from each other. As in Raymond Carver's fiction the essential condition is one of *aloneness*. And thus the way in which virtually no one looks at the camera. There is, of course, a rich tradition in American photography of the candid public shot (one thinks of the New York photographs of Paul Strand and Walter Evans, for example). But Frank achieves something beyond the candid. I can call it only a quality of intense isolation. The camera 'observes' unobtrusively and informally, but it equally renders human eyes which look nowhere except into their interior emptiness; hence the poetic intensity of the images as a collective experience. The general effect is a kind of Eliotic 'hollowness' – the very ennui of which that very Whitmanian poet, William Carlos Williams warned in 'To Elsie'. In Frank's photographs the 'pure products of America' so to speak, have indeed 'gone crazy'. Everybody exists in a seemingly endless sadness and, by implication, imminent death. *The Americans* thus pictures states of being. The external space of the continent mirrors an internal space so that each image suggests not so much a geographical as a psychological picturing of the USA's condition.

In a very different way Diane Arbus (1923–71) is another central photographer who exemplifies this condition. As Patricia Bosworth's biography makes clear, here is a diffident, distressing and disturbing photographic undertaking. Arbus (much like Sylvia

Plath's quasi-heroine in *The Bell Jar*) begins her career in the fashion business; but rapidly rejects its surface constrictions. And yet 'apparel' and the cosmetic remain basic to her imaging. Arbus negotiates the line between surface image and interior being – the codes of private and public *telling* in which one's self is as much fluid as it is repressed. But unlike Avedon and Frank, she renders this vision in relation to her native habitat: New York City. 'Space' in this sense is paramount. Unlike the images of the west, for example, her New York is made up of restricted spaces – interiors in which individuals squeeze into the terms of their being (thus 'New York Giant' is emblematic of her entire undertaking). Her subjects exist under enormous psychological and social pressures – distorted into the extreme corners of social and sexual behaviour: of a bizarre lifestyle. Hence the way it has become relatively easy to dismiss Arbus's images as exploiting their subjects. As Boswell notes, one of Arbus's favourite films was Tod Browning's 1932 *Freaks*: 'She was enthralled because the freaks in the film were not imaginary monsters, but *real* – midgets, pinheads, dwarfs had always excited, challenged, and terrified her because they defied so many conventions.' [21] *Freaks* 'fascinated' her and offered a parallel to New York City which increasingly offered itself as a literal extension of the world of the film: 'She had begun to prowl the city at all hours. ... She saw hunchbacks, paraplegics, exhausted whores, boys with harelips, pimply teenage girls.'

Arbus, of course, was influenced by Lisette Model and Weegee (Arthur Fellig) whose night-time excursions into the underside of New York City relish a fearful fascination. And in many ways Arbus, like Weegee, borders on the voyeuristic – drawn, as it were, to outsiders and the city's 'invisible' inhabitants. Hence the extent to which she photographs so many of her subjects within private spaces: a transvestite in suspenders and stockings in his bedroom, an hermaphrodite in his/her dressing-room. The photographs invade as they expose these private spaces and moments: giving us access to the unmasking of the individual identity (masks and 'veils' are basic to the whole play of public and private selves in Arbus's vision). Significantly, these are never furtive. When Arbus insisted that she 'knew' her subjects she made a basic claim to the *kind* of photography she sought. And this is what makes her so different from Weegee. The Weegee vision is surreptitious and sensational – a photography made 'on the run' and to the moment. Its level of exposure is akin to the newspaper. 'Love in the Cinema', for example, or 'Legs at a New York Bar' [22] are emblematic of Weegee's *oeuvre*. These are stolen images, literally imposing on the private and flaunting the voyeur's thrill of the hidden glance.

In Arbus there is nothing of this. An image in Arbus openly confronts the viewer; her subjects invariably pose and look directly at the camera. Any sense of confrontation is with us – for we are often so close to the subject as to make us question our own motives for judging and 'looking' at another figure. Hence the effect of the photographs' square format, a polaroid-like image which ironically suggests the snatched and forbidden.

The substance of an Arbus image is achieved precisely through its studied formality. The photographs seek not so much to expose and intrude as to measure the terms of an individual's life. Thus the ways in which detail is so crucial to their effect: a cigarette, a letter and an envelope, a photograph on the wall, or clothes on the floor. These become extensions of the self as photographed; part of the autobiography being mapped by the single image. We read these images slowly as they emit a poetic intensity which renders them as icons rather than photographs of a deep sense of sadness and loneliness. Collectively they constitute a chilling record of urban and suburban America.

The Arbus approach thus achieves a very specific vision – dangerous as it is empty of feeling. Indeed, one often obtains the sense of individual feeling so hidden as to be frozen. Subjects speak to us from a cadaverous state, as if belonging to another 'favourite' Arbus environment: the New York morgue. Like Frank's images, many of these photographs suggest an incipient emptiness: a vacuum in which the surface structures of the culture operate without reference to its inhabitants. Two of the central images from the Arbus Aperture monograph are of a Hollywood house (a film-lot front) and of Disneyland. The iconic references are full of secondary resonance and point-up the terms by which Arbus undermines cultural myth. But they equally insist on a sense of 'America' that Nathanael West expressed in *The Day of the Locust*: all those 'sad' and 'lonely' individuals adrift in a 'dream dump'. Thus the sense of emptiness and, like the conclusion of West's novel, the sense of anguish. Indeed, one Arbus image, 'Xmas tree in a living room' (1963),[23] exemplifies her 'view' of America. This is a photograph *sans* figures: a frozen time-capsule almost redolent of absence. It is a middle-class suburban living-room literally stuffed with objects. There is a Christmas tree with a stack of carefully wrapped and placed presents around its base. In the corner is the ubiquitous television. On top of the television is a clock, as sterile as the room's atmosphere. The carpet has a deep pile; a table lamp is still wrapped in cellophane. The whole scene is one of orderliness in which nothing is out of place. But equally this is not a room in a house so much as a 'museum'. Arbus has offered an almost bizarre image of suburban style (and kitsch) as a still life – a frozen life in which all is surface. One wants to see the inhabit-ants of this room but one senses that they are in other rooms, separate as they are alone, living out precisely those 'hidden' selves that Arbus characteristically images in bedrooms and dress-ing-rooms. Here the 'living-room' is the very opposite: an ironic freak show of absent feelings. Objects constitute an atmosphere of death – a condition basic to her view of family life and relationships. It is perhaps sadly ironic that the only community group Arbus photographs are the retardents from New Jersey. These images show a rare sense of play and simple joy; but their simplicity is of course qualified by the psychological limitations of their subjects. They exist outside any awareness of their individual selves and individual histories – the very opposite to the Ameri-can figures Arbus portrays. Almost like her suicide they represent an alternative to the bleak world of her photography. A 'human' community is imaged within the confines of an asylum which, paradoxically, keeps the outside at bay. Once again the assumed terms of reference have been turned upside down.

Arbus thus returns us to Lowell's sense of 'lost connections' as pervasive to the culture, but she does so through the formal individual portrait. Her images probe the basis of identity and the limitations of personal expression. In the work of Lee Friedlander (b.1934) there is a similar response but the fragmentary and discontinuous state he explores foregrounds the very terms by which the camera, and the eye, seeks meaning. His images of urban spaces consistently break up any easy or assumed point of entry into the scene/seen. The surface of the photograph renders a world at once discontinuous as it is diffident. Figures (often Friedlander himself) will be reflected in windows and mirrors just as lines of 'communication' – roads, fences, telegraph wires – seemingly conspire to break up any sense of continuity. In many ways a Friedlander image is so fractured and discontinuous as to suggest a series of visually semantic questionings, reproducing photographically Lowell's predicament in 'Memories of West Street and Lepke'.

'Newark, New Jersey' (1962),[24] for example, is a typical Fried-lander image. Two figures stare out through the window of an ice-cream parlor (we are in the world of 'Bobbysoxers') at a street parade, perhaps on Independence Day. But the image refuses to celebrate or to validate the scene in any way. Rather it establishes its meaning through a series of implied gaps and spaces in its terms of reference. It reflects upon the scene and increasingly splits up the photographic space into a fragmented series of public codes and questionings. As in this image, Friedlander's photographs will often glut the eye in a deceptive richness of detail and imagery as everything is reduced to a spectacle at once enigmatic and tendentious. Thus, the act of looking is basic, but 'knowing' is problematic. The public America Friedlander photographs exists as a kind of archaeological site full of relics and codes from an earlier period. And hence the effect of 'Newark, New Jersey', for this is not so much a celebration of a public event as a stern reflection of emptiness and displacement. The two figures exist within the ghost of a previous world, of familiar spaces now made strangely anonymous.

This is especially obvious in the way once again Friedlander makes use of advertising imagery as characteristic of this play of presence and absence, surface and substance. In 'Newark, New Jersey', for example, there is a plethora of Coke bottles and an American flag – homely and safe 'signs' of significance. In turn they are bolstered by typologies from an older America as we read on the window 'FRENCH FRIES, CHEESEBURGER, ICE CREAM'. The play of image and word here is akin to what Dos Passos referred to in *Manhattan Transfer* as 'scrambled alphabets' of meaning; vocabularies of displacement in which meaning is always transferred but never achieved. The camera can no longer read the environment it photographs, it can only affirm perplexity. Thus, the distinctive quality of a Friedlander image is one of a discontinuous space; a literal world always distanced from the eye. America exists as a series of codes and surfaces which are now fragmentary: lost connections. The eye can only reflect, not confirm, the experience.[25]

In many ways Friedlander's images parallel Pynchon's concerns in *The Crying of Lot 49* but the difference is that one feels there is no hierophany. The camera now registers an endless series of images which, in their lost connections, form part of a fragmentary but pervasive discontinuity. Hence the irony of Gary Winogrand (1924–84) who, before his death, stored up thousands of photographic images without even bothering to develop the films. Merely the 'act' of photographing was sufficient; the image had become secondary. In a perverse sense, Winogrand has taken this kind of American photography to its ultimate conclusion: a photography so concerned with absence is itself absent – it remains a literal *negation*, a negative in an undeveloped film. The photographer refused to produce a positive print. It is perhaps the ultimate irony but one given a consistent rationale in the light of so many photographic developments. Lowell's 'lost connections' have been more and more affirmed. As Ronald L. Haeberle noted about his Vietnam war photograph 'People about to be shot' (*Life* magazine, 1969): 'Guys were about to shoot these people ... I yelled "Hold it" and I shot my pictures. M16s opened up and from the corner of my eye I saw bodies falling but I did not turn to look.' [26]

6

Paradigm Regain'd: Alistair Cooke, Disneyland and the Ideal of America

Robert Giddings

A historian has to be treated as a witness, and not believed unless his sincerity is ascertained. The maxim that a man must be assumed to be honest until the contrary is proved, was not made for him.

John Emerich Edward Dalberg Acton,
The Study of History (1907)

Before the Revolution, American history tended to be no more than the history of each original founding state. The historical tradition was thus originally promotional, antiquarian and, in both a literal and figurative sense, provincial. A truly 'national' history was long in coming – not, in fact, until after the Civil War.[1] Americans, furthermore, relied heavily on Englishmen for the telling of their history; even accounts of the Revolution were borrowed from Edmund Burke's brainchild, the *Annual Register*. A focus for a national sense of history was eventually provided by the establishment of the American Historical Association in 1884. This is not to deny the sure and steady growth of a sense of the national past in the popular consciousness: the Revd Jeremy Belnap, Chief Justice John Marshall, Parson Weems, William Wirt, Jared Sparks, Ralph Waldo Emerson, the Sanderson Brothers, William and Frederic Tudor, all attempted in their various ways the enormous task of wresting the nation's history from the hands of such English historians as George Chalmers. The mythologising of American history thus has early origins. It continues to surface in the rhetoric of national politics. Little better evidence of its persistence, however, exists than in two of the best-known examples of the post World War II entertainments industry: Disneyland and the broadcasting career of yet another English-born interpreter of America, Alistair Cooke.

On examination we can see that each relates closely to the other. The Disney theme parks present in tangible, visitable form the basic themes that have been the lodestar for America's journey through history. There are three of them in the USA (Anaheim, California, opened in 1955; Walt Disney World, Orlando, Florida, opened in 1971; and the EPCOT Center, adjoining the site at Orlando opened in 1982), as well as Disneyland settlements overseas: Disney-Nippon in Japan and Disney-Monde just outside Paris. Despite local variations of theme and activity, it is nevertheless possible to see Disneyland endeavour as a collective metaphor for America's dream of America. Each, essentially, is based on a model that epitomises the 'small town' in America of the kind immortalized by Norman Rockwell on the covers of the *Saturday Evening Post*, and familiar and loved Main Street USA. This is the kind of small-town America conjured up in hundreds of Hollywood movies, as well as in dramas by the likes of William Inge. From Disneyland's Main Street various attractions lead off: Bear Country, the Rivers of Mark Twain, Fantasyland, Futureland, Frontierland.

There is a strong ideological thread holding these various elements of Disneyland together, reaching back not only into a fabricated historical past, but into an equally constructed present and future. One is invited to contemplate the fulfilment of a faith in human perfectibility: decent, respectable, communal America. And it is just this populist version of America that has been consistently peddled by one of the twentieth-century's great journalists, Alistair Cooke.

Backed by the massive capital resources of Time-Life, Rank Xerox, the big American banks, in turn a winner in 1978 of the Imperial Tobacco Gold Award for the most outstanding contribution to radio broadcasting, Honorary Knight Commander of the British Empire in 1973, the prestigious columnist of the *Manchester Guardian* and the *Listener*, regularly listened to in her bath by Queen Elizabeth II, frontman of America's PBS's Masterpiece Theater, Alistair Cooke has had one of the most significant and consistently successful careers in modern mass media.

Cooke's career has also been deeply portentous. Culminating in the much acclaimed 13-part television series, 'America: a Personal History of the United States', which has been shown in 28 countries and was named by *Newsweek* 'the finest gift to the nation for its two hundredth birthday', his career seems consolidated and perpetuated in the book of the series, *Alistair Cooke's America*, which continues to sell well, especially at Christmas: worldwide, its sales in hardcover top 2 million. Cooke was invited to address a joint session of Congress on 25 September 1974, which marked the 200th anniversary of the first Continental Congress at Philadelphia on 25 September 1774. The University of Cambridge honoured him with an honorary doctorate. His 'Letter from America' is broadcast to more than 30 million listeners on BBC Radio 4 and the World Service, and has had the longest run of any radio series.

When Kingman Brewster, as President of Yale University, bestowed the Howland medal on Cooke, he called him 'the most authoritative interpreter of the American scene and American mores'. The press, radio broadcasting and finally the massive complex of transatlantic media imperialism have thus made Alistair Cooke into a powerful 'historian'. He was described by Sharon Churcher in the *New York Magazine* as 'perhaps the most successful and certainly the most ubiquitous one-man enterprise in the thinking media'.[2]

Under the guise of a beloved idiosyncrasy, Cooke indeed peddles a particularly powerful mythology. We may take the book, *Alistair Cooke's America*, as our best evidence. It is in this convenient, portable form that consumers are most likely to come across it, reinforced as it is by the steady drip-drip-drip of the weekly 'Letter from America'. For the book presents, crystallises and perpetuates the leading myths of American history. It tells Americans just what they want to hear and does not tell them things they do not want to know. It tells the world what the Americans want the world to hear about America – and no more.

Anthony Burgess in the *New York Times* magazine wrote that when Europe, after millennia of war, rapine, slavery, famine, and intolerance

> had sunk to the level of a sewer, America became the golden dream, the Eden where innocence could be recovered. Original sin was the monopoly of that dirty continent over there; and back across the Atlantic, in America man could glow in an aura of natural goodness, driven along his shining path by divine reason. The Declaration of Independence itself serves as a monument to reason. Progress was possible, and the wrongs committed against the Indians, the wildlife, the land itself, could be explained away in terms of the rational control of environment necessary for the building of a New Jerusalem. Right and wrong made up the moral dichotomy; evil – that great eternal inextirpable entity – had no place in America.[3]

Burgess is unmistakably, even heavy-handedly, ironic. But Alistair Cooke tells you the same story straight: he really means it.

Alistair Cooke's America offers a fascinating twentieth-century artefact. The cover shows him as Time-Life's Livy, and located in the background, misty but clearly discernible, is a globe turned to display the American continent. On the back cover, each with an appropriate graphic image, are given the chapter headings that purport to landmark the US's course through history: The New Found Land (American-Indian face, black-and-white photograph); Making a Revolution (George III, oil portrait); Inventing a Nation (Colonial troops, painting); Gone West (bison, horse, Indian painting); A Firebell in the Night (slaves and cotton, black-and-white photograph); Domesticating a Wilderness (prairie family homestead, black-and-white photograph); The Huddled Masses (immigrant family, black-and-white photograph); The More Abundant Life (street scene, modern urban America, with neon signs and automobiles, coloured photograph).

It all seems to be there. Flip through the pages, and the balance of text and illustrations seems a convincing mixture of fairness, informality, lucidity and learning lightly carried. Above all there is the apparent sincerity, the resolve to produce the best analysis from the available sources. 'Americans are taught a very simple view of their revolution,' he writes of the colonists' crisis with the British government.[4] Unconsciously we respond by thinking, well, here at last, in this treatment, we have the promise of *real* history. *America* was not brought into being as a rush job, but was long in the meditative pipeline: 'Very often', writes Cooke in apparently contemplative vein, 'when I was on the road and writing or pondering all this.' [5]

A major quality of Alistair Cooke's (and, I am convinced, one of the essential explanations of his enduring success) is to be located in his style. This might seem a nebulous quality to point to, but it is unavoidable in any serious attempt to analyse Cooke as a media phenomenon. For Cooke is at once far more than just a presenter; yet he is not what you might call a real historian, as can be borne out by consultation of the bibliography of virtually any serious work on American history: seldom does Alistair Cooke's name feature.[6] Cooke's style has regularly been described as witty, urbane, civilised. The *New York Times* called him 'a conspicuously reasonable, cultivated and civilized man'. Leslie Halliwell's *Television Companion* praises his 'incisive wit' and 'urbane manner'.

Several of the style's ingredients are worth looking at in more detail. First, there is the charm. It is singularly persuasive. An unnamed media industry observer quoted in the *New York Magazine* said of Cooke: 'he could be a judge and deliver the death sentence on you and you'd still like him.' [7] The style also contains a cunning alchemy of asserted professionalism ('as a historian I'm not sure that an integrated society will work') [8] and assertion interlarded with cracker-barrel philosophy ('one of the oldest chestnuts seemed newly roasted. It is that line of the Italian immigrant asked to say what forty years of American life had taught him: "There is no free lunch"').[9]

The whole performance is held together in layers of bland, polystyrene prose, topped with a rich sauce of quality-by-association: Samuel Johnson, Edward Gibbon, Oliver Wendell Holmes – the names tumble out. In *Six Men* (1956), which is supposed to be about 'gods' that he had 'come close to' and who had 'demonstrably' taken to him, Cooke writes a whole chapter on Edward VIII on the strength of having been shaken by the royal hand as a Cambridge undergraduate and having sat a few rows away from Edward in a cinema. The quality might be demonstrable, but the association is sometimes a bit far-fetched. Style is indeed everything: the magic passes of the master magician who masks from the audience the method used to produce the rabbit from the hat. And yet as history it is junk, or, as Americans would say, schlock, but it is schlock superbly gift-wrapped. It is texture without substance. The minute it is subjected to examination it falls apart. It is not history, but mythology.

Alistair Cooke does not exactly 'lie'. What one gets is the selective truth. The result is a confection of the most dearly-held myths the Americans have evolved, together with those they would dearly want others to believe. Like the master illusionist he is, Cooke seems to be doing one thing while really doing another. Examine any of the pinnacles in his narrative of the great nation's history, for example Christopher Columbus and 1492, the Revolutionary War of 1776, the Civil War of 1861–65 or the Opening of the West and the Huddled Masses.

As far as Columbus is concerned, Cooke seems happy to rely mainly on Admiral Samuel Eliot Morison:

> Of all the standard historians, both classical and revisionist, I have been most grateful to that venerable Admiral of the Ocean Sea, Samuel Eliot Morison, who threw me a lifeline when I was floundering in whirlpools of competing 'facts and theories'.[10]

In Cooke's version the story bodies forth one of the most dearly-held American myths: the Herbert Spencer/Samuel Smiles/Horatio Alger myth of the self-made poor boy who makes it through nerve, hard work and 'enterprise'. America, Cooke tells us, was itself named for 'a Florentine businessman and promoter' and set on the path to its modern achievements by Christopher Columbus, 'a giant of a redhead, six feet tall at a time when the average virile male was about five foot four', who was also 'fast talking' and an 'egomaniac who combined in curiosity, romantic stubbornness, and sense of mission something of Galileo, of Quixote, and John the Baptist'.[11] It makes for a quite hopeless romanticism.

With the American Revolution Cooke again insists that his will be a no-nonsense treatment of the facts. He actually decries the superficial way in which Americans are usually taught about 1776: 'that it was a straightforward crusade against a tyrannical Parliament and an hysterical king an ocean away.'[12] His own account, however, offers exactly more of the same. It is essentially the familiar tale of no taxation without representation. The complexities of whether it was a revolution, of property in the new order, of the creation of a new market – all go by the board.

There is the same mixture of elegance and superficiality in his treatment of the Civil War. In Cooke's version the Civil War was about black slavery and mass production. These issues, for him, are indeed to be understood in black and white. The main issues as defined by Cooke are reductive to a degree. There is the men-of-their-time thesis ('men of all sorts belong always to their own time'). But if this was so, how do 'times' ever change? For an historian, even a self-styled one, this is naivety itself. The climax lies in the claim that things were not as bad for the blacks as they might have seemed.

In Cooke's account of the opening up of the west the really horrifying facts behind the Great Western Land Grab are scarcely touched upon. The stark facts are that the land was thieved from the Indians by lies, broken promises and ultimately genocide. The wildlife was destroyed and the wilderness colonised by means of a fur trade based on whisky. Those who really want to read the facts about the founding of the west are fortunate to have as a corrective the works of writers of the integrity of John Upton Terrell or Dee Brown.[13]

Nor does Cooke make any effort to explore the economic consequences of the western expansion, which were disastrous. The market was rapidly glutted with agricultural machinery. In the 1880s agricultural prices fell when high European crop production coincided with very high American wheat harvests. The result was collapsed prices. Farm bankruptcies between 1888 and 1892 resulted in half the population of Kansas leaving their farms to search for new opportunities. By 1886 the American railroad system was virtually finished, and then 200,000 workers were laid off. In addition, this meant a huge decline in the need for steel.

Cooke's recycling of the Huddled Masses myth is simply a matter of supply and demand. There was a lot of work to be done in the USA; there were a lot of people in Europe having a rough time. So they went to America to get a better share of the cake. 'Why did they come? ... The most powerful reason was hard times in the homeland.' Whenever life could hardly be worse at home they came to believe that life was better in America. The Irish came because they were starving. Jews came because they were persecuted. Relatives who had made it wrote back home and their practical accounts

> of an attainable decent life were read aloud in cottages, markets, and factories. The word spread beyond the factories and the ghettos to the farmers of southern and central Europe. And whereas before 1890 the immigrant stream had flowed out of Scandinavia, Germany, Ireland, England, Canada, in the next thirty year the mass of immigrants came from Italy, Austria-Hungary, Russia and again and always Ireland.[14]

Great excitement is whipped up: the bustle of 'as many as fifteen thousand ... arriving in one day, and the ships had to drop anchor and wait. But eventually the engines would rumble again ... Soon the newcomers would be on the docks sorting their bundles and baggage in a babble of languages.' What did they find? 'Markets groaning with food and clothes. There were streetcars all over town. You could watch the automobiles.' [15]

Cooke does not touch upon a number of important factors which are not simply additional details but rather the socio-economic deep structures that account for the surface quality of the narrative. Cooke gives us the hoary old myth about the melting pot of nations. A little matter that he omits to mention is that in 1864 Congress passed an Act that allowed American contractors to import foreign labour. The American Immigration Company was set up and their agents toured Britain, Germany, France, Belgium to encourage the low paid to come over. Those who took up the offer turned over a percentage of their wages until their fare to America had been paid up. This was nothing more than wholesale exploitation of cheap labour.

It was not as if these immigrants were entering an economic/industrial paradise. Apart from their working and housing conditions, they faced life in a roller-coaster economy. Domestic overproduction created economic depression, bank failures, wage cuts, unemployment, strikes, demonstrations. Between 1880 and 1884 business failures tripled to approximately 12,000 a year, while between 1880 and 1900 there was a total loss of $45 million as a result of numerous strikes. But these clouds do not trouble the blue skies of *Alistair Cooke's America*. There is no mention of the Great Railroad strike of 1877, which spread from West Virginia, to Baltimore, Pittsburgh, Chicago, Buffalo, St Louis and San Francisco, and cost over 100 lives. A silence is maintained about the garment workers' strike of 1883. No mention made of the strikes and disturbances of the 'Great Upheaval' in 1885–86. There is not a word of the Chicago Haymarket riot of 1886, the

Homestead Steel strike of 1892, the Pullman Palace strike, Coxey's March of the Unemployed in 1894.

And so it goes on, to its selective conclusion, 'The More Abundant Life'. Many things are simply not mentioned. No organised crime, Scottsboro boys, no Sacco and Vanzetti, no crisis over civil rights, no McCarthyism, no power politics behind the dropping of the atom bomb – the list goes on. A college friend once told me that if you do not understand American mythology, you will not understand either American history or make sense of American politics: 'Abraham Lincoln', he told me, 'was born in a log-cabin he made with his own bare hands.' *Alistair Cooke's America* is mythology posing as history, but it is from the pinnacle of this mythological pile that Cooke scans modern America. And how does he describe the sights?

The first thing to be grasped is that the celebrated series of 'Letter from America', which has run on the radio since 1946, were not really intended as serious, in-depth political journalism. From the start their originator had in mind much more impromptu weekly chats than anything in the nature of a 'report' from the US on a weekly basis by some kind of correspondent. We should not misread the title: these *are* letters; they are personal and informal. In the 'Preface to the British Reader' of a collection of these broadcast missives published in 1951 Cooke sets a tone we should not mistake:

> it would be a crime against Nature for any generation to take the world crisis so solemnly that it put off enjoying those things for which we were presumably designed in the first place ... I mean the opportunity to do good work, to fall in love, to enjoy friends, to sit under trees, to read, to hit a ball and bounce the baby.
>
> The suspicion that these things are what most men and women everywhere want led me to suggest, in London in 1946, that Britons might be more honestly enticed into an interest in America and Americans by hearing about their way of life and their tastes in these fundamental things than by suffering instruction in the procedures of the American Senate and the subtleties of the corn-hog ratio.[16]

The Director of the BBC Home Service, Lindsay Wellington, responded to the concept wholeheartedly, and further urged Cooke to 'forget politics altogether' and to talk about anything in America that interested him. He was to do this for a large and mixed audience ranging from 'shrewd bishops to honest carpenters'. The subject-matter was defined as 'the passions, the manners, the flavour of another nation's way of life'.[17]

The beginnings of this enterprise hold the key to the entire Cooke case. What was initially conceived and perceived as harmless broadcast chat and blather, has gradually and imperceptibly assumed the stature of serious journalism, if not 'history' on the wing. To purloin and distort that comment of Dr Johnson's about Milton, we have elevated Alistair Cooke from one who could probably carve heads upon cherry-stones into a genius that could cut a Colossus from a rock.

It is no wonder that when we examine Cooke's attempts to deal with weighty matters of the post-war period we find him seriously wanting. One method he adopts is to ignore embarrassing stories, no matter how big they are. Thus Cooke makes no effort to explore the extraordinary story of Paul Robeson, a genius of blues and spirituals, and whose performance in *Othello* gave Broadway the longest run of any Shakespearean production (296 performances) but whose passport was revoked from 1950 to 1958. Normally Cooke loves rehearsing stories of the stars, and this one had everything: the son of a runaway slave who made it to college, who gave up law to go on the stage, whose voice was described by Alexander Woollcott as 'the best musical instrument wrought by nature in our time', whose peace and civil rights rallies attracted thousands – but Cooke recognised a hot potato when he saw one.

We have only one extended example of Alistair Cooke's treatment of a contemporary political issue, *A Generation on Trial: USA v. Alger Hiss* (1950), his eye-witness account of the Hiss–Chambers case. It is still readable, but time has not improved it as journalism or vindicated it as history. It is vintage Cooke, a colourful, idiosyncratic, lapidary description of the surface quality of an extraordinary moment in American post-war history, which fails to dig beneath the topsoil or detect the serious signs and portents. The House Committee on Un-American Activities was established in 1938 to probe subversive activities. Under its early chairmen, Martin Dies and J. Parnell Thomas, it was supposed to concentrate on fears of fascism, but soon directed its focus to organised labour, supposedly 'communist' movements, and, latterly, to the civil rights movement.

The Federal Theater, Writers' Projects (such as the state 'Guides') of the Works Progress Administration, and such individuals as Harold Ickes, the New Deal Secretary of the Interior who ran the Public Works Administration, and Harry Hopkins, who ran the Works Progress Administration and was President Roosevelt's most trusted adviser on foreign affairs during the war, came under attack. The Committee's activities slackened during 1942–45, but after the war became a well-established and maintained piece of armoury for deployment in the Cold War. The enemy was now communism, the world communist conspiracy, reds under the bed and, above all, the communists and their fellow-travellers in the State Department.

Cooke fails to portray the Cold War period in America as anything very wild or demented. This is a Cold War without its chilling insanities. The trial proceedings are no madder than, say, Mencken's account of the Scopes Trial. But this was not an example of boondocks judicial farce; this was a great nation turning obsessive, demented. In Cooke's view, things are so simple. The atom bomb had been dropped, not just to bring the war to an end and save Allied lives in an invasion of Japan, but – as was widely rumoured even at the time – for reasons of international power politics: to show Stalin that the US had the bomb, and *would use it*. Cooke was to be found writing: 'The decision to drop the bomb was made on the fearful calculation that an invasion of Japan might confront five million defenders and five thousand suicide aircraft and cost up to two million American lives.' [18] This might do as a comment from the man in the street, or one of those voluble, opinionated taxi-drivers Cooke always seemed to be lucky enough to talk to before recording one of his broadcast 'Letters'. But a real journalist would do some research before repeating such an assertion. He would have discovered that President Truman did not ask the opinion of the military adviser most directly involved. General Douglas MacArthur was merely informed of the decision shortly before the bomb was dropped on Hiroshima. The US Strategic Bombing Survey reported: 'Japan would have surrendered even if the atomic bombs had not been dropped, even if Russia had not entered the war, and even if no invasion had been planned or contemplated.' [19] J. Robert Oppenheimer is on record as saying that the development of the bomb was important in order to 'get less barbarous relations with the Russians'. Vannevar Bush, chief aide on atomic matters to Henry L. Stimson, Truman's Secretary for War, said: 'That bomb was developed on time ... It was also delivered on time so that there was no necessity for concessions to Russia at the end of the war.' [20]

These views were current before the time Cooke wrote *A Generation on Trial*. They had been discussed by, among others, Norman Cousins and Thomas Finletter in the *Saturday Review of Literature* in June 1946.[21] The very foundations of the Cold War are thus not even laid out in *A Generation on Trial*, and so as a serious study of major events in the period the book gets off to a shaky start. The Soviet Union is 'a society under the dictate of a combination elite corps, priesthood, and prison guard' – an enemy we had failed to recognise. The Russians had always been the bad guys:

The fact we have just wakened up to (which the military alliance of the Second World War made it essential to overlook at the time) is that nothing has ever been further from the Russian purpose, their history, or their temperament than Protestantism, humanitarianism, liberalism, or the golden rule.[22]

In 1948 Whittaker Chambers, journalist and an editor of *Time*, came before the committee and stated that Alger Hiss, an official in the State Department, had given him classified information to transmit to Soviet agents ten years before. Hiss denied the accusations. When Chambers repeated his statement in proceedings that were televised, Hiss filed libel charges. Chambers was able to produce seemingly valid documentation, and the federal government then prosecuted Hiss for giving false testimony in denying that he had ever handed over State Department documents to Chambers, and for denying that he had ever seen Chambers since early 1937. The first trial of 1949 was a deadlock, but in 1950 Hiss was given a five-year prison sentence.

Cooke's purpose was to put down a 'record of the trials of Alger Hiss, from the first accusation to his conviction', which he hoped people will turn to 'in order to make up their own minds about the proper verdict'.[23] This is vintage Cooke, with the emphasis on story-line, courtroom drama, personality clashes, atmosphere, but showing weaknesses when it comes to historical or political analysis. It is so unworldly, so unaware of darker issues, and of the serious crisis in America and its possible impact on the 'free' world that it is like a school history book written for adults.

Reading it today, one major impact, one especial failure is the absence of insight into the significance of Richard Nixon. This apparent blindness to the darker side of domestic politics is a marked feature of Cooke's coverage of the 1950s. The sheer amount we are not told is overwhelming in its absence. We might have benefited from hearing from a keen observer on the scene about Nixon's career before he entered the race for major public office. A little something about the Californian proving ground, his grooming by Murray Chotiner, for example. Chotiner was a Los Angeles lawyer who was employed as Nixon's adviser and consultant for the congressional election of 1946 and stayed with Nixon for the rest of his career.

Chotiner's strategy was simple, and based on the insight that elections are not so much won by the victor as lost by the opposition. Chotiner's aim was always to seek to destroy the enemy. Rather than expending too much time and money on pushing your own case, think of ways of publicly destroying your opposition.

Nixon's opponent in the election of 1946 was the Democrat Jerry Voorhis, a very popular legislator and, it was widely felt, a man who truly represented his constituents in Washington. Voorhis had begun to alarm the real estate, insurance and banking interests, and many were suspicious not only of his record of avid support for the New Deal but also of his sympathy with organised labour. The final blow was his wartime proposal during the grain shortage that alcohol production should be reduced. The big money and commercial fraternities looked for a new candidate. Republican leaders found a willing Richard Nixon.

Voorhis was the strong candidate; Nixon the unknown. Chotiner resolved to damage Voorhis's reputation in a carefully planned campaign. Initially he circulated the rumour that Voorhis was a PAC-backed candidate (backed by the Political Action Committee of the National Trade Union Alliance, CIO). Great play was made of Nixon's war service. Voorhis had stayed safely behind the lines in Washington politicking. The leaflets described Nixon as: 'The clean, forthright young American who fought in defense of his country in the stinking mud and jungles of the Solomons.' 24

Records in fact show that Nixon's actual job lay in organising supply facilities behind combat lines. Nixon himself even referred to mixing with his men in 'foxholes' during the war. Great play was again made of the false assertion that Voorhis was a PAC-supported candidate, with the clear innuendo that the PAC was supported by the communists. Nixon's campaign manager went as far as to say on 24 April 1946: 'Now that the Political Action Committee has publicly endorsed the candidacy of Jerry Voorhis ... American citizens who resent the efforts of a minority group to control the people's representatives have the opportunity to rally to the support of Richard Nixon.' 25 By September an advertisement in the press read: 'A vote for Nixon is a vote against the Communist dominated PAC with its gigantic slush fund.' Gradually the information fed to the press by Chotiner and his team – several of whom stayed with Nixon right up to Watergate days – began to filter through to the news pages.

In an address given in his home town of Whittier, California, Nixon told his audience that he would not stand idly by in the face of this attempt by high-powered pressure groups seeking to seize the people's government from the majority of the people. The smears against Voorhis continued and were a very marked feature of this campaign. The details are astonishing, including telephone calls to voters during the final days asking: 'Did you know Jerry Voorhis was a communist?' Nixon won with 56 per cent of the vote. These events tell us much about Nixon and American politics that Cooke, to his discredit, never mentions.

Even when Nixon became a figure in international politics, not a word was uttered by Cooke about his curious political past.

The election of 1948 showed a revival of support for the Democrats. This was the year in which Truman defeated Dewey in the California primary. The cross-filing law in California, which allowed candidates to run in primary elections without revealing their party allegiances enabled Nixon to conceal that he was a Republican. One of his mailshots was addressed to 'Fellow Democrats' and was published by 'Democrats for Nixon. J. R. Blue, Chairman'. Nixon won the primary with slightly over 50 per cent of that vote, in turn.

It was at this stage that Nixon began to figure in the nation's media through the confrontation with Alger Hiss, though, once again, shadier aspects of his involvement in Californian politics are not discussed by Cooke either in *Generation on Trial* or the broadcast 'Letters from America'. Nixon was elected to the Senate after a campaign against Helen Gahagan Douglas in which he managed to get his opponent smeared as a communist. The sobriquet 'Pink Lady' was securely attached to her by constant repetition. Nixon asserted that if she had her way the communist world conspiracy would never have been exposed and Alger Hiss would still have been influencing the US's foreign policy.[26] Attacks on Douglas were the daily diet of this campaign: she gave comfort to Soviet tyranny; she would end the draft; she supported communist endeavours in Greece and Turkey; she would have abolished the Committee on Un-American Activities; she voted with known communist supporters in the Congress; she supported recognition of China and China's entry to the UN; and she favoured giving away atom secrets. Nixon had obviously learned his lessons from Chotiner. The trump card was to use Joe McCarthy himself in a speech in Los Angeles, widely broadcast on regional radio: 'The chips are down ... between the American people and the Administration Commicrat Party of betrayal.'

The Archbishop of Los Angeles, J. Francis A. McIntyre, threw in his support by ordering his priests to preach anti-communist sermons. Some zealous men of the cloth even urged from their pulpits that women standing for high office should be defeated. Anti-Semites had a field-day. Communism was part of the Jewish world conspiracy, and the real name of Douglas's husband, the actor Melvin Douglas, was Hesselberg. Nixon this time carried 56 per cent of the vote.

He was now seeking to secure really high office and stood as Eisenhower's running mate in the 1952 presidential race. It was rumoured that Nixon was using a secret fund contributed by Californian businessmen with oil, real estate and manufacturing interests.[27] The story was written up by New York journalist Peter

Edson. Nixon tried to dowse it down by claiming that it was part of a communist smear campaign, but in the end he was convinced by top men in the Republican Party that he would have to clear his name or leave the race. On 23 September 1952 he appeared on radio and television and gave the famous 'Checkers' speech, in which he denied that one cent of the $18,000 – the figure widely bandied about – had gone to him for personal use. He stressed the comparative poverty the Nixon family had always had to endure. He could have got money by putting his wife on the congressional payroll, but had not even done that because there were so many deserving stenographers and secretaries in Washington that needed the work. He denied that his wife even had a fur coat, but wore a plain 'respectable Republican cloth coat'. He played the role of a poor country lad who worked his way through law school, and compared this with Adlai Stevenson who had inherited a fortune. Of his war service, he said: 'I got a couple of letters of commendation, but I was just there when the bombs were falling.' (He was not.) He was not a quitter, and neither was Mrs Nixon, the former Pat Ryan, who he alleged had been born on St Patrick's Day. (She hadn't.) Then came Checkers. This was the one gift the family had received from supporters. It was a spaniel given to the children: 'And the kids love that dog and I just want to say this right now, that regardless of what they say about it, we're gonna keep it.' (No one had mentioned the dog.)

This maudlin and self-pitying performance did the trick. Darryl Zanuck, the Hollywood producer, telephoned Nixon after the broadcast and said: 'That was the most tremendous performance I've ever seen.' [28] Nixon was welcomed back with open arms by Eisenhower, on whose shoulders he publicly wept. Thousands wrote in urging him to stay on the ticket. At a lunch given by the Radio and Television Executives Society on 14 September 1955, the vice-president admitted that he had 'staged' the Checkers speech. 'Now don't get me wrong,' he said, 'I meant every word of that speech. I loved that dog ... But let's be realistic: a dog is a natural.' The dog and the coat, he admitted were 'props'. It had taken him days to prepare the speech: 'I'm a firm believer in the off-the-cuff speeches that take a lot of time to prepare.' [29] This is clearly the embryo of the great Nixon joke: 'Sincerity. That's the thing. Once you can fake that, you can fake anything.'

The style was to be consistent. In the 1960 campaign against John F. Kennedy he played the poor boy made good for all it was worth. He told crowds in Chester, Pennsylvania, on 22 October 1960:

I grew up in a little country store. Saturday was a long day because that's the day we started at 8 a.m. My mother used to get up at 5 a.m. and bake pies ... cherry was my favorite. Boy, she could make the best.

At a rally half an hour afterwards, the pies had become 'apple pies' and Ma Nixon's apple pies were 'mighty good'. He knew poverty so severe that customers would buy 'hamburger rather than steak, stew meat rather than the chuck roast that was a little more expensive, no strawberries out of season.'

As he whistle-stopped through Michigan and Illinois the stories were embroidered and embellished. By Danville, Illinois, he was mincing the hamburger himself. Later he talked of family poverty that had denied him the kind of toys American kids were really entitled to: 'I wanted to get an automatic train, not an electric train, but just one that would wind up.' His brother wanted a pony, but his poor old father had to say no. Later he wanted it more than anything in the world but his mother and father could not buy the pony as there would not be enough money for food, as the family was now in dire straits. The money was also required for 'the shoes that my other brothers needed'.[30]

We see none of this side of Nixon in Cooke's coverage, even during the massive exposure during the presidential battle with John F. Kennedy. As always, Cooke gives an account of the surface qualities of the political scene. When he comes to report on Nixon's election campaign of 1968, the main point he stresses is that Nixon is a unique candidate in American politics insofar as he is making a 'come-back'. He has nothing to say about what kind of politician he is, or anything about the darker side of his previous political career.

It is clear that politics do not really hold much interest for Cooke. Even when Nixon gets to the White House and Cooke has the duty to tell listeners what kind of politician he is, we find his interest is drawn to 'what [Nixon] does with his day, the gadgets and objects he likes to have around him, the sort of midnight snack he chooses to steal from the icebox'.[31] The Nixon he constructs for us is worth savouring:

> Mr Nixon has taken over a small office, where he can put his feet up and [a moving touch] have a fire, with the air-conditioning turned way up ... Nixon is a small-town boy, and in spite of the trappings of power ... he likes small surroundings and homely things.[32]

The bombing of Cambodia and the Watergate horrors must have really shocked Cooke. Watergate began – and this is his phrase for it – as 'an absurd late-night movie'.[33] With that monumental lack of suspicion that so characterises the way he looks at the world, when this appalling story first started to break he told us in Britain that the 'Democrats think they have found a big scandal, though it is no bigger than a Molotov cocktail'. As he unravelled the opening intricacies of the matter in September 1972 he asked: 'Is this already confusing? Do I sense the first polite suppression of a yawn? If so, your instinct is a healthy one and may soon be shared by the American people.' [34]

Even as the details accumulated he was still protected from believing the worst by his long apprenticed unworldliness. We should wait for proof, he advised:

> It is surely no excuse that in the Watergate case an over-whelming amount of the stuff printed by way of allegation is turning out to be true ... It is on the basis of newspaper reporting, and the leaked grand jury testimony, that over half the American people ... now believe that the President was involved ... The flurry of charges is so serious that we should all take a deep breath, wait for the indictments, wait for Senator Ervin's committee findings ... wait for the trials, and then come to a conclusion. This self-restraint is long over-due. It is not, I admit, a good recipe for selling newspapers. [35]

For those who took a real interest in politics and watched politicians carefully, the nemesis of Nixon would not have been the scandal, or at least not the surprise or shock, it seemed in Cooke's eventual coverage. He would have seen it for what it was: the full realisation of the promise Nixon had always shown.[36] Just how little of this Cooke previously admitted (or was aware of) may be gathered from reading his coverage of the Kennedy – Nixon battles in 1960. In a piece called 'The Unexplained Mr Nixon' he was telling readers of the *Manchester Guardian*, as it then was, all about Nixon's early struggles against poverty (even though he does not actually mention the famous fruit pies or even the hamburger), the hard college days, marriage to a miner's daughter, the 'stint' in the Navy, the 'tough campaigning' in California and his own amazement at the 'dislike' that Nixon arouses.[37]

Huge socio-political complexities have thus been matters of heart-stopping simplicity to Cooke. Civil rights and the violence that attended the movement were thought by him to be caused by a particular kind of 'Negro trouble-maker':

> Let us be clear about the kind of Negroes we have in mind. We are not talking about decent Negroes hungry for a decent house and a place in society. We are not talking about the people who long for a vote or a seat on a jury ... We are talking about people who long for a television set, a

case of bourbon, a girl, a cool car, and a wad of folding
money ... I believe the seed of this anarchy, and it is nothing
less, is in the poor Negro's envy not of the white man's vote
or his education but of the white man's fancied wealth and
the baubles it buys.

It is revealing to note that when he published this broadcast in
his collection *Talk About America* it had been deliberately edited.
In the broadcast he said:

Let us be fairly clear about the kind of people we are talking
about. We – as distinct from Pravda and the African radio,
and I regret to say quite a few otherwise intelligent liberals –
are not talking about decent Negroes hungry for a decent
house and a place in society.[38]

The Watts riots he is here describing began on 12 August 1965.
Now, it must be remembered, 1965 was a crucial year for black
consciousness in the US. During February and March Selma,
Alabama, had attracted national attention. It was here that Martin
Luther King Jr and 770 other civil rights leaders were arrested on
1 February during demonstrations about state regulations on
voter registration. Malcolm X was assassinated in Harlem on 21
February immediately prior to a rally in support of black and
white coexistence. Black marchers left Selma on 7 March after
2,000 prospective voters had been arrested in registration lines or
demonstrations. The marchers intended to go to Montgomery, the
state capital, but were attacked by 200 Alabama state policemen,
using whips, batons, tear-gas and dogs. Governor Wallace refused
a second march protection, accusing the federal judge who had,
in fact, approved this second march, of 'prostituting our law in
favour of mob rule'. President Johnson sent in 3,000 National
Guardsmen and military police. The marchers arrived at Montgomery on 25 March and on the same day civil rights leader Viola
Liuzzo was shot dead by Ku Klux Klansmen outside Montgomery. In June, Martin Luther King led a protest march of
20,000 in Chicago after the arrest of 526 anti-segregation demon-
strators. The cartoon strip *Amos 'n Andy* was withdrawn from
syndication after protests that it negatively stereotyped blacks. In
Watts over 10,000 black rioters burned and looted an area covering 500 blocks. Forty million dollars' worth of damage was done.
Fifteen thousand police and National Guardsmen were involved in
restoring order; 34 people were killed (28 of them blacks) and
4,000 arrested. Was this really caused by blacks wanting television sets and wads of folding money?
    Lacking the tenacity, or even the desire to know, which
energises a journalist such as I.F. Stone, Cooke's coverage of the

really major issues of the time read like skilled revamps of official press releases. In a 'Letter from America' as late as 1968 Cooke was peddling the orthodox view that the Vietnam war:

> crept up on us with no more menace than a zephyr. South Vietnam was only one of many strange place names that joined the noble roll call of countries which America, in the early glow of its world power, swore to protect and defend.[39]

War in Vietnam, he asserted, was the price of the Kennedy inaugural speech: 'we shall pay any price, bear any burden, meet any hardship, support any friend, oppose any foe to assure survival and the success of liberty.'

But what was he really saying? Does this statement mean that the USA got involved in the Vietnam debacle because John F. Kennedy proclaimed that his country intended to protect 'liberty'? In the face of the evidence available – not all of it hindsight – we can only draw one of three conclusions: this is either ironic, cynical or naive. As Cooke seems incapable of irony, and few would be ready to accuse of him of cynicism, we have to conclude that these views are simply uninformed. Now a professed journalist should be informed. It was not a matter of US government secrecy that American foreign affairs as conducted in South-East Asia were part of a considerable and elaborate strategy to maintain economic conditions favourable to the USA, and that these policies were to be furthered by physical means if necessary.

Post World War II Indo-China was an area of considerable interest. It was next door to Thailand. However politically regrettable much of Thailand's internal politics may have been, the country had always remained a bulwark against the eastward expansion of communist ambitions. Vietnam was making very determined efforts to rid itself of the presence of French imperialism. Ho Chi Minh declared a Vietnam Republic on 2 September 1945, and even though the French recognised it, they made every effort to limit its success. By the end of 1946 guerrilla war had broken out in North Vietnam. Next year China and the USSR recognised Viet Minh and began active military support. These events were watched carefully in Washington. It was at this stage that the massive US invoice – the price eventually to be paid by the US – was prepared. It was at this stage that the US began military aid to French Vietnam. In spite of the command of France's greatest soldier, De Lattre de Tassigny, French control gradually declined. In 1952, on the way back to France after having been relieved of command, de Tassigny pleaded in the US for more American aid in Vietnam. Between March and Septem-

ber 1953 US aid was massively increased. By 7 May 1953 the fall
of Dienbienphu brought total defeat to the French – of the
garrison of 15,000 men only 73 escaped; over 10,000 were taken
prisoner. The solution that emerged was the creation of North
(communist) and South (anti-communist) Vietnam. France with-
drew forces from Indo-China, and the US, although accepting the
agreements, significantly refused to sign them: reserving the right
to take any action ('bear any burden') deemed necessary should
the agreements be breached.

Vietnam, Laos and Cambodia, having signed agreements with
France, were now free of foreign control, and free to trade on the
Mekong. As the communist North Minh took control of North
Vietnam in late 1954, the US increased military aid to South
Vietnam. The South Vietnamese army was reorganised with 100,000
active troops and 150,000 reserves. The US sent a training mission.
Insurrection continued and in April 1956 the US Military Assist-
ance Advisory Group assumed responsibility for troop training, all
under Eisenhower's presidency. One could have legitimate grounds
for wondering if Cooke ever read the newspapers.

As early as 12 July 1960, before Kennedy had been elected
President, Khrushchev told a news conference that the Monroe
Doctrine had died a natural death. Immediately the US State
Department reaffirmed the Monroe Doctrine and accused
Khrushchev of attempting to establish a 'Bolshevik doctrine' for
worldwide communist expansion. Ngo Dinh Diem, the President
of South Vietnam, regained power in November after a coup at
Saigon. On 20 December various dissident groups met and organised themselves into the National Front for the Liberation of
South Vietnam – the Viet Cong. On 11 October 1961 the US
pledged assistance to South Vietnam should they be attacked by
the North. General Maxwell D. Taylor was sent to prepare for the
worst, which came in due course. Kennedy sent a personal
message to President Diem on 26 October 1961 pledging further
assistance, and on 11 November the first US Support Units
arrived, and by February next year the US Military Assistance
Command had been established.

Do these developments really bear any resemblance to
Cooke's terms of something creeping up with no more menace
than a zephyr? Cooke's journalism is like the man who shouts
'Fire!' as the brigade arrives and uncoils its hoses. He could have
told us how the involvement in Indo-China had been carefully and
officially engineered since the mid-1950s. Instead Cooke chose to
tell everybody what they already thought they knew – that the war
was a surprise to all, and especially to all the powerful politicos in
Washington. No wonder they did not know what to do about it.
Yet, as he interprets things, the US's reasons for being involved

in Vietnam were as clear as could be. He told listeners in 1965:

> The United States decided, after it had shored up eastern
> Europe in the nineteen forties, that it must try to back up
> non-communist countries on a continent which has been an
> American concern since sea-power made the Pacific Ocean a
> threat to the United States.[40]

Having given the impression that the whole thing was simply
drifted into, just one chapter of accidents after another, Cooke
can then go and leave us with the picture of poor old confused
President Johnson, at his wits' end, happy to take advice from
anyone prepared to give it:

> To some of us any end, by peaceful means, is a good end.
> But do not suggest this point to the Australians or the
> Malays. If Vietnam goes, there is no question we shall suffer
> a Munich that will instantly turn Cambodia, Burma, Thailand
> ... towards the communist side. It will look as if we jibbed ...
> From Pakistan to Hawaii, we could see another lost conti-
> nent, at the mercy, surely, of China. This ... is the root of
> the problem. All piety and proclamations of virtue aside, any
> intelligent solutions that you may have in mind will be
> gratefully received by President Lyndon B. Johnson, The
> White House, 1600 Pennsylvania Avenue, Washington,
> DC.[41]

In December 1977, marking the occasion of the 1,500th 'Letter
from America', George Scott remarked in the *Listener* that Cooke
had an unquenchable curiosity and 'the gift of talking about
serious subjects in easy palatable language, without ever trivialis-
ing them'.[42] It is a major part of the enchantment that that is
what he *seems* to be doing. Suspicion is aroused, and then
seriously deepened, only when one begins to make investigations
and the omissions, distortions and paperings-over begin to
become evident. This is the essence of Cooke as media-historian.
He *seems* to be dealing with the complexity of things; nothing, in
fact, could be further from the truth.

Cooke never took it upon himself to dig very deeply into
Reaganism, finding it much more congenial to describe the symptoms than diagnose the condition. During Reagan's 1980 campaign
he told listeners that Reagan loves homespun simplicities:

> Reagan ... has gone round the country ... for many years,
> saying over and over: 'We are not the party of big business
> and the country club, but the party of Main Street, the small
> town, the shopkeeper, the farmer, the cop on the beat, the

guy who sends his kids to Sunday school, pays his taxes, and never asks anything from government except to be left alone.' It sounds like a speech from a Warner Brothers movie of the 1930s ... Those Warner Brothers movies had immense appeal in the days of the Depression, the appeal of small-town paradise lost ... for all the seeming naivety of Reagan's visionary picture of the paradise he'd like to regain, he is on to something that touches the hearts of the many frustrated Americans who have seen the Carter administration expanding the bureaucracies ... increasing the dependence of the poor, the blacks, the dispossessed on the government, by way of welfare, a dole.[43]

To a real observer such nostalgia for so irretrievably lost a small-town America (did it ever truly exist?) at a time when US capital reached the sophisticated legerdemain that gave the world the term 'junk bonds', when financial hegemony strove to be global, when big business, finance, commodity trading and cartels sought ever more to dominate the US domestic situation, might seem worth examining. But Cooke has never been one with an inclination to examine the deeper structures. He has shown little interest in the chronic socio-economic ailments of which 'Reaganism' was only the display behaviour.

Take but one dimension of the Reagan 1980s: the fate of America as a debtor nation with regular budget deficits and a serious balance of trade problem. Such, however, had been America's political dominance of the 'free world' and its global financial hegemony that it was able to get other nations to fund its expenditure. By the end of the 1940s the US held three-quarters of the world's gold. Ten years later it was a debtor nation. But it has turned itself into the supreme super-imperialistic power. The concentration of international finance capital has achieved far more significance than private, monopolistic finance capital. Old 'colonial' imperialism – such as that supremely achieved by Britain and for a time emulated by the US – has become obsolete. Government finance capital now dominates all other forms of capital.

Since the beginning of the century war had been the main element in international balance of payment relationships. World War II had shifted financial power from the Old Powers to the New World. This situation was changed for ever by the Vietnam War. The Korean War had been financed by deficit funding, shifting the cost on to wealth to be created by future generations. This time US strategy was, in Michael Hudson's phrase, financing America's wars with other people's money. It was European financiers who forced an end to the Vietnam War and made

Johnson stand down.[44] But a 'free world' led by the US represented a desirable arrangement of political realities, and US hegemony seemed essential for its survival. Builders and architects of world order were prepared to dismantle the IMF and the rest of the global capital apparatus, and

> all ... constraints were removed upon US economic profligacy. The US budget deficit for the fiscal year ending June 30 1972 was quite calmly forecast by the Treasury at close to 39 billion dollars ... not only had the US compelled the other nations of the West to pay for the overseas costs of the US war in Asia, it had accomplished something of far greater significance. Those overseas military costs were now the central banking assets of the non-US members of the IMF.[45]

The unthinkable had happened: the US was maintaining its power through bankruptcy. The American Dream that Reagan promised to make true amounted to unveiling a future in which the US gave up the products of its vast industrial muscle in exchange for the paper the nation had printed and persuaded other countries to accommodate as banking assets. In this respect the falsity of Reagan was not only physically apt but symbolically appropriate: plastic surgery, make-up, hair dye, cue-cards – the whole performance of the presidency attempted to body forth economic and political power that was other than pretended. The style had no content.

The picture of Reagan's first election to presidential office in 1980 that Cooke gives us is style devoid of content. The result, he told listeners, was one 'unhindered movement of the landslide, first in the South, then through the Mid-West, then into the North-East and, finally, across the West to make the map one sheet of uniform blue'.[46] This is by no means a valid comment on the election. When we look at the results from the Electoral College, Reagan won 44 of the 56 states, with 489 of the possible 538 votes. But only 54 per cent of people eligible to vote had bothered to go and vote at all. Of that total 54 per cent, Carter got 41.7 per cent and Reagan 51.6 per cent. (The remaining 6.7 per cent went to the independent candidate, John Anderson.) In essence Reagan's 'landslide' amounted to no more than 27–28 per cent of the vote – not what might be called a continental shift.[47]

Cooke's off-the-hoof journalism has never been noticeable for its controversy. Scepticism is a required element of a journalist's equipment. It is of no small significance that Alistair Cooke's initial exposure to practical journalism was as a film reviewer. He is very good at describing what he sees. His is not an inquiring mind. He tends to take the world on face value. The *New Statesman* recorded in 1978 that he wrote his copy on the democratic convention by taking quick notes about the bunting, then watching the event on the television in his hotel room. It is symptomatic that he called Woodward and Bernstein the 'ditch-diggers of the *Washington Post*'. It is, furthermore, quite difficult to locate Cooke ideologically. He frequently acknowledges his debt to H.L. Mencken. Is one alone in wishing he had learned more from his master, and cultivated a real scepticism, a readiness to doubt popular opinion and the goodwill of office-holders? Cooke's inclinations seem to lie somewhere between a Roosevelt New-Dealer and the authors of the *Daughters of the Revolution's Manual for US Citizenship*.

I once had a feeling of *deja vu* so deep that it was almost vertiginous. It was while watching the pageant 'America on parade' at the end of a fun-packed day at Disneyland. It was a thrilling presentation of the energy and skills of the early colonists, the courage of the revolutionaries, the enterprise of the homesteaders, the spirit of the western pioneers, the creative drive that built the railroads, invented the telephone and the phonograph, and the bravery of the armed forces who went everywhere to make the world safe for democracy. (The selection and omissions are arresting.) Over the years Alistair Cooke has selected a set of units from past history and present events with an overall generic unity – an harmonious mixture of convenient memory and well-judged observation – an ideal of America past and present. It is a theme park of the mind, a dream world. It is the thinking man's Disneyland.

7

Michael Cimino's America

Brian Lee

Cimino's two major films to date, *The Deer Hunter* (1978) and *Heaven's Gate* (1980), both directly confront complex and troubling issues of race and class in America. They do so, moreover, within a variety of contexts that constitute a broad picture of American society, past and present, rural and urban. In addition to these Cimino has made three minor films in which the same themes are obliquely introduced, but are subordinated to the demands of popular genres. It is for that reason that I designate them as 'minor'. The term is in no sense meant to imply any adverse valuation. These are: *Thunderbolt and Lightfoot*, (1974) *The Year of the Dragon* (1985) and *Desperate Hours* (1990). In 1987 he made a sixth film, *The Sicilian*, which also relates tangentially to concerns of this essay, but which demands to be discussed in connection with Francesco Rosi's great precursor, *Salvatore Giuliano*.

Re-viewing this body of work and rereading the substantial criticism and commentary that it has attracted, it is impossible not to conclude that Cimino's impressive achievements as a film-maker have been almost universally misunderstood and unappreciated. At one superficial level it is easy to see why this has happened. *The Deer Hunter* fell victim to the retrospective political debate about the Vietnam War and was used indiscriminately as a weapon in the hands of battling factions from the left and right. *Heaven's Gate* suffered a similar fate when its spiralling production costs became the occasion for the demise of United Artists. Steven Bach's account of all this in *Final Cut* [1] is painstaking in detailing all the petty politicking and financial mismanagement indulged in by crass studio executives, but it has nothing to say about the masterpiece that those same executives attempted to suppress or butcher.[2] Like *Citizen Kane*, 40 years earlier, the manner in which the film survived the death throes of departing studio dinosaurs is little short of miraculous, and the fact that Cimino, unlike Welles, continued to work in Hollywood reflects no credit at all on those who would have stopped him if they could, but testifies more to the changed economic conditions of film production there.

At a different level, the misreadings of Cimino's films are more disturbing and cannot be dismissed so cursorily. They stem from a set of radical misconceptions about the nature of and relations between genre, narrative and cinematic realism. And while the critics who make them are sometimes sensitive and sympathetic to Cimino's art, they nevertheless do him a disservice by misconstruing the identity of the object he creates. So that when Richard Combs talks of 'the undoubted failure of *Heaven's Gate* as a conventional narrative' [3] or Ryan and Kelner deplore the same film's avoidance of 'more politically valorized urban industrial class struggles of a later era',[4] it is apparent that the film is being judged in relation to abstract and wholly inappropriate models.

In some respects *The Deer Hunter* suffered even more at the hands of critics unwilling to see it for what it is. By the time of its release, ten years after *The Green Berets* (1968), it had become virtually impossible for any serious film-maker contemplating Vietnam to follow the old prescription for World War II combat films. The eventual triumph of freedom and democracy brought about by charismatic leaders and their socially diverse GIs, moulded into efficient fighting units, may still have represented Washington's aims and coloured government rhetoric during the war itself, but by 1978 even the most hawkish politicians were admitting that the war had been lost and that American 'democracy' had taken a severe blow. More significantly perhaps, the signifiers that were used to construct this outmoded scenario – freedom, democracy, individualism, equality – had lost much of their descriptive utility and evocative power during the previous decade, and were heard much less frequently than such terms as patriarchal oppression, multinational capitalism, racism and imperialism. Even if America had won the war the prevailing climate of thought in 1978 would have made it virtually impossible for Cimino to create a film in which a hero endowed with superior skill and moral power defeats an evil or inhuman other. As Jeanine Basinger points out in *The World War II Combat Film*,[5] there are very few differences in genre between World War II films and those set during the Korean War. But apart from John Wayne's *The Green Berets* (1968), films about the Vietnam War – even *First Blood* (1982) – have had to incorporate an entirely new myth about war and more particularly about war as it expresses contemporary attitudes to race and class.

It is around this issue that the most interesting critical controversy has gathered, often generating more moral heat than aesthetic illumination, and sometimes confusing one with the other. *The Deer Hunter* has been described as a fascist film in its use of images ('*The Deer Hunter's* mountain landscapes are, so to speak, "white", "Aryan", a distillation of elemental purity, both natural, and, by a subconscious extension, racial') and also in its use of the motif of 'one shot':

the movie's pivotal metaphor, to be developed through its scenes of Russian Roulette, is unquestionably linked to the historical ideology of Fascism: killing as an elitist, almost Godlike rite, legitimised by a spurious affinity with gladiatorial combat and medieval knight-errantry. It seeks to invest killing with the lonely nobility of suicide, another act requiring no more than one bullet.[6]

These statements contain very obvious rhetorical tricks and false arguments. The 'so to speak' white mountains are transformed 'by a subconscious extension' (whose?) into a racial image, and the 'It' of the second quotation is placed in such a way as to refer both to the ideology of fascism and to *The Deer Hunter*, thereby changing what was merely a tenuous link to an identification. And even if the fascist images and metaphors are present in the film, surely the nature of Nick's suicide, portrayed neither as lonely nor noble, and Mike's eventual inability to kill the deer, would constitute a most damning criticism of that ideology. In point of fact it seems inappropriate to call Cimino's work either fascist or even reactionary – such labels serving only to flatten out and simplify the complexity and density of his work.

The same is true of the argument about Cimino's realism, though here the issues are more tangled and subtle. *The Deer Hunter* has been both praised and blamed for its realism and its lack of it, as well as for its refurbishment of classical American myths and motifs. With one or two exceptions, the critics who have entered upon this debate have merely confused realism with reality, and this elementary error can easily be dealt with, though again it is instructive to notice how critical sleights-of-hand are employed to obscure unreliable thought processes. John Pilger, writing in the weekend *Guardian* about Vietnam movies in general (24 February 1990), castigates Cimino for his use of the game of Russian roulette in the film. He says that he can find no evidence to show that the Vietnamese forced their prisoners to indulge in this barbarous sport, and concludes that Cimino invented these episodes for his own dramatic purposes. Indeed, he quotes the director as saying that 'the fine wires have got really crossed and the line between reality and fiction has become blurred'.

Pilger then goes on immediately to say:

Cimino's discrepancies might not have mattered had he not insisted that his film's most memorable moments were based upon fact – 'meaningful horror' he called them – and had his film not been regarded virtually as documentary and had he not been elevated to a champion of America's 'new patriotism'.

Whatever status we accord to Cimino's own statements, it is difficult to make 'meaningful horror' stand for 'based upon fact'. And if there are people who regard the film 'virtually' as documentary, and Cimino himself as a 'new patriot', that is a sad reflection, not on Cimino but on his public. Moreover, as Robin Wood points out: 'If it were proved tomorrow that, after all, Russian roulette was practiced by the Vietcong, this would not make *The Deer Hunter* in the least a better film than it is.' [7] This seems indisputable to me, though I am not sure that Wood has addressed the main issue here. The question is not so much about the film's quality as about its pretension to realism.

A more interesting debate, and one that takes us closer to the main critical issue, has centred upon the film's presentation of its main locales and characters, especially the contrast between the Vietcong in and around Saigon and the Ukrainian/Americans in Clairton, Pennsylvania. I propose to look closely at a few of these recent interpretations, not because they are intrinsically significant, but as a way of approaching one of the problems that has dominated much of the best recent writing about genre films, realism and ideology.

It has been argued by Antony Easthope [8] that by 'stretching narrative realism to its limits' the film 'manages to reproduce almost all four of the features in the structure of the traditional war film. The hero, collectivity, the enemy as other – only victory is missing (and is replaced with mourning).' Leaving aside for the moment the astonishing phrase '*only* victory is missing' (as if it didn't make much difference to the meaning of the film), I want to explore the idea of narrative realism being stretched to its limits.

For Easthope, the film's realism is 'troubled' by the fact that 'this film about Vietnam doesn't show Vietnam until 1 hour and 10 minutes into the action' and because 'the two halves of the film are only tenuously and somewhat enigmatically held together across the story of four shots from a gun'. First, *The Deer Hunter* is not about Vietnam in the way Easthope implies. It is a film about American society and the American psyche and the ways in which these relate to the war in Vietnam. Exactly the same point could be made about Norman Mailer's novel *Why are We in Vietnam?* which doesn't mention Vietnam until its last page but is nevertheless one of the most trenchant analyses of American involvement in the war. Second, the four shots that link the major episodes are enigmatic only for those who do not know what the film is about. Mike's 'one shot' that kills the deer enunciates his moral code while those fired by the Vietcong and by Nick demonstrate its futility and underlying barbarity; a fact recognised by Mike himself when he returns to the mountains and refuses to fire the fourth shot at the deer. If anything remains enigmatic it is only the failure of hostile critics to make plain the nature of their objections to Cimino's film. With a little more pressure, however, I think that they can be persuaded into clearer view.

As a matter of fact, Easthope's next sentence begins to uncover his critical position: 'The constraints set by the attempts to reproduce ideology as a unity and so without contradiction are well seen in the way community is portrayed in the text.' The community in question is that of Clairton, a Pennsylvania steel town populated by Americans of Ukrainian stock, a choice that, according to another of Cimino's critics, Mike Westlake, 'allows both the plausibility and the distance necessary for it to function as a representation of the American essence'.[9] In his view, other possibilities, such as a small mid-western town or a New York Italian community, would have been either too realistic or too much of a special case. What we are given instead is a community with

> no generation gap ... no teenage delinquency, no racial problems (because all come of the same stock), no decaying city centre, and prosperous suburbs, no nearby campus with protesting students ... and interestingly in the face of the evident poverty of the community, no urge to better themselves, no unions, no bosses, no police, just folk.

I think that what Westlake and Easthope are implying in the passages I have quoted is that Cimino is portraying an ideal (false) community, and that what he has a duty to locate are the contradictions and conflicts inherent in capitalist culture. These, it is further implied, are what lie behind America's desperate imperialist adventure, and are the source of its failure. Now while this is a perfectly tenable political position, it is possible to respect it without also accepting its use as a yardstick to measure the success or failure of bourgeois art representing a liberal humanist, or indeed any other philosophical or moral position. What is at issue here is not just a reading of a particular film, but the wholesale rejection of Hollywood genre films as ideological manipulation. These essays, stemming as they do from the ideas of Horkheimer, Greenberg and MacDonald, remain unconvincing as criticism because, as I propose to show, they signally fail to come to terms with the text Cimino creates.

The same is true of critics who attack the film from a different political angle, in this case one that defines popular art in terms of its audience's ritual gratification. Gilbert Adair is representative here. He calls *The Deer Hunter* a 'servile barometer of its audience's aspirations', and conveniently for my purposes bases his view in part upon a reading of Cimino's portrayal of Clairton:

Here, in short, in a close-up of that America which Michael, Steven and Nick (Christopher Walken) have been called upon to defend, and it would be churlish not to admit that Cimino has recreated the texture of a small, tightly knit industrial community with an almost novelistic wealth of detail: the local supermarket where Nick's girlfriend Linda (Meryl Streep) works, the masculine clutter of the bungalow shared by Nick and Michael, the dark silhouette, both ominous and reassuring, of the iron foundry, and the entanglement of the television aerials and bulbous church domes peacefully cohabiting the town's skyline. This part of the movie is bathed in the Edenic atmosphere of a huge, extended and classless family (as rarely in the American cinema, one has the impression of everyone knowing everyone else), felt most strongly during the wedding party itself, a spectacular set-piece of dancing (both Russian heel-dance and American rock), singing, eating and drinking, with neatly laundered children, plump Slavic grannies and garrulous old American legionnaires packing every corner of the screen.[10]

In their different ways, these readings of the film seem to be equally misguided; Adair's because he fails to perceive the tensions and contradictions in the contrasting images on the screen, the others because they imagine that the lack of institutionalised conflicts in the foreground of the film implies ideological unity. What Cimino is giving us, both in his general *mise-en-scene* and in the long wedding sequence that stands at the centre of the film's first section, is a carefully constructed picture of a society losing its former homogeneity as it is absorbed by the undifferentiated dreck of contemporary American culture. The cupolas of the Orthodox church do not peacefully cohabit the skyline with television aerials and the supermarket. As the camera angles make clear, the church is losing its prominence as it is hemmed in by a mass of modern clutter. And the foundry where Mike and his friends are first seen is important, not because of its ominous or reassuring silhouette, but because the inferno inside points us insistently towards Vietnam and the fires of Saigon. The wedding party extends and emphatically establishes the same theme of a culture clinging unsuccessfully to the vanishing signs of its ethnic origins. The marriage itself is based upon a deception with the pregnant bride carrying another man's child, and the couple's uncertain future is clearly indicated by the drop of wine (blood) spilt on her white wedding gown. The party following the ceremony quickly degenerates into uncontrolled, formless dancing and violence, and ends with Mike, the film's 'hero' running naked down the street. Before that he and his friends confront the 'uninvited' guest, a soldier returned from Vietnam, whose only reply to their questions is 'Fuck it'. The atmosphere created in this early part of the film is anything but Edenic.

The same is true of the first hunting sequence where the idealised romantic imagery and the grandiose score have to be read in juxtaposition with the crude attitudes, language and behaviour of Mike's friends. They have no appreciation of either the landscape or the rituals of hunting, and Mike's attempts to impose order and control lead to a rupture within the group, with his motives being questioned, not merely by his companions but inevitably by the viewer as well. More importantly, the first hunting trip must be read as a prologue to the Vietnam episodes, just as the second one serves as an epilogue to them. Once again Mike stalks a deer, but when he has it within his sights he lifts the rifle and fires above it's head. Returning to the hunting lodge he finds Stanley brandishing a hand-gun. In a cold fury he disarms him, forces him into a parody of Russian roulette, and finally hurls the gun down the mountainside. These rejections are absolutely crucial to the film's meaning and to its implicit commentary on an American tradition which embraces Hemingway as well as such film genres as the Western and the war film. Cimino's affinities here are with Mailer's *Why are We in Vietnam?* or perhaps more closely with the text that hovers behind both of them, Faulkner's *The Bear*. Mailer's account of the pilgrimage made by Tex and DJ up the Alaskan mountain has some similarities – the rejection of weapons, the description of the sunset, and the appearance of the moose – but the use Mailer makes of this episode, the significance he draws from it, is quite different: more Lawrentian than Faulknerian.

> God was a beast, not a man, and God said, 'Go out and kill – fulfil my will, go out and kill,' and they hung there each of them on the knife of the divide in all conflict of lust to own the other yet in fear of being killed by the other and as the hour went by and the lights shifted, something in the radiance of the North went into them, and owned their fear, some communion of telepathies and new powers, and they were twins, never to be near as lovers again, but killer brothers owned by something, prince of darkness, lord of light, they did not know.[11]

As Richard Poirier points out, this landscape might, in its self-sufficiency, be free from human 'shit' or from any kind of human genius in the form of technology (and just before Stanley has his gun taken from him he is told that he is 'full of shit'), but finally its beauty is inhospitable. No one could 'relinquish' himself to it, as in Faulkner.[12] In point of fact, Mike does not exactly relinquish himself to nature in this sequence either. After he spares the deer, his shouted 'OK' hangs in the air more like a question than an affirmation, and marks his troubled ambivalence for us.

The status of Mike as 'hero' is crucial to any reading of the film. Superficially he appears to conform to Robert Ray's definition of the traditional Western hero as a man who combines the qualities of the Outlaw and the Citizen to assert an American exceptionalism.[13] Like his fictional predecessors, Mike is endowed with unusual skill and courage which he uses individualistically to restore and heal the community. Unlike them, however, his attempts end in failure. Nick is dead, Steve is a paraplegic, and the war is lost. The important, unmotivated shot that introduces the final sequence of the film underlines this last fact. We see a television screen showing pictures of maimed American helicopters being pushed over the side of an aircraft carrier, presumably to make space for fleeing refugees. It is an eloquent symbol of the failure of American technology in the war. As the friends then gather to attend Nick's wake, Mike is deliberately marginalised. He sits looking ill-at-ease and out of place in his military uniform, and when he attempts to help with the preparations he fumbles with the knives and forks, dropping them on the table. And as they uncertainly join together in singing 'God Bless America' one is reminded that it was Nick who had earlier accused Mike of trying to usurp God.

It would be difficult to think of a film more unlike the traditional combat movie than *The Deer Hunter*. I would suggest that of the four essential elements attributed to the genre by Antony Easthope (a hero, collectivity, the enemy as other and victory), *The Deer Hunter* contains only one, and it is this, the presentation of the Vietcong as stereotyped Oriental villains, that prevents it from completely fulfilling its ambitious aspirations. Nevertheless, it remains the most comprehensive artistic statement about the war to come out of America.

I suspect that this limitation in Cimino's vision derives from his inability to wholly free himself from the form of what Leslie Fiedler calls 'the disguised Western'. Many critics have compared *The Deer Hunter* with Westerns ranging from *My Darling Clementine* to *Rio Bravo*, and while those comparisons have some point, I think that his indebtedness to the genre is less self-conscious, and as a result not sufficiently critical of it. He certainly remedied that mistake, though, in *Heaven's Gate*, by confronting the traditional Western head on and subjecting its supporting myths to the kind of exhaustive analysis which ought to have rendered the form obsolete.

In choosing the Johnson County wars for his subject Cimino

removed the American Indians from consideration altogether, focusing on the power of class rather than on race, and though his portrayals of both new immigrant communities in Wyoming and individual immigrants is dense and grainy, giving the film a feeling of historical authenticity, his prime concern is to expose the roots of American capitalism, blackened by the bloody conflicts between individual robber barons and newly formed, uncertain democratic communities. There is a very obvious continuity of theme running from *The Deer Hunter* to *Heaven's Gate* that encompasses more than just the inability of skilful, courageous idealists (Mike/Averill) to save the community, but also the nature of the values that are put under threat by the relentless drive of capitalism.

Robin Wood, in praising the film (he calls it one of the supreme achievements of the Hollywood cinema),[14] suggests that its values are refreshingly naive, especially when contrasted with the weary cynicism of so much contemporary cinema. This, I would suggest, is the inevitable consequence of viewing its events through the accumulated layers of completed history to catch a glimpse of a moment at which it could all have turned out differently. What I think is more to the point is Cimino's indictment of those representatives of eastern and Old World power and privilege who failed to prevent American society from taking the direction it did. This is why the prologue and the epilogue of the film are so important. Like the opening and closing sequences of *The Deer Hunter* they point to the causes and consequences of the hero and his culture's failure, moving from exuberant activity and ritual celebration to isolation, defeat and passivity. The Harvard sequence is a brilliant visual encapsulation of the film's main themes both sexual and social; the waltz foreshadowing the great roller-skating sequence and contrasting with it, and the mock student battle rehearsing the final, climatic encounter between Canton's mercenaries and the immigrants, a battle which ends ironically when the mercenaries are saved at the last moment by the US cavalry. Like the wedding party sequence in *The Deer Hunter*, the Harvard ritual goes awry; the students are boisterous, disrespectful, and slightly out of control. Billy Irvine's (old) world weariness, the Reverend Doctor's ineffectual platitudes, and Averill's disengagement, all point to the ultimate failure of the Brahmins to save their society from its rape at the hands of the ruthless Canton. Averill's lack of commitment is also manifested in his personal failure with Ella, who is also raped by Canton's men, and comes to understand that she cannot depend upon Averill for her security and protection. The epilogue, in which we see Averill as an older, bored figure, trapped in the cage of his expensive yacht and his empty marriage, is an integral part of the film; essential to our understanding of his failure, and that of his class.

It is hardly surprising that Cimino's films have not been great successes at the box office, nor that they have ruffled the sensibilities of his employers. In departing from the reassuring tutor code of Hollywood he has baffled audiences expecting more guidance through his films. And in daring to question such sacred cows as the success ethic and American Exceptionalism, he has proved too subversive for executives who want only to reproduce proven formulas. It is not too much to hope, though, that eventually his time will come and his genius will be more widely recognised.

8

The Politics of Formalism in Post-war American Poetry

David Murray

The test of a 'politics of poetry' is in the entry of poetry into the world in a political way.

Barrett Watten

A revolution involves a change in structure; a change in style is not a revolution.

Jerome Rothenberg

If you decide to do something politically, you do something that has political efficacy. And if you decide to write poetry, then you write poetry, not something that you hope, or deceive yourself into believing, can save people who are suffering.

George Oppen[1]

This essay is partly a response to a recurrent problem I have encountered in teaching and discussing modern American poetry, and partly an attempt to connect this to the wider political issues of community and pluralism posed by ethnic and other pressure groups. Put simply, the poetry I find most challenging and interesting often fails to engage the students' attention and emotional engagement. This is likely to go to poems which they can respond to as personal, autobiographical, Confessional. The easy answer (leaving aside the question of my teaching competence) would be to say that they are responding to content, and to things that they recognise and are confirmed by, rather than to the complexities and uncertainties of form, and its interplay with content. But increasingly a lot of these poems are also the affirmative expression of a particular group, and their broadly political dimension and intention complicates the issue. Accessibility and popular appeal are seen as positive attributes, and the appeal to personal experience as a powerful political tool. The argument for the importance of the Language Poets, or Charles Olson, over, for instance, Adrienne Rich, must not, then, set them up on one side of an aesthetics – politics divide, but demonstrate the ways in which their poetic concerns are inextricably linked with a redefined politics.

The well-worn and sterile debates of the 1930s tended to set up art-as-weapon against art-as-retreat or enclave, and see a concern for form as a distraction from the political, and it is possible to see my impasse with students in these terms, but my aim here is to undermine that distinction. To do this I use the writings of the Language poets, who are particularly interesting, in combining uncompromisingly experimental poetry with an explicit Marxist political orientation.[2] Through them I explore the dangers and possibilities of the uses of the personal and subjective both in poetry and in political analysis, within a society which has increasingly shown the capacity to commodify and assimilate all oppositional stratagems. Much of the discussion about the concept of a postmodern condition has centred round the assumption of just such a society and has concentrated on the role of the local and the decentralised as reflecting a rejection of grand narratives or unifying ideas. At the same time the challenge to the idea of a pluralistic but unified society found in political and ethnic groups is reflected in the questioning of any overall consensus or criteria for literature, and the nervous inclusiveness of recent anthologies and courses. The idea of an inclusive America, and what cultural forms it would express itself in, has been subjected to a prolonged and fascinating critique in American poetry since at least Whitman, and it is worth looking briefly at the earlier dimensions of the poetic/political self, in order to isolate the key terms of this essay, which are self, form and audience.

'What is that aboriginal self on which reliance may be grounded?' Emerson's question was asked in the context of an argument about the competing claims of a religion wedded, as he saw it, to second-hand revelation and social conformism, versus a personal power and vision gained through first-hand experience of nature and its transcendental properties. It was also asked in the unsettling knowledge of the difficulties of being sure that what one was setting up *against* society in the name of the self, and of personal experience, was not in fact merely a distorted and monstrous version of it. What was needed, then, was, as Thoreau later described it, a fulcrum outside society, from which it could be moved. Later formulations of this opposition have taken a multiplicity of forms, but while the confidence in a Romantic or Transcendental self may have been discarded, the fundamental opposition has persisted, and with it the idea of a place beyond or prior to the social, which can be invoked not as an *escape* from the social and political but as a resource, a source of strength to oppose it. Emerson's doubts also persist, of course, though more likely now to be phrased in the language of Marx.

The question then becomes the extent to which an appeal to a subjectivity, or transcendence, can be a resource against the commodification and reification of modern society. The danger is that it is just itself a by-product of society's power, an illusory and entirely safe and harmless area of freedom without effect or consequences. Put like this, the sterility of the opposition and the necessity of some middle terms become clear. In particular we can introduce the nature of a public space, as a basis for a model of politics, the activity of a polis or community.

Given their generally low view of the social it was inevitable that for the Transcendentalists true art would be seen as the expression of a fundamental self. Poetry would be original when it came directly from our origins. For Whitman this did not necessarily exclude society, because in America, at least potentially, he found a material expression of his self. Thus he invoked an organic community, for which he claimed the right to speak. As his extensive political writings show, he was fully aware and critical of the rifts and inequalities in a changing America,[3] but the America celebrated in *Leaves of Grass* is based on a consensus and a totality which is achievable through an idea of democracy. It is democracy which is 'the password primeval', the reconciling of the one and the many, and also, as the word primeval suggests, of origins and goals. In a manoeuvre to be repeated many times, change and invention, the modern is linked back to, and validated by the primary, the ahistorical and mythic.[4] Form is very much the issue here, in that the breaking of forms is in the name of something new, but also of something more fundamental, more primary. So invention becomes a finding of what is already there to be found. The dynamism of a new nation becomes justified by seeing it as an unfolding out of the past, a revealing of a pattern already there in essence. So dead and rigid forms need to be swept away, and change and invention are justified.

Whitman's synthesising vision, manages not only to transcend or elide the opposition between the one and the many but also, through his taking on a bardic and public role, bridges the gap between poetic and social forms. Emerson's statement that 'it is the property of the imagination to flow and not to freeze' also involves a concept of the Imagination from Kant and Coleridge, which places it as a unifying force, which links the transient with the fundamental and unchanging. It flows, rather than explodes or breaks. So in Whitman's America of *Leaves of Grass* the conflicts his political prose struggles with are healed or transcended. Later poets have been unable to find such a perfect fit between poetic and political form, but the relation between the two has continued to be an issue. Just as, in political terms, an absolute opposition between a free self and an imprisoning society provides no answer to the question *how* the values of the free self can take effect in society, and needs some mediating conception of the public and political, so in literary terms any claim to be able to change society by art needs to be able to explain the mechanism by which this happens, particularly if it is working with a view of art as autonomous and separate.

Trying to deal with the related issues of the uses of various aspects of the personal and subjective, and the political implications of poetic form in the period since World War II means having to take account of the persistence of oppositions, which manage to obscure the complexities of both the poetry and the politics. The New Critics codified aspects of Modernism in order to separate out the realm of the aesthetic as an area of impersonality, and to stress the autonomous and free-standing nature of a work of art. In doing so they excluded politics as antithetical to poetry, and in the process led to a marginalisation of whole areas of poetic experiment, and achievement, as Jerome Rothenberg demonstrates in his anthology *Revolution of the Word*.[5] Perhaps the most serious effect of the simplifying oppositions of art-as-weapon of the 1930s Marxist ideologues and art-as-autonomy of the New Critics, was not just the totally inadequate response to important political poets of the 1930s and later, like the Objectivists, but the long-term distortion of political and aesthetic debate in the Cold War period, in which the difference was reduced to a matter of complexity. Politics was simple-minded and direct, propaganda, and art was complex, ironic self-referring. The row over the Bollingen award to Ezra Pound for the *Pisan Cantos* revealed both the difficulties of arguing in these terms and the unavailability of any others.[6]

When critical opposition to such aestheticism came, though, it was not in the form of a reinvigoration of any political dimension, but in the name of the personal. The development of the idea of the Confessional managed to pit the personal against the impersonal and ironic mode championed by New Criticism, but to do so in a way which, true to Cold War rhetoric, kept it very separate from the political. In fact the advent of Confessional poetry still tends to be told as a narrative of liberation, an escape from restrictions, a new finding of self, though the nature of this liberation is confusing. Confession might imply a therapeutic coming into the open, but the nature of that open space is not clear, since we often seem to be eavesdropping on something private, the Catholic confessional rather than speech in a public place.

So politics was again avoided, through an ideological rejection which saw individualism as being the only locus of value and of freedom. This is itself deeply ideological, and in placing the area of freedom in the private and subjective it in fact restricts it, conferring a sort of absolute power, but in an area which by definition has no public space or audibility. It also diminishes the political by discounting any possible role for the subjective within it. An associated critical manoeuvre was to use the term Confessional to describe poetry which in fact used the personal and subjective but in quite different ways, with M.L. Rosenthal in one critical study even corralling Allen Ginsberg into the group, for instance. Of course there are no clear demarcations between different presentations and uses of the self, and of subjective experience, but one of the things at issue could be identified as the degree to which the subjective experience is itself transformed and re-viewed by the formal processes of the poem, or whether the poem is a straightforward medium for the expression of a view.

If the reintroduction of the personal is merely to turn the writing of poems into realist descriptions of angst, or whatever emotion seems appropriate to poetry rather than prose, then even when the political is reintroduced, as in the large number of poems produced under the personal-is-political banner from a wide variety of groups, what we have is writing which often leaves intact the very subjective experience which should be questioned by the particular resources made available by poetry, those of language and form. Instead the most we are likely to find in the way of using the properties of the form is a series of metaphoric or metonymic connections to link private experience and general political situations in a non-exploratory way.

It could, of course, be argued that the straightforward language was a positive political advantage in making the poems available and accessible, and the objections to it dismissed as elitist, which would be a re-run of the 1930s' positions. But the more fundamental criticism of such poems is that in using language uncritically as a transparent medium, and in seeing personal experience as the solution rather than the problem, they produce bad politics as well as bad poetry. The most explicit critiques of this kind, and the most consciously developed alternative poetic strategies, come from the Language poets, with their scepticism about referentiality and the expression of subjectivity. Robert Grenier, for instance, in a discussion with Bob Perelman and others on the use of the 'first person', criticises poems which offer a reassuring sense of self

> that you can project yourself onto and identify with as a kind of locus of sensibility that you'd like to be possessed of, at least while reading the page, to give the world a center of feeling it might not have in the flux of shifting phenomena. [7]

Instead of language and the formal properties of the poem being used to *explore* such certainties they are merely affirmed, and Ron

Silliman makes explicit the connection with other unreflexive poetry. A William Stafford poem is discussed and unfavourably compared with one by Frank O'Hara, where, as Barrett Watten puts it: 'O'Hara reinterprets literary forms in terms of the sub-jective I. But he doesn't propose that subjective I as the final result.' [8] In Stafford, though, 'What makes the poem work is that same sense of agreement you get in bad didactic writing, whether it's talking about the individualized subjective I or the People or Logos.'

What is crucial about O'Hara's use of a self in his poetry, and so strikingly absent from so many of the imitators, is the fluidity of the self, the sense of its creation and dissolution in the poem itself. This goes with a mistrust of all permanencies and abstractions:

> The only truth is face to face,
>   the poem whose words become your mouth
> and dying in black and white we fight
>   for what we love, not are.[9]

This poem, 'Ode Salute to the French Negro Poets' is a good example of what Watten refers to above, in that although it is self-consciously using a lyric voice at times, and asserting its value politically, the poets he is addressing, like Aime Cesaire, point towards both surrealism and a world of politics beyond the self-imposed limitations of the lyric. What could be a cosy reduc-tion to the personal ('the only truth is face to face') is under-mined by the way the self is inextricable from the poem, the words from the mouth that utters them, so that uttering becomes othering in language, a giving up rather than a holding on and defining of self (dying in black and white). The black and white of print is of course also that of racial difference, and the parallel is clear in the destructive effects of prejudice in fighting for what we are, what keeps us separate, rather than for something beyond which unites us. This political point is actually exemplified in the way we are not allowed to rest in a style or attitude for long in O'Hara's poems.

O'Hara's reference to Cesaire points to his long-term interest, in common with other 'New York poets', in Dada and surrealism, and also in a whole range of French poets. These offered possible models for writing which avoided high seriousness and a tight sense of a controlling ego, and there is a clear continuity of concern here with the Language poets. In general they pick up early Ashbery, particularly the more clearly surrealist poems of *The Tennis Court Oath*, rather than his later work, and while the O'Hara of 'Second Avenue' would also fit this surrealist model, even the 'I do this, I do that' poems of the *Lunch Poems* can be seen as closer to surrealism than to the Confessional, in the terms I have outlined above. André Breton's 'For Dada', for instance, gives a clear sense of the liberating effects of a release from a controlling and ordering sense of self:

> I speak for the pleasure of compromising myself ... The obscurity of our utterances is constant ... The Dadaists from the start have taken care to state that they want nothing ... What is myself? Don't know, don't know, don't know.

This passage is quoted by Barrett Watten, but for him surrealism's ultimate recourse to a subconscious implied the danger of reinvoking a unity. At the level of content it was 'above all a defense of the self and its value in art'. In breaking down established orders it still implied a more fundamental (subconscious) self.

> One of the problems with the attack on normative grammar, which would break it down into bits and pieces of verbal rubble which might then release libidinal flux, is that it demands a prior value, 'a whole person in a whole world'.[10]

Since this is not possible, as far as Watten is concerned, 'we have to go back to the original impossible act'.

Watten's rejection of surrealism here can also apply much more widely, in that fragmentation and disruption as a step towards a larger reincorporation, a revealing of a larger whole, is a constant theme in American poetry. If the purpose of breaking into pieces is not to reassemble in a larger or fuller order, what is it? Watten is interested in the point of overload, the point when a unifying principle breaks down, and his account of Olson's Berkeley reading stresses this aspect. The reading has often been seen as a quintessential Olson performance, where his precarious ability to incorporate and synthesise materials from an ever-increasing range, while never coming to rest, was actually demonstrated in performance.

> Olson's refusal of closure gives the effect of presence, and this imagistic 'stand' appears as the 'solution' to a lifelong public and political dilemma. In fact, the theme of Olson's political experience, the failure of liberal politics from the Roosevelt era to the present, is central to Olson's assumption of the hero-poet.[11]

Rather than go along with this, though, Watten concentrates on a different effect on the listener, which leads away from the person holding the materials together, and towards the materials themselves: 'The availability of materials in the discourse – the *linguistic* present created – far outweighs the "in-time romance of self" in importance.' For Watten this moment can be compared with an earlier point of poetic breakthrough. 'Just as the phenomenon of *zaum* poetry in the Russian Futurist movement, so the mass of contingent detail that could not be integrated into the prior American modernist models produced the "superinduction" of Olson's Berkeley reading.'

By concentrating on the point at which an overload of meaning topples over into something else, and seeing it not as incoherence or failure, but as encouraging or enabling an attention to the medium itself, Watten might be seen as offering a way of *reading* as much as anything else, but this raises a problem of intention, as is clear in an exchange over Pound's later *Cantos*. Ron Silliman describes how

> Kenner was sitting down there trying to figure out 'Angold *tethneke*' and everything else like that, and I was learning how to read words without feeling anxious about the fact that I didn't know perhaps the language they were written in.[12]

Watten's uneasy response to this ('How did you decide that that was good enough?') points, I think, back to a Formalist respect for the terms of operation of the text itself, and crucially this respect involves the *content*. As he says elsewhere: 'I don't see that an open text, one that isn't organised around content, doesn't run similar kind of risks [of creating a power imbalance between reader and writer] in terms of overcoding or blanking out (undercoding).' [13] At the same time Watten is concerned to distinguish this from a New Critical emphasis on the autonomy of the work of art which would cut it off from politics.[14] What he finds important in Russian Formalism, Futurism and, in different ways, in surrealism is a way of claiming political relevance for what was dismissed by others as mere formal experimentation. So the importance of the Olson reading was that it represented the move from politics-as-theme to politics-as-form in Olson himself, and was not just a result of how Watten as auditor chose to respond to it.

The main criticisms of Formalism have centred round the extent to which, in its concern for *ostranenie*, estrangement and the laying bare of the device, it ignores any aspect of the text which cannot be handled in terms of formal codes and expectations, since these, in their breaking, are what constitutes it as an aesthetic phenomenon. This can be seen as producing a version of the text which is autonomous, but also cut off from change and history. The defence would be that the aesthetic effect in fact *depends* on change, the making strange, but, more fundamentally perhaps, that this change is always a response to content. As Watten puts it: 'a new technique is the demand of a new content.' *Zaum*, or transrational poetics, is caused not by an escape from meaning, but by an overload of content. Zaum is more than just a formal device, it is 'a basic response to unassimilated content'.[15] The claims go further than this, though, in that the influence goes the other way too, since the importance avant-garde artists have claimed for themselves is based on the importance of their changes in form in political terms, and this is where the Language poets' relation to Marxism is of real importance.

The dominance of a crude socialist realism, propagated through the Party apparatus of Writers' Congresses, printing presses and so on had the effect of marginalising the stubborn and continuing presence of left experimentalism, and of course the mainstream American criticism, dominated by New Criticism, was also happy to accept a parallel simplified opposition of experiment versus propaganda, which it could fit into an overall opposition of freedom versus State control. The renewed attention to the debates of the 1920s over Modernism and Marxism has tended to present Walter Benjamin and Brecht as outright winners over the Stalinism of Lukács, but this is to ignore the importance of Lukács' analysis of reification and commodification, without which concepts, certainly, the Frankfurt School's key analysis of the culture industry would be impossible.

In America the real debates can be seen not in the rather thin critical and polemic writings of the 1920s and 1930s but in the poetry of the Objectivists and the still ignored experimentalists represented in Rothenberg's *Revolution of the Word*. It is this body of poetry, via a Marxism informed by the Frankfurt School, which forms an important context for the Language poets. The Objectivist concern for direct reference, and a language cleansed and transparent, may seem a long way from the work of Silliman or Bernstein, but if the Objectivists insist that language can tell the truth ('that the nouns do refer to something; that it's there, that it's true, the whole implication of these nouns')[16] they are quite clear that this truth does not coincide with the version of reality current in society. One of the definitions Zukofsky gives of the objective is 'desire for what is objectively perfect, inextricably the direction of historic and contemporary particulars' [17] and this is very close to one of the key elements of Lukács' requirements for realism, that it should get beyond the commodified and false view of the world as split between what he identified as impressionism and naturalism, or a world of absolute ahistoric subjectivity and of absolute determinism and fatalism, and represent change and development. The repression and philistinism exercised under the name of socialist

realism should not obscure Lukács' main point here, which can be
used to develop a scepticism about modes of representation without rejecting the whole idea of it. Heller argues that 'the Objectivist
poem does not enact a mimesis but mediates between representa-
tional systems'.[18]

It can be argued, then, that there has always been a clear and
even a necessary connection between Marxism's demonstration of
the ideological character of much that had been considered 'natural'
and a critique of language itself, as a prime site of ideological
investment, but rather than arguing for the cleansing of language so
that it acted more reliably as a neutral and transparent medium of
representation, the Language poets see the referential capacities of
language as themselves taken over by the pervasive commodity
fetishism which affects the rest of the society. Language, then, if
used referentially and 'naturally' can only reduplicate the reification
and commodification of its society, not because of any inherent
repressive or restricting qualities in normative grammar but because
we have become unable to see it as production rather than as a
transparent and inevitable form. The alternative, though, needs to
be more than absolute non-meaning, a form of freedom without
political significance, and the problem, according to James Sherry,
'is not how to create an undifferentiated "libidinal" mass, but how
to avoid it as an alternative to the oppressiveness of normative
grammar'.[19] The original destructive moments of the earlier avant-
garde are not usable, and forms must be developed rather than
destroyed: 'Everything is already destroyed around us. Yet what can
we do to rebuild when the old forms are radioactive with the
half-lives that constructed them?'

So the making strange, the defamiliarising involved in zaum,
those very qualities which seemed to separate it from the real world
and confine it to the aesthetic, now return specifically as *political*
resources. One thing that distinguishes them from the earlier avant-
garde, though, is their greater awareness of the mechanisms and
institutions which control the circulation and distribution of cultural products. Certainly, as Peter Burger has argued,[20] the older
avant-gardes challenged those very categories of art which had
obscured its place as material production, within an economic and
political system, but any optimism that revealing this would itself
constitute a decisive political intervention, with real social consequences, was unfounded, when we look at the processes of marginalisation and assimilation that have taken place since.

A great deal of the renewed critical interest in the political
possibilities of the avant-garde has come out of French post-
structuralism. While the Language poets are clearly familiar with
this material, it is significant, however, that their critique is generated out of Marxism and out of the avant-garde itself, and perhaps

as a result tends to see the problem in more culturally specific terms. In poststructuralism a general and pervasive assumption about the assimilative and cooptive power of modern society sits rather uncomfortably with a celebration of the liberatory power of language when set free from reference; it is difficult to find any conception of a public place where this liberation is to take place, or a politics that would go with it.

The Language poets face up to the power of the culture industry to turn opposition into commodity and its power to render ineffective alternative or subversive positions, so they are acutely aware of the dangers of assuming a causal or even a homologous relation between artistic and social change. Allen Ginsberg's use of Blake's 'When the mode of the music changes, the walls of the city shake' was in the context of a belief in social change and of a public role for the poet for which the turmoil of the 1960s and his own high public profile seemed to give him some justification. In contrast the Language poets inhabit a world in which they see no immediate cracks in the city walls of controlled language, and are suspicious of accommodation and compromise, preferring the historic role of the avant-garde as separate, small and unassimilable.

In 'The Political Economy of Poetry' Ron Silliman analyses the way poems, which 'both are and are not commodities', are produced and circulated, with a view to defining their actual and potential political role: 'Limited and partially determined by economics, the social organization of poetry in the modern period is characterized by two primary structures, the network and the scene.' [21] Large public readings, as part of more general political demonstrations, have given way to smaller and more specific groupings, with poetry directly related to the specific concerns of the group. Silliman's description of the interactive nature of poetry entails a clear awareness on the part of the poet of the audience and its role:

> The goal of the poet who would consciously use the ideological component of her work is to make her audience recognize their own presence in the world as part of a dynamic and structured series of relations, to which a variety of options can be applied. Yet what this recognition entails, and what these options need to be, depends largely on integrating composition of the audience into the field of the writing.[22]

So the poet is offering a way for the audience to see the limits and constructedness of themselves as subjects of/in normal language and the ideological categories it supports, *and* the existence of options, but these options are specific, and related to their actual situation. In other words total freedom is not the issue here, and this would be the answer to the criticism of Altieri who, in an

exchange with Jerome McCann, argues that a reliance on the
reader's sense of interpretive freedom to produce meanings

> comes dangerously close to relying on the idea of the free
> pleasure-seeking consumer that L=A=N=G=U=A=G=E Writ-
> ing's doctrines so pompously revile. After all the basic dodge
> of capitalist advertising consists in promising an undefined
> freedom that depends on a person's thinking that he or she
> is the only one on the block to compose a social order or
> possess a certain way of arranging his or her world.[23]

While this charge is answered, I think, in Silliman's model of the
interactive network, it retains some of its force when we look at the
ways in which Ashbery's later poetry has been read as just such an
invitation, and has been assimilated into a postmodern elevation of
freeplay. The freedom in the freeplay of poststructuralism is very
different from any understanding of what freedom could seriously
mean in a political sense. As McCann insists: '"Audience freedom"
in these texts is to be experienced as one experiences "political
freedom" in any communicative or agenting framework.'[24] He goes
on to point out that in contemporary society this cannot be unproblematically equated with pleasure, given the way instant gratification
of created needs can operate as a political distraction. This argument can, of course, slip into using difficulty and unpopularity as in
themselves guarantees of ideological integrity, and the combination
of scepticism over the culture industry and an ultimate belief in the
oppositional power of art owe more to Adorno than to the celebra-
tory tones of postmodernism.

Nevertheless, while insisting on the need for localised and
unassimilable groups and networks, Silliman is also aware of the
limitations of fragmentation. While this problem is being addressed
politically it also needs to be faced in terms of poetry and audience:

> Different groups exist for real reasons and will have different
> poetries. Oppressed groups have, in a very general sense, a
> similar direction of struggle which permits coalition building
> across group borders. The problem for aesthetically defined
> networks and scenes is how to do likewise.[25]

One of the difficulties is that the Language poets' suspicion of
language as an area of false consciousness rather than of self-
expression would involve a high degree of scepticism about the way
most other political groups use language to develop and valorise a
sense of personal or group identity, but Jerome Rothenberg's view
stresses a different sort of possible unity. His term for a situation of
uniformity and the removal or assimilation of opposing views or
practices is monoculture, which he takes from Claude Lévi-Strauss.

For Rothenberg, the way to keep in touch with what we all have *truly* in common, and not what unites and homogenises us as consumers, is the local and specific:

> There's a problem of creativity becoming unlocalised and broadcast from a few dominant central points until we're all hooked into the great communications network which tends to make our art and our music for us. In terms of the monoculture our way of looking at ourselves in the world is conditioned for us from a greater and greater distance. And the worst thing about it is we don't know it's happening. We get to like it and think it's a creation we share. [26]

For Rothenberg there is a resource which is presocial, or at least prior to *this* society and its values, and to be found in those areas of ourselves and our culture which connect up with the most archaic elements, but he rejects the idea that this involves a mythic and timeless and somehow ahistorical approach.

> I see the process in time as non-linear and multichronic (including but not dominated by dreamtime), though synchronic and simultaneous in consciousness; i.e., the mind bringing together a number of elements from culturally and spatially separated chronologies ... The idea has been to intensify our present consciousness – our sense of past and future not as distant and ourselves as alienated, but as open to our immediate and useful apprehension. [27]

What is really nostalgic is not this, but 'clinging to the older linear model, feeling that if that goes, history itself goes'.

Here Rothenberg can be seen as continuing and restating Olson's wish to 'disclose the intimate connection between personas-continuation-of-millennia-by-acts-of-imagination-as-arising-directly-from-fierce-penetration-of-all-past-persons, places, things and actions-as-data'. [28] Crucial here, though, is the sense of person not as just an accumulation, a product of a process, but an active part of it; not just a user of forms but a creator of them. Situating himself in Gloucester, in the *Maximus* poems Olson presents the geography and history as in the process of discovery. Not the inert facts but the 'finding out' of them, makes up his self:

> the precessions
> of me, the generation of those facts
> which are my words, it is coming
> from all that I no longer am, yet am,
> the slow westward motion
> more than I am. [29]

Olson's etymological tracing of history to 'istorin' ('finding out for oneself') means that he starts from the particular and local, and can use this against the numbing generalisations and definitions of the past ('No Greek will be able/to discriminate my body') and, combined with his physical sense of himself, his 'proprioception', this resistant 'finding out' can constitute a way of being in the world, and in America, which constitutes a public space.

> I have this sense
> that I am one
> with my skin
>   Plus this – plus this:
> that forever the geography
> which leans in
> on me I compell
> backwards I compell Gloucester
> to yield, to
> change
>   Polis
> is this. [30]

9

Entre Americanos: Cuba and the United States

Jacqueline Kaye

> The most ruthless killers ever encountered in Miami arrived among the Mariel refugees. Some men who would have, should have died in Cuban prisons or mental wards will open fire on strangers in crowded bars or cafeterias to simply prove quién es más macho. They consider killing an accomplishment.
>
> Edna Buchanan, *The Corpse had a Familiar Face*[1]

If national identity is itself a kind of fiction, which certain communities agree to believe about themselves, then nations' views of one another are doubly fictitious. Where such views involve hostility and aggression, then we are in a realm of powerful fantasies. Benedict Anderson's *Imagined Communities* [2] captures many of the elements of the fiction of twentieth-century nationhood. The strands of this tapestry of the desired are particularly sought after in post-colonial countries where flags, anthems, languages, religions and rituals of all kinds may have to do duty for the absence of shared experience or to vault the gap in continuity caused by colonial rule and the ossification of tradition and custom.

I am concerned here with the relationship between myths and national identity in two close but profoundly unequal political communities: Cuba and the United States. Neither of these nations is an old one. Cuba's independence from Spanish rule came late and after the War of Independence in the 1890s it passed, effortlessly it seems, into the US sphere of influence. Teddy Roosevelt's Rough Riders and the Platt Amendment were the double face of US imperialism: help the struggle for freedom from European domination on the one hand, and on the other bring Cuba under US control. From 1898 onwards the US freely intervened in Cuban affairs, sometimes at the invitation of Cuban politicians. The constitution of 1940 gave Cuba the option of a liberal democratic path. This is a fact to which anti-Castro historians and politicians often refer. But the corruption of post-1940 politics led to Batista's coup of 1952, and wholesale torture and intimidation led to the revolution of 1959.

At which point, of course, according to one imaginary scenario, the US should have welcomed the 26 July movement's taking of power, encouraged the reintroduction of the 1940 constitution and established friendly relations with the new regime. This scenario, however, fails to notice the fact that by 1959 the Cubans had in fact run the gamut of a whole series of political possibilities in less than a hundred years: colonialism, imperialism, dictatorship, bourgeois democracy. They had known it all – except socialist revolution.

The close ideological and economic ties which Cuba established with the Soviet Union did not however guarantee cultural sympathy with that nation. Cubans generally found Russians and east Europeans cynical, greedy and even smelly. Nor did they find the Vietnamese particularly appealing, although Havana and other major cities were full of Vietnamese in the 1970s; they were being educated, healed, cared for by the Cubans. Cubans were creating new connections which denied the 'naturalness' of previous ones.

This was not an easy task. I have lost count of the times I have been told by Cubans in the years between 1968 and 1985, when I variously lived in and visited Cuba, that it had been a 'mistake' for Cuba to alienate the US. On the other hand, I have been told many times by Americans how surprised they were that the Cubans had 'got away with it'. The harsh fact is that once Cuba had become a 'communist' country, it hardly counted at all. What mattered was the Soviet Union.

Robert Kennedy's book on the misnamed Cuban missile crisis shows a keen awareness of the *quién es más macho* syndrome:

> The final lesson of the Cuban missile crisis is the importance of placing ourselves in the other country's shoes. During the crisis President Kennedy spent more time trying to determine the effect of a particular course of action on Kruschev or the Russians than on any other phase of what he was doing. What guided all his deliberations was an effort not to disgrace Kruschev, not to humiliate the Soviet Union.[3]

President Kennedy apparently spent little time wondering how to avoid humiliating Castro or the Cuban people. Nor indeed did the Soviets, a point not lost on the Cubans. Never at any time were those missiles 'Cuban'. The backdown by the Soviets, whatever deal was done behind the scenes, enabled the US to recover some of the status lost after the 'Bay of Pigs' fiasco of the previous year which had first led Castro to proclaim Cuba a socialist country. The invaders were all Cubans and they were swiftly abandoned by their US patrons when the expected anti-Castro rising did not happen. The captured prisoners had to be ransomed by private subscriptions.[4] On his first day back in Florida, one member of Brigade 2506 was refused service in a restaurant because he was black.[5]

Until 1959 Cuba was highly influenced socially and culturally by the US – particularly urban US – and Cubans generally looked north, not to Latin America, the Caribbean or Africa, for cultural inspiration and contacts. Cuba's ethnicity, if I can for a moment use a term which causes me great unease, was Spanish and African. But these ethnic origins had very little meaning for most Cubans to whom Spain and Africa were vague concepts. Such ethnicities were more important for artists who liked to play around with them in their works. Guillén's work is one example; so is that of Alejo Carpentier, although a more sophisticated achievement than that of Guillén; the paintings of Wilfredo Lam would be another. In music, however, Cuba had produced its own style which had influence throughout the Americas.

I have to say that I have personally never been convinced by arguments about the 'mulatto' nature of Cuban culture. Its origins appear to be in the work of José Martí, a man given to biologising and whose main contribution to the development of the idea of a separate Cuban identity was his warnings against the power and influence of the US.

Even Cuban creole links with Spain were weak by the nineteenth century as Cuba was the powerful colony of a country which was feeble and corrupt. Cuban Spanish is far evolved from the Castilian and even the *gallego*, the language of Galicia where most Spanish immigrants originated.

The 'African' elements of Cuban culture, although even more tenuous than the Spanish, have come to be stressed in Cuba during the last 20 years. There may be two reasons for this: one is that Cuba, like many post-imperialist societies, sought to retraditionalise itself and that it has thereby run the risk of folklorisation and auto-exoticism; the second reason might be that in the early 1970s the Cubans mistakenly believed that Black Power movements in the US were a truly revolutionary force there. The support for the Black Panthers and the appearance in Havana of exiled black leaders unleashed a wave of auto-africanisation among the black petit-bourgeoisie in Cuba. Some of this was viewed with alarm by the Cuban authorities, especially when accounts denouncing Cuban racism like that of Carlos Moore appeared or when books like John Clytus's *Black Man in Red Cuba*[6] were used to attack the revolution.

Gradually, however, anthropology and folklorisation gained official approval. The government in Cuba has even approved 'santería', a pagan religious system of possession and animal sacrifice based on gross superstition which is widely touted as an

'African' survival. Artists like Rogelio Martínez Fauré, whose
work on African cultural origins was originally viewed with some
scepticism, are now officialised. Cuba has African dance groups;
but it also has classical ballet which, despite its aristocratic
connotations, survived under the formidable guidance of Alicia
Alonso: and it also still has half-naked beplumed women dancing
at the 'Tropicana' nightclub. This syncretism or 'pachanga' is what
is regarded as special about the Cuban Revolution, but its ideological origins are literary and come from the novels of Alejo
Carpentier with his concept of 'lo real maravilloso', a phrase
meaning not 'magical realism' as it is often mistranslated but 'the
magic of reality'. Its influence has also been mainly literary and
vast: extending to García Márquez and Salman Rushdie and
Isabel Allende, and it has now spread, ironically, to Africa where,
among others, it is doing the rounds in the novels of Tahar Ben
Jelloun.

This is not the place to discuss the political implications of 'lo
real maravilloso' except to say that it seems most often to be
found in those countries where reality is anything but magical. In
the Cuban context, it is the idea of syncretic survivals which is
most important; it implies simply not having to choose and it has
an obvious appeal to people who have lived politically on the edge
for the last 30 years and where every day has seemed to demand
a strenuous ethical commitment.

This is the official version, as it were. But there is another side
which is harder to plot. United States influence does survive in
Cuba and has increased, just as Cuba has, in a sense, inserted itself
more strongly into the US since the revolution and has now in fact
colonised part of that country. Before the revolution the US was
viewed by Cubans in a favourable and attractive light. Those who
knew of Martí's strictures against the 'colossus of the north', and no
one who has visited Cuba since the revolution does not know of
them, were in a minority. Even Martí's position was not clear-cut.
He lived most of his adult life in the US, preferring it to the Latin
American countries he had visited, and his writings are unsystem-
atic and contradictory, turned out as journalism to keep himself
alive. I have elsewhere analysed in detail the most important of
Martí's writings on the US.[7] He is the major pre-communist ideo-
logue of the Cuban Revolution. He is its 'apostle' and shrines to
him are to be seen throughout Cuba. He is in fact a less charismatic
but also less complex hero than 'Che' Guevara whose determination, on purely ideological grounds, to Africanise and Latin Ameri-
canise the Cuban Revolution has still not been confronted by the
Cubans. Che exists on two levels in Cuba: the public level of
martyrdom and sacrifice, of the long hair and faraway look in the
eye; and the subversive level of his scurrilous and witty attacks not

only on the Soviets and the Chinese but also on the Cubans themselves, which survives only in anecdotes like the one about his television appearance when, having failed several times to light his cigar with a Cuban match, he cried to his millions of viewers: 'Damn it, they can't make anything right in this country!'

Martí's death at Ocho Rios in 1895 at the beginning of the final push against the Spaniards, saved him as a hero for the Cubans. Among contemporaries, unpublished documents show, he was known as the 'little tax collector' and despised for his lack of military prowess. Martí was no Marxist. He had read Marx but loathed the emphasis on class struggle. He was in fact a Krausist, a Spanish offshoot of Kantianism which stressed the need for harmony in human affairs. Martí's radicalism lay in his warning about the danger that the US represented to the rest of Latin America and his fears about the failure of the US to create a harmonious society out of the many cultures which made it up, its failure to develop a spiritual dimension and his fear that immigration would pollute and corrupt the achievements of American democracy. In this respect, he particularly feared the Germans and the Irish. Eventually Martí's dislike of the discordant aspects of US life developed into a full-blown xenophobia which took the form of hatred of immigrants because they lacked 'patriotism':

> En otros lugares, lo traído de Europa, violento y criminal, predomina en el movimiento obrero, y lo mancha y afea ... las tierras despóticas de Europa, se han venido de allá con un taller de odio en cada pecho y quieren llegar a la reorganización social por el crimen, por el incendio, por el robo, por el fraude, por el asesinato ...

> Esa Alemania, y Polonia, esa Noruega y Suecia, toda esa espuma, se ha derramado por el país entero, y no se sabe si los trabajadores del país serán más poderosos que ella.[8]

> In other places, the outcasts of Europe, violent and criminal, control the workers' movement which they stain and spoil ... the despotic countries of Europe, they have come thence with breasts full of hatred and a desire to bring about social change through crime, arson, robbery, theft and murder ...

> That Germany, and Poland, that Norway and Sweden, all that jetsom has been carried over the whole country and there is no way of knowing if the nation's workers will be able to survive it.

Note the phrases 'lo traído' (outcasts) and 'toda esa espuma' (jetsom): insulting and frightened turns of phrase which express all Martí's fastidiousness and his late-nineteenth-century fear of racial mixing. It was 100 years later, in 1980, when around 120,000 Cubans left the port of Mariel for Miami that banners inscribed 'L'escoria que se vaya' (Let the shit leave) appeared in the streets of Havana and even one which read 'Cuba, territorio libre de negros' (Cuba, a land free from blacks). I learned this, by word of mouth, when I visited Havana in 1982; on the same visit I read an article by the highly respected Cuban anthropologist and historian of music Fernando Ortiz called 'Entre Cubanos'.[9] Ortiz's most well-known writings deal with the idea of the happy syncretism of the European and the African in Cuba. This essay, never republished in Cuba, and hard to find, confides his fears that the Cuban mentality is basically criminal as a result of the degradation created by slavery and racial mixing. This is the dark side of syncretism and the desire not to choose, and it coincides pretty closely with Martí's essays and with myths of race and race-mixing in the US. In fact, Martí's language of inundation echoed the xenophobia he found in the US and it is the common currency of racism today.

Prosperity and education should, in theory, compensate for cultural differences in the US. The Cuban Revolution attempts also to create a cohesive community through 'culture'. The word 'culto' is to be found throughout Martí's writings and was often on the lips of Cuban communist party officials in the 1970s. 'Culto' does not mean educated, it is a highly hispanic word which carries with it the implication of 'cultivated', refined and well-mannered. It was surprising to discover that groups of workers on visits to the 'Tropicana' were given lessons on how to behave, which knives and forks to use and how to dress. It was apparently the task of the revolution to teach table manners. This could be seen as the influence of the Spanish element in Cuban culture and it has been used to combat yanqui casualness and informality. Castro has always remained formally if militarily dressed. Hemingway is remembered as a man who appeared in the streets of Havana wearing shorts and sandals. When I lived in Cuba, men who wore sandals in the street were regarded as homosexuals. Women were not allowed to enter hospitals wearing trousers and, at the University of Havana in 1971, it was declared in a large gathering of students and teachers held in the Humanities Faculty that miniskirts and beards were counter-revolutionary unless worn by those who had been in the Sierra Maestra – the beards that is, not the miniskirts.

This is important, though apparently trivial, because it illustrates the extent to which the revolution wanted to create or sustain a certain Cuban style. The pre-revolutionary style had either been an imitation of the US or geared towards fulfilling US myths about Cuban identity. Cuba may not have had much political importance for the US prior to 1959, but it had an existence as a leisure area. Pre-revolutionary Cuba was, for the US, a nation of pimps and prostitutes and Havana was one of the major operating theatres for the Mafia. The Cubans were seen as natural entertainers and criminals. Cuba had provided boxers, dancers and musicians and, pre-1959, its most famous son was Desi Arnaz. We can immediately see therefore that post-revolutionary Cuba had a serious image problem. Replacing Arnaz with Fidel Castro has been one of the unsung achievements of the revolution. Arnaz, as Ricky Ricardo, was a stupid but handsome and musical fall-guy for Lucille Ball's dotty, eye-flutterer, Lucy. This was what not only Cuba, but indeed the whole of Latin America was for the US audience – a place where everything and everyone was for sale.

This is the context of the revolution's sweep against prostitution and homosexuality, including the misconceived UMAP which crowded thousands of supposed homosexuals together in concentration camps where some were tortured and killed in a scenario to be repeated during the Peruvian embassy siege of 1980. It is also the reason why the words *dignidad* (dignity) and *serio* (important) were so often on the lips of Cuban officials.

It is hard to say whether the US had any ideological influence on pre-revolutionary Cuba. The spirit of free enterprise was certainly everywhere as stall-holders, shoeshine boys, bartenders as well as whores, gamblers, sportsmen and musicians tried to hustle a living from the tourists. The first wave of Cubans to leave after the revolution included many belonging to this undignified element as well as the bourgeoisie in full flight. It was the Cuban, especially the Havanese, bourgeoisie, which was most influenced by the US where they had often lived for long periods and whose language they spoke. The nostalgia of Edmundo Desnoes's *Memories of Underdevelopment*[10] and the film that was made from it dramatised the double allegiance of this class.

In the film, co-produced by Desnoes, one scene is set at Hemingway's finca Vigia and René Villarreal, one of Hemingway's servants, appears in the film. An off-screen voice accuses Villarreal of having been a 'slave'. He had been taken off the streets of San Francisco de Paula and brought up by Hemingway. When he saw the film, he got a gun and went looking for Desnoes and the film's director Tomás Gutiérrez Alea. 'The man didn't seem to understand that the film was a work of fiction,' Alea is quoted as saying.[11]

Desnoes' debunking of Hemingway in his essay 'El último verano' [12] was one of many attempts by Cuban writers and intellectuals to disembarrass themselves of their debt to the north. Officially Hemingway has always remained very persona grata in Cuba. He is probably Cuba's most famous writer – he lived there for over 30 years. When he returned to Havana after the revolution everyone knows he kissed the Cuban flag, he cried 'Venceremos' and declared 'I'm not a Yankee'.[13] For most Cubans, this was enough. Castro won a fishing prize instituted by Hemingway and after his death his home was turned into a museum so sacred that no one was actually allowed to set foot inside it; viewing is strictly through the windows. In 1972, Hemingway's cabin cruiser 'Pilar' was restored at the government's expense. Desnoe's essay represented a rare dissension from the heroic fiction of Hemingway:

> [H]ay que admitirlo: Hemingway no compra una finca en San Francisco de Paula y ancla su yate de pesca en Cojímar porque sencillamente le gusta Cuba es porque le recuerda España, es que está lo suficientemente aisládo y cerca de los Estados Unidos para refugiarse aquí y escribir en inglés sin visitas inopurtunas, es que puede seguir pescando agujas en el Caribe.[14]

> It has to be admitted: Hemingway does not buy a farm in San Francisco de Paula and anchor his fishing boat in Cojímar because he sincerely likes Cuba, it is because it reminds him of Spain, it is because it is isolated enough yet near to the United States for him to hide away here to write in English without unwanted visitors, it is so that he can go on fishing in the Caribbean.

In other words, Hemingway was a tourist. The Cuban characters in *The Old Man and the Sea* and *Islands in the Stream* are servants, bartenders and prostitutes. The heroes who accompany Hudson on his hunt for the German submarine crew are Americans or Basques. While Hudson may note the poverty of Cuba as he drives from his ranch to Havana, he salves his conscience with handouts just as Hemingway himself was generous in individual acts of charity.

According to Desnoes' essay, Hemingway announced firmly on his return to Havana that it would be his 'last summer' there, and told his wife to pack up their immensely valuable collection of paintings, which were in fact taken back to the US. On her return in July 1977 to visit the museum Mary Walsh asked for a Gordon's gin, 'but none could be found in any bar in Havana'.[15]

In the early 1970s I was offered a contract by a US-based publisher for a book on Hemingway in Cuba, but it was clear that such a work would not be welcome in Cuba and that I should not get access to the finca Vigia papers. Fuentes' excellent book shows that things have changed, and it contains a mass of new material. Fuentes shows that Hemingway in his own life was, to some extent, integrated into Cuban culture although he was never able to convey this in his works. When he was awarded the Nobel prize he announced: 'This is one prize that belongs to Cuba, because my work was created and concerned in Cuba, with my people of Cojímar, where I'm a citizen – here I have my books and my home.' [16]

It was possible before 1959 to be a citizen of both Cuba and the US – if not literally, then figuratively. It was no longer possible after 1959. After 1959, a choice had to be made. The Cubans did not really need Hemingway, but they wanted him as a totemic figure. What they did not want was Hemingway-style prose, nihilism and mordant desperation. In an extraordinary interview in 1978 with two American journalists, Castro claimed he had learned guerrilla tactics from *For Whom the Bell Tolls*.[17] I have even met otherwise sane students at the University of Havana who assured me that Henry Morgan's 'No matter how, a man alone ain't got no bloody fucking chance' was evidence of Hemingway's commitment to socialism. Yet writers who imitated his style were attacked as counter-revolutionary, as was the case with Eduardo Heras León's *Los pasos en la hierba* which won the Casa de las Américas prize in 1970 only to be subsequently denounced by the journals of the Revolutionary Armed Forces; as was the case with Fuentes himself in his description of the anti-bandit campaign in Camagüey, *Los condenados de Condado* (1968).[18] Both of these writers suffered marginalisation for producing Hemingway-style prose versions of episodes from the revolution. This, they were told, represented bourgeois reaction and despair.

The blockade against Cuba by the US cut the island off from its greatest cultural-exchange area. The continued presence of US cultural influence from the 1960s onwards was either fossilised or clandestine. Fossilised, that is, like the cars made in the 1950s, huge machines of chrome with tail-fins, like a certain middle-class style of dress for women which always included stockings and crimplene in 90 per cent humidity, like the way women would wear full make-up and rollers, like the architecture of downtown Havana, including the famous Hilton renamed the Habana Libre, like the outdated slang and constant showing and reshowing of old movies on television. A 1970s Cuban joke was that a Cuban millionaire was one who had seen *Casablanca* a million times. Clandestine contacts might include Allen Ginsberg and Eldridge Cleaver, a smuggled copy of *The Chase*, those economists and brigadistas who made their way through Canada for brief, officially-sponsored visits. To all intents and purposes the intimate intellectual and cultural links between the two countries were severed and they addressed each other over a barricade of propaganda and sloganising.

Wanting to turn away from the US and shake off its influence, the Cubans used the writings of Martí to assert their essential Latin Americanness and also developed investigations into the African origins of Cuban culture beyond Guillén's tinkering. Prerevolutionary Cuba appears in semi-documentary work like Miguel Barnet's retelling of the life of a runaway slave in *Cimarrón*; in Enrique Cirules' talks with the sole survivor of an attempt to transplant a colony of poor United States settlers at Gloria in the early part of the century, told in *Conversación con el último norteamericano*; in Moreno Fraginals' detailed exposition of the importance of technological innovation in the sugar industry in *El ingenio*.[19] Such works create a sense of a unique Cuban experience away from the *pachanga* and bullshit.

The Latinamericanisation of Cuba is an interesting study still waiting to be done. Although many Latin American writers have at some time or another supported the Cuban Revolution, few have been quite as loyal as García Márquez who keeps a house in Havana. But in fact restrictions on travel have meant that very few Cubans have any first-hand experience of Latin America. Views of Latin America are based on films, books and cultural delegations which have been freely available and widely disseminated to counterbalance the hegemony of the US. This identity was based on Martí's polarities. Latin rather than Saxon, Catholic rather than Protestant, African rather than Nordic, generous rather than rapacious etc. Now that the US is itself being Latinamericanised such polarities are rather threadbare. Some aspects of Latin America puzzled or alienated Cubans: they were perplexed by the Mexican obsession with death, and the highly Europeanised creole culture of countries like Chile and Argentina had little to offer Cuba. On the other hand, as Cuba's Indians are a sentimental memory, Cubans have little in common with the *indio* cultures of central and mid-Latin America.

Africa was another matter. As the flight to the US continued throughout the 1970s Cuba became more Africanised – at least until Mariel. But this Africanisation was a highly folklorised version: carnival, santería, music, dance and food. The real African experience was quite different and decisive.

In October 1975 Castro sent Cuban troops to support the MPLA government in Angola and SWAPO in Namibia. Troops were also sent to Ethiopia. For the next 13 years the Cubans at any one time had upwards of 30,000 troops in the frontline in the fight against South African sponsored terrorists. During this period, the whole of the Cuban merchant fleet, a not inconsiderable number, was engaged in ferrying military and medical supplies to Africa. It is not known how many Cubans were killed; there is practically no town or village in Cuba which has not lost someone. Every town big enough to have a museum has a war memorial in it to those killed in Angola. Of all those countries throughout the world which opposed apartheid, Cuba was the only one which fought against it. Because of Cuban efforts, South Africa was unable to create a buffer zone of influence between it and black Africa. Maybe as a result the tide turned, apartheid was abolished and the ANC will one day take power in South Africa. No one talks of this – neither the Cubans themselves, nor the US whose opposition to African communism was combatted in a conflict still to be chronicled. The impact on Cuba itself has been enormous, but also, for obvious reasons, largely undocumented. Angola was not the Africa of 'Sensaymaya'. It had nothing to do with singing and dancing. This was the real Africa as stunning to Cubans as Vietnam had been to the US. Angola was disease, immense ignorance, poverty beyond socialist dogma. And the Cubans fought and gave their lives to defend it.

The shifting fictions of national identity cannot be reduced to a coherent narrative, or even coherence. It seems that certain fictions achieve a mythical status that takes on a life of its own. The Mariel exodus reproduced the Cuban criminal in the heart of the US: *Scarface* and *Miami Vice*. Meanwhile in 1991 Cuba struggled to host the Pan American Games while the ghost of the old Cuban holiday resort reappeared in Redford's ghastly *Havana*. Cuban businessmen in Little Havana showed that the spirit of Franklin is not dead; while Cuba itself seemed to stand alone against the fall of communism, being more communist than the communists. Castro, now completely grey, must be about the same age as the vibrantly blonde Celia Cruz, the Queen of Salsa, one of whose hit songs is called 'Canto a la libertad'. Martí is a hero not only to the *fidelistas* but to those who plan to take their place and who broadcast from the US to Cuba over Radio Martí. Oscar Hijuelos's *The Mambo Kings Play Songs of Love* [20] won the Pulitzer Prize for a novel about two Cuban brothers who made a name for themselves as musicians in New York in the 1940s and whose greatest claim to fame was, yes, that they had once appeared on the 'I Love Lucy' show. One of Celia's songs is an 'Afro-Cuban' lullaby called 'Babalao' but she sings it wearing a sequined flamenco dress, a style originally from Moorish Spain, and her hair is an uncompromising yellow.

I once met a New York Jew who had lived for 30 years in Cuba and who had been active in the 26th July movement before that. He wanted to leave. Since living in Cuba he had become more Jewish, insisting that Matzos biscuits be supplied on his ration book and commemorating the Passover. Before coming to

Cuba he had been a Marxist. He spent a long time telling me, one hot afternoon at the Patrice Lumumba Beach Club, that the Cubans remained basically traumatised by the Moroccan occupation of Spain. He believed that this accounted for the Cuban's fascination with homosexuality. It was a complicated argument involving voyeurism and repression and many dark, dark references to highly placed military personnel. It was the Jamaican writer Andrew Salkey who pointed out to me the similarity between Castro in full flow and Mick Jagger on stage.

National identities, an agreed exchange of fictions. If you decide to do away with one set you have to replace them with another. 'No one has changed more than us – now what we're not going to do is change back,' Castro was reported as saying during the Ibero-American summit in Guadalajara, Mexico, in 1991.[21] Yes, it's no longer Latin America.

In one of the more intelligent books recently published on Cuba, Jacobo Timerman writes: 'Vegetation and landscape Caribbean; music and sensuality, African; language, deriving from Spain; but the daily lifestyle is as American as the glass dome allows.' [22]

Cubans have lived under a glass dome for 30 years, observing and being observed. As Timerman points out, waiting has become the condition of being Cuban. It is hard to say how Cuban identity will re-emerge. It may even be that the revolution will turn out not to have been that important in the elusive fantasy of national identity.

The Cuba-in-exile which is developing in Florida is a kind of grotesque mirror image of the pre-Castro Cuba so beloved of the United States and maybe, as Don DeLillo suggests in *Libra*, it has already played a sinister role in the fantasy world of US politics. In any case, it is a most bizarre phenomenon. Is the United States really so powerful that it can summon up the dead? Meanwhile, if you think that Cubans have a wonderful sense of rhythm, then *The Mambo Kings Play Songs of Love* is the book for you.

10

'This Uncertain Content of an Obscure Enterprise of Form': Eric Mottram, America and Cultural Studies

Clive Bush

It was in 1964 that I was first invited to tea by Eric Mottram to discuss possible graduate work in American literature. He lived in a basement flat in Church Street, Kensington. The ghosts of Ford, Pound and Joyce hung over the area and, given that Notting Hill Gate was but a short walk away, they had an improbable rival for genius in the brooding spirit of Tony Hancock. London-style, Mottram's kitchen (a place of at least equal importance to the study) was in the bricked-in right side of the well which permitted light from the street. The flat was dark, the table and typewriter shoved up under the grimy-grilled window. To the left was an expensive stereo system with an early SME arm which later would be scratched merrily back and forth in search of that significant track (guided lowering of the stylus was mercilessly delayed on Mottram's system) over the protesting vinyl surface of 'The Rite of Spring' or a Bach Cantata. Wagner, for obvious reasons, posed the worst problems.

I first connected Mottram with music.[1] It was in this room I first heard many of the great jazz and blues musicians, Wagner's *Parsival, Tristan and Isolde*, the works of Charles Ives, Walter Piston and many others in the American tradition, and the musicians who were then shaking the musical world of the 1960s: Boulez, Henze, Stockhausen, Berio, Cage, Ligeti and Xenakis among many others. I had a reasonable listening knowledge of the classical repertoire but Mottram seemed to have several performances of any major work, and hours of comparisons compelled one, in Ives's words, to stand up and use one's ears like a man. The other side of the room which darkened lengthily backwards was largely occupied by a couple of big stereo speakers. Books crammed available space. Cardboard boxes sat around, filled with records of the entire range of 'classical', contempory classical and jazz music. Piles of *Time* magazine, the *New Republic* and the

Socialist Worker competed for space and ideology on the floor.

'You had better not become an academic,' was the advice. 'It's a lonely life, it's very hard work, it's unbelievably badly paid, and no one in this God-forsaken country gives a damn.' The advice seemed sound, there was a picture of Bosch's less-than-ambivalent 'Garden of Delights' pinned over the boarded-up fireplace and the floor space between it and Jeff Nuttall's visceral sculpture combining a rubber ball and tube for a syringe and coloured anatomical drawings seemed unsettling to say the least. Trophies (masks, spears and poisoned arrows) from a Conradian past in the Malayan seas also hung on the wall. But Mottram had one supreme advantage over most other academics I had met: he wasn't boring.

Some perverse twist of fate, or some sense of moment, man and milieu, however, held me there. More pragmatically, none of the jobs I had interviewed successfully for suited my restless sense that I had hardly begun an adult intellectual life. Premature burial in the British Council urged on me by my genial and somewhat waspish Shakespeare Professor, Geoffrey Bullough, was out. 'Well,' said Mottram, 'if you insist, but don't blame me, you'd better read these two books and come back and see if you're still interested.' The books were Hawthorne's *The Scarlet Letter* and Dreiser's *An American Tragedy*. The two books changed my life.

Certainly I had enjoyed Old English poetry (for all the sweat on the language), Chaucer, the Elizabethan poets, Shakespeare, the odes of Keats. From 1961 I had been mostly extremely lucky in my undergraduate teachers at King's College, London. But even so I still knew virtually nothing of the great European literatures since the French Revolution. Contemporary poetry in English, whose modernity was then exclusively represented by T.S. Eliot, Robert Frost or, even worse, by Robert Graves, left me cold, and politically and intellectually insulted. The kind of public-school England and its conflicts, as represented by Auden and others, I had never experienced, hardly knew existed, and when I came to know of it I was appalled by its ability, with obvious notable exceptions, to turn out mechanical nincompoops whose most profound characteristics were social incompetence at any level of society except their own, and a chilling synthesis of pompous (and sometimes vicious) confidence and half-knowledge. I was mercifully spared public-school leftism until I had had a chance to read the great socialist writers for myself. None the less, in Mottram I found a teacher who understood, and who could articulate clearly, the profound disquiet I felt about the relation of literature to politics and culture. Why did my teachers not talk about the things literature was so obviously about?

Mottram was clear:

> The majority of educators, journalists and other rulers of
> taste and distribution in our society are conservational classi-
> cists. They assume, and continually attempt to maintain,
> poetry as a rapidly consumable entertainment article on a par
> with cigarettes, newspapers and booze, a source of quick
> minimal kicks which does not interfere with the stability of
> class divisions and rigid labour/leisure proportions in the
> Security State.[2]

That seemed a good place to start.

Hawthorne's *The Scarlet Letter* was of a type of literature
which plumbed artistic, political and emotional depths. It showed
that the heart of another, in Ford's phrase, was indeed a 'dark
forest', and suggested that only a lifetime of reading and rereading would reveal this particular book's richnesses both technical
and human. I would recognise the same intensity later in
Dostoevsky, Kafka, and in Conrad, Ford and Lawrence.

Dreiser was different. Beneath the awkwardness of a natur-
alistic and psychologically naive style was the first sense of
modernity I had felt in literature written in English. It was the
crass, materialistically glittering, publicity-haunted, emotionally
shallow and melodramatic world of permitted twentieth-century
experience. All values danced to money or exploitative sexuality
and hence lacked the very significance of profound conflict itself.
It had the honesty of showing that democracy and law in America
rarely worked in fact, and that no one was in the hand of God.
Things were not all right. You needed guts, or luck, or cunning,
and preferably all three, to survive emotionally and physically.
Dreiser's power was the ability to communicate this world with
an integrity which was thoroughly secular.

I had audited some of Mottram's classes in the preceding
three years, 1961–64. I had been immediately taken by his
lectures on Winthrop, Charles Brockden Brown, Melville, Emily
Dickinson, Faulkner, and a writer nobody had heard of called
William Burroughs. I held off, as if sensing that going into that
area would need a big commitment and there were many other
areas of reading I had not yet caught up on. My provincial
grammar school (that current site of right-wing nostalgia) had left
me very unprepared. At King's College, the drama course (unusu-
ally badly taught) at least let me read Ibsen, Strindberg, the
German Expressionists, Brecht and, above all, the plays and
writings of Sartre who demonstrated the most profound political
and artistic use of the European intellectual tradition by a single
author in the twentieth century.

What attracted me to Mottram was, in the 1950s' existentialist catch-word, 'authenticity'. This was not some manifestation of a contentless Platonic secret centre of truth, but a way of being in the world in which imagination, intelligence and commitment to action (which included all kinds of serious writing and the arts) were primary. Literature, art and the life of the mind mattered. They were not a social luxury, but virtually as much a necessity as food, decent housing, medical and educational services. They certainly played a major role in understanding and resisting the absence of those things in any culture or country. Real things and real values were at stake. They were achieved only by enormous effort. The capacity of human beings for evil was infinite, and twentieth-century human history seemed to confirm the darkest visions of a Swift, Twain or Kafka.

A younger contemporary of Sartre, Mottram's young manhood was the world of fascist Europe. His coming of age was not simply the Navy but the horrors of war and the isolation of young men denied the chance of a steady emotional, social and sexual life. Crucial lessons in survival and key life experiences had to be sorted out later against crippling nostalgia, and physical and psychological damage: themes which would give Mottram's poetry an extraordinary range and sense of urgency.

It was also a world of crumbling British power, and the emergence of a second-rate culture where an Elgar or a Britten seemed provincial against a Stravinsky or Messiaen, and where an Arnold Wesker paled before the intensity and innovativeness of a Brecht. After the war British film-making would not match its continental rivals. Only the theatre in the 1960s, with the productions of Peter Brook and Peter Hall, showed real if fleeting sings of life. A Kingsley Amis, an Iris Murdoch, a John Betjeman, a Philip Larkin which delighted the generation immediately before mine in its search for mildly ironic and vaguely social quietism in the context of imperial exhaustion were simply not even marginally interesting. Even the angry young men had no imagination of form, and seemed more trapped in (and therefore 'liberally' reinforced) the kinds of damage English class society routinely inflicted, than offering any way of imaginatively working their way out of it. Surely someone somewhere in the world was writing literature that had both formal imaginative and political ambition.

Unlike every other country in Europe, Britain's illusions about itself remained, as they still do, at least on the surface, comfortingly undisturbed. The heroism of the British people during the war was not to be rewarded economically, culturally or politically, as the United States put the economic brakes on Attlee's government, thereby guaranteeing the return of a post-imperialist and nostalgic conservatism which was to find its apogee in 1980s

Thatcherism at home and a snuggling up to America's super-power, in lieu of its own departed glory, abroad.

The Leavises left their mark on the young scholar who went up to Cambridge after the war. The 'seriousness', the care for non-western cultures, the sense of the intergenerative activity of all the arts, the taken-for-grantedness of 'literature and society', the fury against the establishment and propagandist incompetencies of the British Council, the BBC, the Sunday newspapers, the so-called serious newspapers, can all be found deeply ingrained in Mottram's work. The Leavises and Cambridge were the demobbed petty officer's hard-earned luck, though they hardly directed his interest in American culture owing to their antipathy to (and general ignorance of) that culture. Nor should other Cambridge influences be neglected. William Empson – 'a dashing modern atheist' as Christopher Hill called him[3] – was at least as important as Leavis, and Mottram will tell, with only half-humorous chagrin, of having to confront the stern discipline of Miss Muriel Bradbrook over a paper on Racine. One deep strand of Mottram's intellectual outlook, in spite of overwhelming American and continental additions, is the Cambridge tradition from the Neo-Platonists of the seventeenth century to Coleridge, and from Coleridge to I. A. Richards, the problematics of Russell and the misunderstood Wittgenstein, Alfred North Whitehead, Basil Willey, Gilbert Ryle, the *Scrutiny* circle and beyond.

Mottram's life and work, as a cultural and literary critic and as a poet, is also deeply embedded in the precise history of the failures and contradictions of British culture during the last 40 years. Belonging to no school, he will leave none. Judging most major publishing houses, reviewers cliques, establishment values, schools and educational institutions in a post-imperialist British culture to be inert and therefore corrupt, he has played the emotionally exhausting role of outsider gadfly in an insider estab-lishment position. His lonely integrity puts him in a very English tradition. Oscar Wilde's words, to a bunch of American reporters in the Aldine Hotel in 1882, are still pertinent. He said he hoped to meet Mr Whitman: 'perhaps he is not widely read in England, but England never appreciates a poet until he is dead.'[4]

Unlike Raymond Williams at Cambridge, or Stuart Hall, formerly at Birmingham, now at the Open University, or the Thompsons (Birmingham, formerly Warwick), or the literary theorists and feminists at Swansea (and every former Polytechnic in the country), or the sociology of literature gurus at Essex, Mottram's academic work in cultural studies is without currently typable and marketable lineaments. Most of his work has been published in small magazines and journals on the principle that you respond without calculation about careers and publicity to whoever wants to publish your work. The result has been that (owing to the big-press consciousness of traditional academics, and the fact that his work was in the contemporary and American fields – if you want to be a professor you had better be 'in Shakespeare', or these days 'in Theory') he received his promotion to a personal chair at King's College at the same time as he received papers suggesting he retire at the age of 60; and this in spite of the fact that the quantity and quality of his publishing output certainly exceeds the combined output of his colleagues many times over.

Even where his reading and interests overlap with the current 'cultural studies' promoters, his practice differs radically from that view of 'cultural studies' which seems destined to become the new academic marketing slogan of the 1990s and which can best be summed up in Brantlinger's recent book, *Crusoe's Footsteps* (1990). This book's historical account of cultural studies in Britain is partial to say the least. Brantlinger laudably wants to defend the humanities against the oversimplifications of neo-conservative views of the 1960s, but has no really positive and recreative sense of what a radical cultural studies might be. In addition, the real world of American and English domestic and foreign politics hardly enters his text, and he has no sense of the complex role of the intellectual outlined, for example, in the radicalism of Sartre's famous essay, and first given in Tokyo and Kyoto in 1965.[5] A mish-mash of quotations from acceptably publicised 'radicals' and publicity-confirmed gurus (apparently Eagleton and Derrida are unconflicted bedfellows in this arrangement) structure a dehistoricised and binary set of oppositions: aesthetic versus engaged, canon versus non-canon, humanism versus post-humanism, classic versus non-classic (Brantlinger never commits the unforgivable sin of giving an example of what he thinks worth reading and defending it), theory and practice, art-for-art's sake versus practicalism, literature as false consciousness versus ideological critique, blacks and women versus the ideological practices of those with power, Arnoldian high culture versus subcultural integrity.

Not for Brantlinger the interdependencies of the discredited Hegelian master – slave relation, nor the psychological complexities of the internalisation of ideological discourses, but the purity of race and sex identifications versus the ideological practices of those with power. It is not the absence of a sense of the actual contradictions of praxis (even while purporting to outline it) which is objected to here, but the reductiveness of the representation of the scene of contradiction. In the latter respect the actual historical power struggles of a Martin Luther King, using Baptist ideological discourse, or a Lech Walesa, using Catholic ideology, to win freedom for the people they represent are condemned theoretically in advance. In my recidivist socialist view, endlessly to elaborate hegemonic controls seems a guilt-ridden exercise characteristic of those whose superior ability to *confess* in esoteric languages structures their drive for academic power.

An essentially behaviourist metaphysic of opposition and assimilation structures Brantlinger's narrative. A key word is, American style, 'redemption'. All previous struggles to critique and study culture anticipate the assumed contemporary status quo of the unquestioned and unproblematised natural radicalism of black and women's studies, and studies in popular culture. Only a minority of books in the bibliography are dated before the late 1970s. The lack of a sense of historical struggle is staggering. Conservative though some of the social judgements in his historical account are, Lepenies's *Between Literature and Science: the Rise of Sociology* (1985) is an essential antidote to Brantlinger's account in its deep sense of historical perspective and range.

Brantlinger's perceived lineages for cultural studies jostle uneasily between Williams, Thompson, the Althusserians, with Eagleton as minimally-critiqued guide. Perhaps the calmness is one of transatlantic perspective and academic comfort. He is not astonished at the real furore that Thompson's *The Poverty of Theory* caused in the late 1970s, but at the fact that Thompson (typecast for academic ease as an empiricist) might use theory to criticise theory. He assumes the liberal 'humanist tradition' never considered political and social issues, or always assumed 'progress'. So much for Marx and Gramsci who had a real respect for the bourgeois period of history. It does not seem to occur to him that 'appreciating great art' (not that he would ever commit himself to an actual definition of what it might be) is a necessary part of a socialist's (not a word he uses) education.

The real world for Brantlinger is bounded by the university. It is also obviously clear that Marx put himself in mortal peril by reading Shakespeare, Lenin by playing Beethoven sonatas, and when Trotsky said 'Since I am not a historian of the Middle Ages, my attitude to Dante is predominantly artistic,' he was clearly betraying the revolution.[6]

There are obviously some excellent things in Brantlinger's book. There's a reasonable outline of intellectual conflicts (he lets one authority modify another, rarely committing *himself* to a judgement) during the last ten years. But the current obsession with theory can obliterate the things which theory is supposed to be about, which is, I take it, art and politics. What is essentially ignored in Brantlinger and most of his cohorts is that the relationship between the arts generally and politics is difficult, and that you may not bury the issues of excellence in the advocacy of liberally correct attitudes. At

one point Brantlinger is back to defending social realism.[7] The
relation between anthropologically-perceivedfolk or ethnic art, and
the deliberate axiom-breaking art of the 'western' modern tradition
is a difficult issue. Mercifully, good artists of all cultures are not
good at insisting on categorical boundaries.

Further, the problem with centralising race, gender and class
in cultural studies is that these are essentially 'social' issues, and
describe structures of hegemonic power often isolated from economics and politics. They are endlessly addressed, of course,
within sociology. Only a few critics (like Hazel Carby) are prepared really to politicise the issues in terms of capitalist economics, actual contemporary history and its foreground. And the key
question remains in relation to the arts: what do you think worth
teaching and defending? How does your school, college or university relate to the general power structure, and is 'correct' politics
an a priori measure of the greatness of art? Does sociology
actually have the means by which to assess art, and do cultural
critics have the means to assess society? What Brantlinger does
not realise is that these two fields have (under different names)
been poaching off each other fruitfully for almost 200 years, and
the culture critics of Birmingham and Indiana are a small new
tuft in a very large historical carpet.[8]

The fact is that class and race questions have to be confronted
in *any* human science (law, literary criticism, political theory,
sociology, anthropology, psychology and the practice of science as
an institutional affair) and all political practice. If these are seen
to define only 'cultural studies' as such, then cultural studies
theorists risk the absolute arrogance of claiming not only a
self-advertising and a spuriously *unique* perception of the historical suffering common to most people in most cultures, but
positing an intellectual feebleness whereby no content of any
political action or achieved work of art surprises a priori identifications. Radicals are rushing to claim Gertrude Stein and
Nabokov now, but they did not do so in the 1930s and 1950s.

As citizens, students in any discipline whatsoever will need
politically educating, and this will certainly include knowing about
feminism, gender and class. But no artistic investigation, as
opposed to a political investigation, can be reduced to a critique
of these issues in terms already identified.

Brantlinger exists with a bundle of quotations and sub-critical
references to Baudrillard and the Frankfurt School, but offers none
of the current critiques of the very idea of 'postmodernism' as a
viable concept. He ends with yet another binary choice. The good
Lord wants you to make a decision: between hopeful mass-cultural
art-forms divorced from commercialisation (a landmark indeed in
the history of patronage) versus art-for-art's-sake modernisms.

Brantlinger can sound like the Billy Graham of the liberal academic world.

I have been tough on Brantlinger because his style is widespread, and absolutely typical (in spite of claims of lone questing) of current Anglo-American radicalism. It leaves many questions untouched. How do you balance the claims of politics and art? What is actually the value of great art? Where does it differ from repetitive ethnic art, or mass-marketed 'popular' art, or art which primarily serves the political interests of women, disadvantaged ethnic groups, lesbian or gay groups, and any political pressure group directly to further its freedom? Also, what is the relation between the funding of universities and education generally, art, politicisation and propaganda? What precise standards (political and literary) do the necessary attacks on centralist and canonical assumptions invoke? Pure anti-canonicalness is pure iconoclasm, and obliterates the very need for judgement. It may even lead to the ludicrous supposition that all art is of equal value. Brantlinger suggests, along with the right-wing, that it is the artist's fault if she/he is ignored and unappreciated by the masses. Does he then really mean that all good art should be immediately understood by the vast majority of people without any training?

And are those who have power over mass-communications systems those who always know what the people 'need'? What are *their* politics? The parade of theory in the services of the masses may lead to paternalism and to anti-intellectualism. As Muriel Rukeyser long ago pointed out, the writing and teaching of poetry, for example, has no role anyway in contemporary mass society, and her plea to reverse this situation was hardly based on values which claimed a privileged class's aestheticism.[9] One of Eric Mottram's favourite teaching lines is: 'I don't know what an élitist is, but I do know what somebody who calls someone else an élitist is. It is someone who says "I can't do it and nobody else shall."'

Mottram's work in 'cultural studies' proceeds in another direction altogether. The artist not the critic, the work of art not the work of theory is primary. His aim is to search out and defend excellence. Mottram has in fact written a great deal on popular culture, and on non-popular culture, but more than that he is also a poet and has tirelessly promoted contemporary English and American poets for 30 years. The perspective that Mottram has, therefore, on his life in the university is that of the practising poet. This makes him as difficult for the academic world as men like E.P. Thompson who do not simply teach history but actively engage politically in the contemporary historical process. The wet and cold Friday night poetry-reading with six people in attendance, has at least a parallel with Thompson's political meetings of similar numbers in similar circumstances.

In all of Mottram's writing there is an urgency which seeks to show the young just what an extraordinarily rich and encouraging culture they have inherited alongside historical failure. There is no such urgency in Brantlinger. In terms of content, right from the beginning in Mottram's work there is a concern with the proper teaching of American Studies (an area Brantlinger constantly sneers at because, alas, it really was first in breaking out of literary criticism aestheticism), and a strong wish that the United States be represented in its richnesses and in its complexities in spite of its social and political failures.

There is also a search for unappreciated figures in the culture with which to restructure a sense of history. Mottram taught the writing of the Beats and Black Mountain writers in the university long before anyone else in the United States or England.[10] His essay on Kerouac is still one of the few to note the complexity of international literary influence on Kerouac's style.[11] He has many first essays on many poets. His lecture on 'Sir George Cayley, a Nineteenth-century Scientific Pioneer: 1773–1857' (a crucial figure in the development of flight) given at both the Polytechnic of Central London (1988) and the RAF College in Hendon (1989) attempted to put this important British figure on the cultural map. In England, he was a very early advocate of Howard Barker's plays, and, in the United States/Mexico, a supporter of Margaret Randall's life and work; a woman who, like Muriel Rukeyser, combined a life of political radicalism and poetry.[12]

What attracted Mottram to Cayley serves to illustrate four major areas of his concerns. The first is to promote the idea of the exemplary working life with its range of intellectual commitments: the second, an ambition to write accurate, unprovincial, socially committed and imaginative criticism. Mottram cites a letter of Cayley to his mother where he states he wishes to renounce his baronetcy:

> I am determined to be the slave of nothing but my reason, for it being the most exalted power of the human being ... I am not tied to England; I am a citizen of the world – I shall settle in that part I like best, if 'Sir' shall be changed to Citizen Cayley.[13]

The third is the relation between technology and culture, and the fourth, the nature of authority and power.

The first two can be summed up in opening paragraph of Mottram's lecture on Cayley: '[Sir George Cayley] acted within the great traditions of the Royal Society, founded in the later seventeenth century – that is of men who termed themselves *virtuosi* not narrow specialists in the later twentieth-century restriction.' It is this English seventeenth-century tradition which had already led Mottram to writers of similar range in the American tradition: Ezra Pound, Lewis Mumford, Edmund Wilson, Buckminster Fuller, Muriel Rukeyser and Charles Olson.

Another theme, whose complex roots can be traced back variously to Mottram's reading of Calvin (of *The Institutes*), the Shelleys, Nietzsche, Hawthorne, Melville, Sartre, Mailer, Burroughs, Norman O. Brown, among many others, is the nature of authority and control. This eventually becomes virtually an obsession with 'the figure of power,' as both a revolutionary and a reactionary possibility in general culture, society and politics. It structures, for example, Mottram's admiration for such polar opposites as John Wayne (for his personal courage and sense of individualism) and Noam Chomsky (for his socialist commitments and politically critical fearlessness). It is a theme which, as will be shown, emerges most complexly in his criticism of fiction and popular culture.

The final area of Mottram's writing, the least known to his students and the academic world, is his poetry. Poetry is the most important and most successful area of all Mottram's writing. The poetry, however, has intimate links with all the other areas of Mottram's cultural investigations. For example, *The Legal Poems* touches on areas of justice, power and authority no less than does his essay 'Laws Scribbled by Lawbreakers', first delivered for his inaugural lecture as Professor of English and American Literature in 1983; and *The Elegies* celebrates exemplary figures of cultural and political life no less than do his essays.

The commitment to an intellectual virtuoso range is most exemplified, in his professional life, in a particular definition of American Studies. And it is evident from the beginning. The influence of the post-war Salzburg Seminar, the brooding presence of Matthiessen, the young R. W. B. Lewis and the man who began to break the power of the New Critics, R. P. Blackmur, and the radicalism of early twentieth-century American culture (in the early 1960s, writers like Jack London, Dos Passos, Upton Sinclair and critics like Emma Goldman, V. L. Parrington and Randolph Bourne were prominent in his teaching) was evident to a young student in the 1960s. His inaugural lecture at the University of Gröningen in 1955 already showed, however, that his own line would be unique and exploratory. He was to take whatever was necessary from the myth and symbol school, the psychoanalysts and the Marxists. Brantlinger seems to assume, in contrast, that the person belongs to the theory. In addition, Mottram was very aware of the resistance in Europe and particularly in Britain to anything to do with American culture, especially in the late 1950s and early 1960s.

In his Gröningen lecture, Mottram took on European anti-American attitudes 'constructing my ideas around facts which I mean to brandish dogmatically in order to attract attention'.[14] Mottram's sarcasm noted that 'the educated Englishman's persistent example of American culture remains the average production-line film from that new Babylon Hollywood, for it is well known that Hollywood films are all beneath the contempt of the educated man.' Mottram made a plea for a complex response, stating the obvious but by no means recognised point that old and new cultures needed each other. It was all the more urgent because 'Pavese's position between America and the Soviet Union is our position in Europe'.[15] Mottram is full of praise for the Salzburg Seminar where 'the mutual concerns of Europe and America obtain their fullest discussion among the younger generation'.[16] Mottram outlined American achievements in painting and music, and quoted Melville's line: 'And the day will come when you shall say: who reads a book by an Englishman that is modern?' [17] Mottram once remarked to me that the British ambassador, who was at the inaugural, didn't seem to enjoy it as much as he should have done.

Mottram set about his task with Victorian vigour. He promoted poetry with one hand and American studies with the other. Five conferences on poetry were organised by him at the Polytechnic of Central London between 1973 and 1976 alone. His lectures at King's College covered not only these areas, but Shakespeare and most periods of English literature since. When he retired last year, Professor Janet Bately at King's College thought she might need four new appointments to replace his teaching alone. From the British Association for American Studies 'Books on America' of 1965 to the largest, last, huge bibliography on 'Culture and Technology', a course given for the MA programme of the Institute of United States Studies for many years to 1989, Mottram's book-lists are worth the entire teaching programmes of most university courses. To be sure you will find your Deleuze and Guattari on the 'Culture and Technology' course but you will also find among the 20 pages of single-spaced lines of the bibliography, Jean Starobinski's *The Invention of Liberty 1700–1789* (Geneva, 1964), Lavoisier's *Methods of Chemical Nomenclature* (1798), Nelson Algren's *A Walk on the Wild Side* (1956), and Woody Allen's *Take the Money and Run* (film, 1969). It makes the literary theorists look anaemic.

Underlying all these programmes is a set of values and principles. Against current trends it insists that individuals are responsible for their own reactions, and for making their responses to the culture as conscious and as explicit as possible. It most certainly engages the humanist position of secularity, individual choice and responsibility, while at the same time acknowledging the post-humanist presence of the involuntary action and the fragility of a self complexly constructed by the unconscious interiorisations of hegemonic controls. It could not, of course, be otherwise from someone who has read literature complexly and seriously. Mottram has always insisted on the importance of theory but Braque's words, quoted as a preface to his book of poems *Homage to Braque* (1976), sum up his attitude to the use of theory: 'you must always have two ideas, one to destroy the other, the painting is finished when the concept is obliterated.' [18]

Where he differs most radically from current cultural theorists is in the non-dogmatic range of information and methods he employs. The latest conference's estimate of the status of a Foucault, or Gramsci, or Shulamith Firestone, Cixous or Kristeva does not interest him; neither does the refining of a particular method of approach, sociological, psychological or post-Marxist.

Mottram has made his own values explicit in many places. And these can best be contrasted with current gurus by analysing his typical procedure. There is space only for one extended example. The essay 'No Centre to hold: a Commentary on Derrida' (1975) is really part letter to friends, part academic essay, and part a review of Derrida's essay 'Structure, Sign and Play in the Discourses of the Human Sciences'.[19] This essay, mid-academic career, marks a summary and turning point in Mottram's output. What he puts together here will inform his teaching and publishing down to his latest graduate seminar 'The History of Creativity' in the early 1990s. The technique is to pick up something from Derrida's text, supply other contexts and materials and then move back again to the text. He does explicitly therefore what virtually every graduate student does *before* she/he totalises the argument in the inevitable drive towards a monological academic style.

Already in 1975 he is decentring Derrida himself by insisting on a much wider cultural map of information with which to approach the kinds of problems Derrida raises. He praises Derrida for insisting that structure exists outside as well as inside given forms, for not to think so interdicts analysis by insisting on centre as fixed. Rather than follow up logically with a critique of Derrida's position within poststructuralist discourse, Mottram typically moves out from Derrida to give a set of contexts for the treatments of the notion of centre within the western tradition.

The method is synchronic and deliberately so. For Mottram the perception of the similar and dissimilar within juxtaposed materials is not a priori organised by a chronology which determines according to value. This method puts him at odds with traditional historical approaches to texts. Nonetheless, at the start of the essay examples of metaphysical centres as historical and political legitimations are given in chronological order. Thus Aristotle's *primum mobile*, and the certitudes of Aquinas's *Summa* appearing in Donne's poetry are given as sequential exempla. Dr Johnson's sneer of 'metaphysical' is seen as evidence of his fear of Jehovah, the ultimate centre. Eliot's Rome is placed against Burroughs's 'continuous show-business of maintaining gods'.

Mottram then moves back to Derrida's choice of words which imply some principle as constant presence. One is *Alethia*, 'that mystique within Bataille's laughter, clearly seen in Sartre's essay "Un Nouveau Mystique".' He then contrasts Olson's use of Ousoos in the poem 'Maximus from Dogtown', remarking that it takes off from White's translation of Hesiod. Olson is seen in exemplary contrast to Eliot who begins in 'Burnt Norton' with the image of the still point and degenerates into 'Little Gidding' of 1942 where 'the generative cannot be imagined beyond the sun-fired-frost'. Mottram does not neglect the politics of Eliot's 'quasi-feudal Christendom'. Yeats's use of Isis and Osiris serves as a contrast, and Mottram then picks up the same myth in the American poets Pound, Duncan and H.D. The tone is not as academic as this summary perhaps infers, for along the way of the critical path are blasts at British Movement poets (whose capacity for self-publicity was in inverse proportion to their importance) and to John Fuller's ignorant dismissal of H.D. Thus the advocacy of centres defended by the second rate in power provides yet another context for the expansive commentary.

Mottram implicitly indicates the political significance of Derrida's work (not a strong point at Yale) because of its attack on certainty. Here he aligns Derrida with the existentialist-absurdists, and cites Bataille's laughter at the moment of the 'suicidal psychosis' which follows such decentring. Wittgenstein's essay on ethics is here cited with approval because of its attack on moralism, and Mottram comments: 'there is only ethical praxis, there are no ethical propositions.'

Mottram further connects Derrida and Heisenberg as seen by the American poet Charles Olson. The infinite play of signification Mottram connects with Heisenberg's realisation that we are at once the instrument of discovery and the instrument of definition. Informing all these discussions is Nietzsche, a crucially important figure for Mottram, both in his attack on ontology and in his concern with the man of power. Robbe-Grillet is seen as continuing the secularisation process in his critique of depth and surface as an inept transcendence configuration falsifying the deep structure of symbol. Mottram quotes from *For a New Novel*: 'Ultimately it is perhaps this uncertain content of an obscure enterprise of form which will best serve the cause of freedom.'

Charles Olson's work (because of its combination of poetry, poetics, myth and history) is seen as part of this enterprise and Olson is probably one among half a dozen figures to whom Mottram constantly returns.[20] Olson is certainly a major contributor to Mottram's perspective on cultural studies, and their meeting in Buffalo in the early 1960s was an important moment in Mottram's career.

Olson's 'brilliance of the going on' is a thickness added to the Whiteheadian metaphysics of process which the poet inherited from the philosopher. Mottram sees certain significant American poets as celebrators of the three historical thrusts at new truth inherited and identified by Derrida: the Nietzschean criticism of metaphysics, the Freudian (and post-Freudian) critique of consciousness/self-identity, and the Heideggerian denial of being as presence.

Michael McClure's view of the body's relation to nature is offered as evidence of the rejection of this traditional transcendentalist metaphysics, for his world celebrates constellations without centre. Nature itself is decentralised 'so that it cannot be returned to a platonic field of descendants from original Forms or Ideas in some symbolic discourse'.

This revised metaphysics, still within the Nietzschean problematic (and Mottram cites Nietzsche's *Beyond Good and Evil* to the effect that freedom is nature itself, defined as in an arbitrary law compelling a long obedience and which results in elegance, boldness, dance and masterly certainty) is paralleled in Duncan's political poems written against United States imperialism in South-East Asia.

> Derrida is of considerable value at this point in showing clearly how ethnology is born as a science only when European or 'western culture' – and within it the history of the metaphysics of centre – is itself '*dislocated*, driven from its locus and forced to stop considering itself as the centre of reference.'

Mottram further politicises the argument by mentioning Césaire, Fanon and Baraka as contemporary agents in helping the oppressed to break away from 'spheres' of influence.

Contemporary art and music assist the enterprise primarily because they celebrate, at a high level of seriousness, an opposition to the inertia of post-imperialist culture from the unconscious to the conscious levels. The interlinked sets of problems, nature/culture, nature/law, nature/art, nature/liberty, are tackled in different ways by Melville, Stockhausen, Xenakis, Olson, Hobbes, Cooper, Thoreau, Snyder, Cage, Sartre, Lévi-Strauss and William Burroughs.

No 'bricolage'-touting critic of the structuralist persuasion ever came near what Mottram did in this essay in the field of intellectual life and culture. Yet Mottram has a word for the would-be *bricoleur* also. Derrida refuses to keep the argument historically placed and Lévi-Strauss courts all the dangers of separating method from truth. The bricoleur, asserts Mottram, runs the risk of the unmoved-mover, as the new god in the machine.

Assisting opposition to the old metaphysics in a new guise are Robbe-Grillet who refictionalises the Oedipus myth away from a unitary universal archetype, and Velikovsky in his account of the relation between Oedipus and Akhnaten which has the same effect. Gilbert Ryle's 'disposal' of the Cartesian inner and outer distinctions is also invoked. Somewhat less successfully, Mottram pitches Piaget against Chomskyan universalist forms, but then recovers to cite Sartre's superb 'Replies to Structuralism' in the famous *Telos* no. 9. piece of 1971. Sartre goes to the heart of the problem when he talks of activity in the world: here attacking Althusser's dominations of ideology: 'What is essential is not that man is made, but he makes that which made him ... Philosophy is that which attempts to think this dépassement.'

Mottram then cites Derrida's use of Lévi-Strauss's *Le Cru et le Cuit,* particularly the sentence: 'Music and mythology bring men face to face with virtual objects whose shadow alone is actual ... Myths have no authors.' This 'new' 'virtual' sense of the world in post-mid-century intellectual thinking is obviously paralleled in the arts, and Mottram cites the 1960s' concern with improvisational and performance-orientated music and drama, citing Webern's principles which look forward to the abandonment of the nature/culture opposition.

Clearly there are dangers. Mottram mentions Derrida's fears that we might be condemned to empiricisms and naivités. Sartre is again invoked to attack totalisation with totalising, and Mottram gracefully concludes and eludes the philosophical impasses by invoking 'supplementarity' which he accurately points out still fails to 'suggest the full process of creative *modification* in the changing paradigm'.

In this essay Mottram is still speaking of the dialectical process (as given in Sartre's *Critique*) in positive ways which he would no longer do in the 1980s. Hegel's negation of the negation can still be invoked as being more radical than anything in the structuralists' non-contradictory overlapping of patterns. Reading Derrida's essay as positively as possible, he cites Derrida's joyous affirmation of a world offered to active interpretation which 'determines the non-centre otherwise than as loss of the centre'.

Nonetheless, as the paper moves into its final section

Mottram becomes more critical. Derrida's contention that choice is impossible because human beings first have to find common ground obliterates the very real set of contradictions and differences that exist with the world, and 'common ground' itself could be seen as yet another drive for a centre. Mottram comments: 'The natural sciences do not search for a constant middle ground: they are founded on an intermodulation between indeterminacy and invariability.'

Does then Derrida entertain the idea of a perpetual mutant within a structure conceived of as a game that is somehow fixed? Mottram cites Hippolyte's criticism along these lines. It is a theme that Mottram will take up again and again in his writings. He will be critical of the romantic body politics of McClure and of the unpoliticised destructive creativeness of Dionysian energy.[21] The necessity of breaking boundaries in the Brownian and Reichian sense must be seen in relation to actual political issues. Bataille's confinement of transgressive principles to the erotic, Mottram sees as an error ('The danger in Bataille is a constant tendency *to reduce* what we can mean in life to the untrained, even untrainable, exigencies of the human body') and becomes less critical in cultures whose relative abundance means there is now less fear of sexual pleasure. This essay is of course written before the identification of AIDS as a world health problem, but even so the point is still valid.

Mottram still sees Derrida as clinging to a kind of centre, and describing it as a function does resolve the dilemma, but fatally separates function from analysis. The final carelessness in the essay is a refusal to define 'perception' positively. Against Derrida Mottram places Merleau-Ponty and Blake: you do not have to have a concept of an object in order to be aware of it.

The guts of Mottram's essay is how to construct (psychically, physically and politically) a sense of self and world without recourse to malign discourses whose aim is to control other people through concepts such as 'origin' and 'centre'. In searching for positive and creative definitions he moves inevitably towards poets and musicians, that is, away from the analytic discourses of the philosophers. He cites Robert Duncan's essay 'Toward an Open Universe' where he states, the poet 'desires to penetrate the seeming style and subject matter to that most real where there is no form that is not content, no content that is nor form'. And Boulez's multiplicity of vertical dimensions (breaking classical binary axes of vertical/horizontal) is invoked for its re-creation of notions of space and sound. Among other examples Mottram cites is that moment when Buckminster Fuller looked at the bubbles bursting in the wake of a ship and realised that 'nature did not use pi as he had been taught'.

The shifting of meanings through the contextual use of relatively constant signs is of course fundamental to language, and
before concluding with the poets Mottram cites two of his most-
used teaching text recommendations: Logan Pearsall Smith's
essay of 1925, 'Four Romantic Words', and William Empson's *The
Structure of Complex Words* (1951).

A moment from 'Ranger', a poem by Theodore Enslin, concludes
the essay:

> Again and again
> the connections.
> there is no absolute
>   centre
> The core of the earth shifts,
> and I see the centering
> of parts.
>   I move away
> to see this one
>   centered
> hold it in my hand.
>   I know the fit,
> not yet the place.
> I cannot rise
> to it – and yet I do.
>   All these
> voices centered in my ears –
> their words.
> What have they said
> to me?
>   The clarity is there
> but not in voices.
>   Simply there ...

Before assessing the major position this essay plays in Mottram's
career, it would only be fair to say that there are clearly gaps,
problems and danger areas in Mottram's approach to cultural
studies. He has a well-known opposition to traditional historians
who have only just begun formally to problematise their own
sense of structure beyond mimetic, social-realist and narrative-
oriented discourses, and who never emphasise the role of technology within politics' relation to the productive process. The
influence of Mumford on Mottram was early and profound.
Neither historians nor historians of technology, or cultural studies
investigators take up the fundamental phenomena of the impact
of technology on all aspects of the historical process. Nonetheless, Mottram's booklists neglect even good history books, and

his written work does not generally draw on this area of information, nor does it draw on feminist writings. While he has not written a great deal about Afro-American writing he has given a course for many years at the London School of Oriental and African Studies on Afro-American writing and culture in the United States.

There are some methodological difficulties even within a general anti-method stance. While it is good and necessary indifferently to take information across sources of variable genre, the difference the generic structure makes to the content of the argument is not always recognised. In other contexts Mottram would fully recognise this. Further, in any one authority cited there may be sharp differences in theory and practice, and difficulties within any one theory. He will in this essay clearly note the problems with Derrida's construction of the non-centre, but sometimes the piling of evidence can reduce important discriminations of differences. Thus the relationship between indeterminacy in Webern, Heisenberg and Fuller's definition of the relation between technology and nature points accurately to a general shift in twentieth-century sensibility and awareness, but may not precisely enough articulate the differences between the areas of, say, politics, formal invention and ethics in any one of them. Mottram does not fully emphasise the drive to authority and control in Fuller's brilliantly inventive technology, nor the simplified and even totalitarian claims in Korsybski's opposition to a somewhat carelessly dehistoricised 'Aristotelian' ideology which underwrites 'commonsense' in western culture, nor the very sophisticated revolution in actual science and method in Darwin's descriptions of variation and natural selection.

The world has moved on from the positivist's fear of 'metaphysics', for there is a 'metaphysics' implicit in any view of the world, and it does not automatically imply, or not imply, authoritarianism. As Greta Jones has shown, for example, natural selection in actual political use could serve any ideological purpose: left and right.[22] To deny metaphysics is sometimes to be blind to your own, and Mumford is on record as stating that scientists, for example, 'are never more engaged in metaphysics than when they deny they have any'.[23]

Third, given that criticism is a type of metaphorical discourse, is there any role for the analytic? What is the relation between the analytic and the metaphorical, and are both necessary in formal terms of current usage even if it is recognised that the analytic is in the end also a different set of metaphoric practices?

Notwithstanding these difficult problems, the essay is dazzling in its range. It picks up the oral tone of Mottram's speaking/teaching style, and makes his cultural studies uniquely boundary-less in terms of nations, in terms of the methodological categories of academic practice, and in terms of the spurious order of sequential time: 'maps rather than chronologies' as he said of Jerome Rothenberg's anthologies.[24] The essay on Derrida represents one of the best examples of Eric Mottram's cultural-studies approach. It is quite unlike any other. The kinds of method, or anti-method, and the areas of information are ones that feed into many other essays by him, and are ones he keeps returning to again and again. The arguments are created about their own moments. Multiplicity extends to both form and content. The sheer range of Mottram's work and reading is of an extraordinarily impressive magnitude: from painting and music to poetry, from the history of technology to political philosophy and psychology, from film to drama through European, American and ethnic cultures. Areas he does not cover are formal philosophy, psychology and, perhaps most obviously, history. Instead of narrative progression, and arguments which proceed along analytical lines, what one has is a collage of issues and information which accretes around a set of deepening judgements, on the basis of what, in Whiteheadian terms, the hand picks up to order at any moment. In one sense there are links with the romantic, transcendentalist essay tradition; a tradition which could only have been reinforced by Olson's critical prose.

Among many issues three broad areas of recurring (rather than progressive) critical interest can be identified: how to organise non-dogmatic critical paths within multiplicity; the attack on metaphysics (here, the lineaments of Marcuse's 'false consciousness'); and the theme of power.

What is most disconcerting for academics is that Mottram avoids hierarchising information according to academic rules. That is, there is a deliberate abandonment of traditional controls of what might go together in any moment of argument. Information from poetry, philosophy, critical prose is deployed across historical periods and across genre. The method is synchronic and metaphoric. In most academic criticism, there is always a drive for an analytic and categorising certainty: the latest definition of postmodernism for example. Such a drive does not exist in Mottram's work. To use Ricoeur's terms, Mottram's critical work hovers between 'rhetoric' and 'poetics'. Mottram knows that what comes together has only virtual and fleeting existence, and rather than build defences against it he acknowledges it as a positive power in his own method.

The emphasis, therefore, is on the liveliness of what can be brought together. The untranslatableness of metaphor, not the reductiveness of critical paraphrase, is what Mottram aims at. Gilbert Ryle's 'category mistake' is precisely the very goal of his work. In an essay on Harry Matthews, Mottram cited Gregory Bateson's and Deleuze's and Guattari's concept of 'plateaux' to describe Matthews's complexities of narrative events: 'A continuous region of intensities, vibrating on itself, which is developed by avoiding any orientation on a culminating point or toward an exterior end.' [25] In that sense it could also describe Mottram's own critical method.

Inside the multiple are ways of rehearsing judgement. The 'virtual' sense of the world must be recognised before any attempt at judgement is made. Indeed, the virtual world is simultaneous with new forms of recognition which are given *with* critical judgement. At its best Mottram's essay style captures the performance of intermodulation between indeterminacy and invariability, thereby aligning the critical act itself with the open forms of twentieth-century poetry.

Describing the shapes of multiplicity is a necessity in whatever he writes about. It is most theorised in his essay on Henry Adams,[26] it is implicit in his huge book-lists, it links with the psychology of his judgements of characters in books. Lee, Amar and Stenham in Bowles's *The Spider's House* he says are alike in 'this desire to exist without dislocation: they are uncreative, static survivalists, sensing that the mid-twentieth century threatens them'.[27]

Then there is the attack on metaphysics. Here Mottram is of the secular humanist generation of the 1930s, and the absurdist philosophers of the 1950s. Mottram's deep interest in 'ethnopoetics', mythological and anthropological issues, however, not only decentres Christianity as governing ideology but saves him from the materialist positivism of, say, an Ogden and Richards.[28] The influence of the absurdist philosophers means that his attack on metaphysics has a political dimension and here he has obvious debts to a tradition that extends back to the European enlightenment. Hence, throughout the essay on Derrida descriptions of spiritual cosmology used to provide alibis for rulers are points of attack, and parallel superstitions are pursued relentlessly in their contemporary avatars.

These issues are linked also to the attack on restrictive certainties which metaphysics legitimate. Therefore Mottram's criticism points towards those values which are necessary for the kind of stability which opens possibility rather than closes it down. Since Mottram's main area of interest is literature, these general concerns can cover the representation of sexual and personal life, politics, social patterns and the manipulations of belief through any type of communicational technology.

The very subject of a falsifying metaphysics seems more pertinent to American society than to almost any other. Mottram

noted in an early introductory essay on Faulkner: 'American
history and geography are re-structured as archaicizing myth with
these epic proportions, as if Americans needed such reference for
their justification and stability.' [29] And there is a difference here,
too, between the Europeans and the Americans. When Twain
writes 'God has forsaken us', it is a moment of despair which has
a weakening effect on his writing, whereas 'for Nietzsche contem-
poraneously, and Camus later, this is a signal to move forwards
into a consideration of the existential situation'.[30]

Intrinsic to this psychological and political area is the question
of ethics, and central to ethics is the question of power and
authority. As he says of Henry James:

> [His] long enquiry almost habitually represents a cage, an
> exploitation, a market of sado-masochistic reciprocities,
> infinite interrogations in a sysyphean drama. Creativity is
> threatened by sexual and market desires to exploit or be
> exploited. Children necessarily live within the parental
> enforcement, the social they are born into, 'Father's Ideas'.[31]

In addition to fathers are confidence men, propagandists, and
those who promise false securities and the compensatory pleas-
ures of discipline and punishment. The literary representation of
the figure of power and its responsibilities, therefore, is central to
Mottram's critical inquiry. In addition, the nature of law as
politics and culture is constantly under investigation in Mottram's
work.

Mottram's critique of the social and political abuse of power was
powerfully aided by his primary recognition of the work of William
Burroughs, in which the Sadean plot is given twentieth-century
significance in innovative writing of high sophistication.[32] It is
something that fascinates him in all literature: 'Burroughs's characters are analogues caught in space-time and briefly emerging like
the performers of *The Tempest*, a recurrent text in his fictions, since
it concerns control and transformation under leadership – including
magic – both usurped and inherited.' [33] It is implicit in his writing
on popular culture: in his critique of 'the luxurious righteousness' of
'individual anarchistic power' of the gun culture in America.[34] And
he can say even of one of his favourite detective novelists, Ross
Macdonald: 'Detective story writers, Macdonald not excepted, tend
to idealise their heroes in order to excuse liability for violence
traded off against violence.' [35] Such judgements become more
complex in more recent fiction. Mottram makes precise our unease
in reading DeLillo, for example, who 'works where utopia and
dystopia are indistinguishable; his plots confer enjoyable reading on
their systems, but also infer our conspiracy to enter their

networks'.[36] In America, though, the tradition has been there since Poe. Mottram observes that among characters in *The Narrative of Arthur Gordon Pym*, 'the closest human relationship is loyalty or disloyalty between shipmates in extreme situations, including cannibalism'.[37] He would also note Poe's influence on Marquéz in his representation of existential and political controls.[38]

It should just be mentioned, however, that underlying the frequent grimness of Mottram's investigations of literature and evil is a sense of, and a strong interest in, comedy. Mottram enjoys a range of comedy from black humour to knockabout farce, even though 'humour and its reliable bases cannot survive humourless wars'.[39] His lectures, with tapes, on American satirists have both delighted and unnerved many student audiences.

Behind the literary representations of psychological disaster, however, is an economics and politics which Mottram rarely lets us forget. In an essay on the American novel in the 1920s, he says: 'In 1926, 207 individuals paid taxes on one million dollars or more in a single year, but poverty was national and largely ignored. Certainly any talk of values in literature and criticism which ignores such facts is valueless.' [40]

What separates Mottram's criticism from others is that its point of value is the creative activity which leads to significant serious work in the arts. The 'creative' alone, he insists, is not a useful term, for human beings are mostly creative in evil ways as the current ecological, let alone the current political, horrors of the contemporary world show. The final triumph of 'capitalist democracy' which saw off 'communism' in the Soviet Union in 1991 began that year with a war in which 100,000 innocent people were killed with precision bombing, in which myriads oil-wells burned for two years, causing incalculable damage, in which a huge section of the Kurdish people have been devastated, and in which the immediate dictator (also a capitalist) who precipitated the crisis was left in power. Even *Time* magazine was moved to ask on its front cover: 'Was it worth it?'

Cultural studies for Mottram is an investigation into what supports the possibility of purposive, creative activity in the actual world in which we live. Opposing (not compensating for) the necessary pessimism of Mottram's critical work is his deep involvement in contemporary poetry. He has written about and encouraged dozens and dozens of poets, mainly American and British, most of whom still have to find their way into the educational curricula. Among the American poets he has papers on are John Ashbery, Paul Blackburn, Bill Butler, Robert Duncan, Theodore Enslin, Clayton Eshleman, Allen Ginsberg, Ken Irby, Jackson MacLow, Tom Meyer, Ezra Pound, Charles Olson, George Oppen, Kenneth Rexroth, Jerome Rothenberg, John Wieners, Jonathan Williams,

William Carlos Williams: and among British poets, Basil Bunting, Paula Clare, Bob Cobbing, Roy Fisher, Bill Griffiths, Lee Harwood, Michael Horowitz, Jeff Nuttall, Tom Pickard. There are also essays on poetry of a more general nature. He has drawn obvious nourishment from the achievements of American poetry in the face of an impoverished British culture. Of Eshleman's *Coils*, he said: 'We have nothing like Coils in British poetry because we have been trained to fear explicit emotion, inventive vehicular forms for the developing of experience, and the communication of abundance rather than scarcity.' [41]

Nonetheless, Mottram's huge effort in assisting the British poetry revival of the 1970s (the volumes of *Poetry Review* edited by him are worth the entire output back to 1945 and since), in which he fell foul of what seemed the entire British literary establishment, is still suppressed as public knowledge, together with the poets he supported.[42]

Yet the real measure of Mottram's involvement in cultural studies is poetry itself. It is here, for example, in *The Elegies* of the mid-1970s, that he creates tributes to those historical and contemporary figures that have given him an idea of human worth which includes invention, radical change and the possibility of real love and comradeship. They include poets like Neruda, Lorca, Vallejo and Rukeyser, composers and musicians like Monk, Lewis, Mingus, Hendrix, Mahler and Webern, philosophers and political activists like Wittgenstein and Gramsci, painters and craftsmen like Samuel Palmer, Courbet and Bernard Leach, comedians like W. C. Fields and Lenny Bruce.

These figures set the kind of standard in art and politics that any teacher would want to pass on. At the beginning of his poem, 'Elegies' (which, he reminds us, the Greeks addressed to war and love not to lamentation), Mottram recalls Muriel Rukeyser's citing of Rosa Luxemburg and it will do, finally, to sum up his own spirit: 'Still elegiac! between two battles, when one is happy to be alive!' [43]

Notes and References

1. I'll Buy That *Ralph Willett*

1. Dale Carter, *The Final Frontier: the Rise and Fall of the American Rocket State* (London and New York: Verso, 1988) p.171.
2. Carter, ibid., p.166. The Mailer references are from *Of a Fire on the Moon* (New York: New American Library, 1971).
3. E.L. Doctorow, *The Book of Daniel* (New York: Bantam Books, 1981), p.302.
4. Louis Marin, 'Disneyland: a Degenerate Utopia', *Glyph 1*, vol. 1 (1977) pp.58, 62.
5. Susan Willis, '*Fantasia*: Walt Disney's LA Suite', *diacritics*, vol. 17, no. 2 (1988) pp.88, 96.
6. Michael Harrington, 'To the Disney Station', *Harper's*, vol. 258 (January 1979) p.39.
7. Stella Shamoon, 'The Billion Dollar Mouse', *Observer*, 20 November 1988, p.64.
8. Ant Farm, *Autoamerica* (New York: Dutton, 1976), p.62. Ant Farm is an architectural design collaborative.
9. Phil Patton, *Open Road: a Celebration of the American Highway* (New York: Simon and Schuster, 1986), p.188.
10. John F. Love, *McDonalds Behind the Arches* (New York: Bantam, 1988), p.437.
11. Simon Frith, 'Rock and Popular Culture' in Donald Lazere (ed), *American Media and Mass Culture: Left Perspectives* (Berkeley: University of California Press, 1987), p.317.
12. Louis Menand, 'Life in the Stone Age', *New Republic*, 7–14 January 1991, p.42.
13. Jill Pearlman, *Elvis for Beginners* (London and Sydney: Writers and Readers/Unwin, 1986), p.97. Records had become a subsidiary interest by the summer of 1956 when Presley left for Hollywood to become its highest paid actor.
14. G.B. Trudeau, *The People's Doonesbury: Notes from Underfoot* (London: Wildwood House, 1981).
15. Rosalind Coward, 'Come Back Miss Ellie: on Character and Narrative in Soap Operas', *Critical Quarterly*, vol. 28, no. 1/2 (Spring/Summer 1986) p.171.
16. Ien Ang, *Watching Dallas: Soap Opera and the Melodramatic Imagination* (London and New York: Methuen, 1985), p.55.
17. Michael Bywater, 'Tastes Like Soap', *The Listener*, 21 April 1988, p.5.
18. Douglas Tallack, *Twentieth Century America: the Intellectual and Cultural Context* (Harlow: Longmans, 1991), p.17.
19. Ibid., p.109.

20. Don DeLillo, *White Noise* (New York: Viking Penguin, 1986) p.19.

21. John Fiske, *Reading the Popular* (London and Sydney: Unwin Hyman, 1989) pp.14, 31.

22. Bobbie Ann Mason, *In Country* (London: Flamingo/Fontana, 1986) p.237.

23. Paul Rudnick, *I'll Take It* (New York: Ballantine Books, 1989) p.248.

2. Self-inscriptions A. Robert Lee

1. James Baldwin, 'Why I Stopped Hating Shakespeare', *Observer*, 19 April 1964.

2. Tomás Rivera: 'Chicano Literature: the Establishment of Community' in Luis Leal, Fernando de Nechocea, Francisco Lomelí and Robert G. Trujillo (eds), *A Decade of Chicano Literature* (Santa Barbara, CA: Editorial La Causa, 1982) pp. 9–17.

3. Gerald Vizenor, *Crossbloods: Bone Courts, Bingo, and Other Reports* (Minneapolis: University of Minnesota Press, 1990), Introduction.

4. Amy Tan, 'Mother Tongue', *The Threepenny Review*, 1990. Reprinted in Joyce Carol Oates (ed), *The Best American Essays 1991* (New York: Tickner and Fields, 1991) pp.196–202.

5. Samuel Eliot Morison, *Admiral of the Ocean Sea: a Life of Christopher Columbus* (Boston: Little, Brown, and Company, 1942).

6. Kirkpatrick Sale, *The Conquest of Paradise: Christopher Columbus and the Columbian Legacy* (New York: Knopf, 1990).

7. As a sample of the recent scholarship and debate, see: Felipe Fernández-Armesto, *Columbus* (London and New York: Oxford University Press, 1991); Jeffrey Burton Russell, *Inventing the Flat Earth: Columbus and Modern Historians* (New York: Praeger, 1991); Jacques Attali, *1492* (Paris: Fayard, 1991); Stephen Greenblatt, *Marvellous Possessions: the Wonder of the New World* (Chicago: University of Chicago Press, 1991); Paolo Emilio Taviani, *Columbus: the Great Adventure: His Life, His Times, and His Voyages* (New York: Orion Books, 1991); John Noble Wilford, *The Mysterious History of Columbus: an Exploration of the Man, the Myth, the Legacy* (New York: Knopf, 1991); William D. Phillips Jr and Carla Rahn Phillips, *The Worlds of Christopher Columbus* (Cambridge and New York: Cambridge University Press, 1992); and Zvi Dor-Ner, *Columbus and the Age of Discovery* (New York: Morrow, 1991) – the companion volume to the seven-hour PBS series.

8. For accounts of recent anti-Asianism, see: Jon Funabiki, 'A Sansei View of Japan Bashing', *San Francisco Review of Books*, vol. 16, no. 4 (March 1992) p.35; and A. Robert Lee, 'America's Other Japan: the Fiction of Toshio Mori, John Okada, Hisaye Yamamoto, Milton Murayama and Jessica Saiki', *The British American*, vol. 4, no. 3 (July 1992) pp. 3–5.

9. Allan Bloom, *The Closing of the American Mind* (New York: Simon and Schuster, 1987); and E.D. Hirsch Jr, *Cultural Literacy* (Boston: Houghton, Mifflin, 1987).

10. Roger Kimball, *Tenured Radicals: How Politics Has Corrupted Our Higher Education* (New York: Harper and Row, 1990); Dinesh D'Souza, *Illiberal Education: the Politics of Race and Sex on Campus*

(New York: Maxwell, 1991); Richard Rodriguez, *Hunger of Memory* (Boston, MA: D.R. Godine, 1981); Linda Chávez, *Out of the Barrio: Towards a New Politics of Assimilation* (New York: Basic Books, 1991); and Arthur M. Schlesinger Jr, *The Disuniting of America: Reflections on a Multicultural Society* (New York: W.W. Norton, 1992).

11. Albert Shanker, 'Courting Ethnic Strife', *Sunday New York Times*, 23 February 1992, p. E7.

12. See, typically, Rick Simonson and Scott Walker (eds), *The Graywolf Annual Five: Multi-cultural Literacy* (Saint Paul, MN: Graywolf Press, 1988); Cordelia Candelaria (ed), *Multiethnic Literature of the United States: Critical Introductions and Classroom Resources* (Boulder, CO: University of Colorado Press, 1989); or a special feature like 'Beyond P.C., the Canon, and Multiculturalism', *Harper's*, vol. 283, no. 1699 (December 1991). Crucial, and symptomatic, anthologies would be: Ishmael Reed, Kathryn Trueblood and Shawn Wong (eds), *The Before Columbus Foundation Fiction Anthology* (New York: W.W. Norton, 1992); J.J. Phillips, Ishmael Reed, Gundars Strads and Shawn Wong (eds), *The Before Columbus Foundation Poetry Anthology* (New York: W.W. Norton, 1992); and Ray Gonzalez (ed), *Without Discovery: a Native Response to Columbus* (Seattle: Broken Moon Press, 1992).

13. Emory Elliott et al. (eds), *The Columbia Literary History of The United States* (New York: Columbia University Press, 1988); and Paul Lauter et al. (eds), *Heath Anthology of American Literature* (Lexington, MA: D.C. Heath, 1990). See also, in this connection: Robert von Hallberg (ed), *Canons* (Chicago: University of Chicago Press, 1984); Sacvan Bercovitch (ed), *Reconstructing American Literary History* (Cambridge, MA: Harvard University Press, 1986); Sacvan Bercovitch and Myra Jehlen (eds), *Ideology and Classic American Literature* (New York: Cambridge University Press, 1987).

14. For a selection of both sides of the issue, see Patricia Aufderheide (ed), *Beyond PC: Towards a Politics of Understanding* (Saint Paul, MN: Graywolf Press, 1992).

15. For general accounts, see: Thomas R. Brooks, *Walls Come Tumbling Down, 1940–70* (Englewood Cliffs, NJ: Prentice-Hall, 1974); Sar A. Levitan et al., *Still a Dream: the Changing Status of Blacks Since 1960* (Cambridge, MA: Harvard University Press, 1975); August Meier and Elliot Rudwick, *Along the Color Line* (Urbana: Illinois University Press, 1975); and Harvey Sitkoff, *The Struggle For Black Equality, 1954–80* (New York: Hill and Wang, 1981).

16. The following set out something of this achievement: Michael S. Harper and R.E. Stepto (eds), *Chants of Saints: a Gathering of Afro-American Literature, Art and Scholarship* (Urbana, IL: University of Illinois Press, 1979); A. Robert Lee (ed), *Black Fiction: New Studies in the Afro-American Novel* (London: Vision Press, 1980); C.W.E. Bigsby, *The Second Black Renaissance: Essays in Black Literature* (Westport, CT: Greenwood Press, 1980); A. Robert Lee, *Black American Fiction Since Richard Wright*, British Association of American Studies Pamphlet no. 11, 1983; Mari Evans (ed), *Black Women Writers (1959–1980): A Critical Evaluation* (New York: Anchor Books, 1984); Keith E. Byerman, *Fingering the Jagged Grain: Tradition and Form in Recent Black Fiction* (Athens, GA: University of Georgia Press, 1985); John F. Callaghan, *In the Afro-American Grain: the Pursuit of Voice in Twentieth-century Black Fiction* (Urbana, IL: University of Illinois Press, 1988); and Elliott Butler-

Evans, *Race, Gender, and Desire: Narrative Strategies in the Fiction of Toni Cade Bambara, Toni Morrison and Alice Walker* (Philadelphia: Temple University Press).

17. James Baldwin, *Notes of a Native Son* (Boston: Beacon Press, 1955); *Nobody Knows My Name: More Notes of a Native Son* (New York: Dial Press, 1961); and *The Fire Next Time* (New York: Dial Press, 1963).

18. Eldridge Cleaver, *Soul on Ice* (New York: McGraw Hill, 1968); Albert Murray, *The Omni-Americans* (New York: Outerbridge, 1970); Alice Walker, *In Search of Our Mothers' Gardens* (San Diego: Harcourt Brace Jovanovitch, 1983); and Toni Morrison: *Playing in the Dark: Whiteness and the Literary Imagination* (Cambridge, MA: Harvard University Press, 1992).

19. Richard Wright, *Black Boy* (New York: Harper and Brothers, 1945); Zora Neale Hurston, *Dust Tracks on a Road* (1942, reissued, Urbana, IL: University of Illinois Press, 1984); Malcolm X, *Auto-biography* (New York: Grove Press, 1964); Maya Angelou, *I Know Why the Caged Bird Sings* (New York: Random House, 1970); Angela Davis, *Autobiography* (New York: Random House, 1974); and Chester Himes, *The Quality of Hurt* (New York: Doubleday, 1972) and *My Life of Absurdity* (New York: Doubleday, 1976).

20. Full references are as follows: Ralph Ellison, *Invisible Man* (New York: Random House, 1952); James Baldwin, *Go Tell It on the Mountain* (New York: Knopf, 1953); Ernest Gaines, *The Autobiography of Miss Jane Pittman* (New York: Dial Press, 1971); Toni Morrison, *Song of Solomon* (New York: Knopf, 1977) and *Jazz* (New York: Knopf, 1992); Alice Walker, *Meridian* (Mew York: Harcourt Brace Jovanovitch, 1976); James Alan McPherson, *Hue and Cry* (Boston: Little Brown, 1969) and *Elbow Room* (Boston: Atlantic-Little, Brown, 1977); Ishmael Reed, *The Free-Lance Pallbearers* (New York: Doubleday, 1967) and *The Terrible Threes* (New York: Atheneum, 1989).

21. Lorraine Hansberry, *Raisin in the Sun* (New York: Random House, 1958); LeRoi Jones/Amiri Baraka, *Dutchman*, originally published as *Dutchman and The Slave* (New York: Morrow, 1964); and August Wilson, *Ma Rainey's Black Bottom* (New York: NAL–Dutton, 1984).

22. Amiri Baraka, *The LeRoi Jones/Amiri Baraka Reader*, ed William J. Harris (New York: Thunder's Mouth Press, 1991).

23. Relevant scholarship on Chicano history includes: George I. Sánchez, *Forgotten People: a Study of New Mexicans* (Albuquerque, NM: C. Horn, 1940); Carey McWilliams, *North from Mexico: the Spanish-Speaking People of the United States* (New York: Greenwood Press, 1948); Matt S. Meier and Feliciano Rivera, *The Chicanos: a History of Mexican-Americans* (New York: Hill and Wang, 1972); Rodolfo Acuña, *Occupied America: the Chicano Struggle Towards Liberation* (San Francisco: Canfield Press, 1972); Matt S. Meier and Feliciano Rivera, *Dictionary of Mexican-American History* (Westport, CT: Greenwood Press, 1981); John A. García et al. (eds), *History, Culture and Society: Chicano Studies in the 1980s* (Ypsilanti, MN: Bilingual Press/Editorial Bilingüe, National Association of Chicano Studies, 1984); Rodolfo O. de la Garza, Frank D. Bean, Charles M. Bonjean, Ricardo Romo and Rodolfo Alvarez (eds), *The Mexican American Experience* (Austin, TX: University of Texas Press, 1985); and Dietrich Briesemeister and Juan Bruce-Novoa (eds), *Missions in Conflict: Essays on U.S.–Mexican Relations and Chicano Culture*

(Tübingen: Gunter Narr Verlag, 1986). For Puerto Rican-American history, see: Christopher Rand, *The Puerto Ricans* (New York: Oxford University Press, 1958); Joseph P. Fitzpatrick, *Puerto Rican Americans: the Meaning of Migration* (Englewood Cliffs, NJ: Prentice-Hall, 1971); Kal Wagenheim, *The Puerto Ricans: Documentary History* (New York: Praeger, 1973); James Jennings and Monte Rivera, *Puerto Rican Politics in Urban America* (Westport, CT: Greenwood Press, 1984); and Manuel Alers-Montalvo, *The Puerto Rican Migrants of New York City: a Study of Anomie* (New York: AMS Press, 1985). For Cuban-American history, see: Carlos E. Cortes (ed), *Cuban Exiles in the United States* (New York: Arno Press, 1980); Thomas D. Boswell, *The Cuban-American Experience: Culture, Images, and Perspectives* (Totowa, NJ: Rowman and Allanheld, 1984); Lyn McCorkle, *Cubans in the United States: a Bibliography for Research in the Social and Behavioral Sciences* (Westport, CT: Greenwood Press, 1984); and Joan Didion, *Miami* (New York: Simon and Schuster, 1987).

24. Oscar Hijuelos: *The Mambo Kings Play Songs of Love* (New York: Farrar, Straus, Giroux, 1989).

25. Tomás Rivera, '... *y no se lo tragó la tierra'/'... and the earth did not part*' (Berkeley, CA: Quinto Sol Publications, 1971).

26. These references in full are as follows: Rudolfo Anaya: *Bless Me, Ultima* (Berkeley, CA: Quinto Sol Publications, 1972); Sandra Cisneros, *Woman Hollering Creek and other stories* (New York: Random House, 1991); Piri Thomas, *Down These Mean Streets* (New York: Knopf, 1967); Nicholasa Mohr, *Nilda: a Novel* (New York: Harper, 1973); Hijuelos, *The Mambo Kings Play Songs of Love*; Cristina Garcia, *Dreaming in Cuban* (New York: Knopf, 1992); Julia Alvarez, *How the García Girls Lost Their Accents* (Chapel Hill: Algonquin Books, 1991); and Alex Abella, *The Killing of the Saints* (New York: Crown, 1991). Relevant literary scholarship and criticism includes Francisco Lomelí and Donaldo W. Uriosto (eds), *Chicano Perspectives in Literature: a Critical and Annotated Bibliography* (Albuquerque, NM: Parajito Publications, 1976); Francisco Jiménez (ed), *The Identification and Analysis of Chicano Literature* (Binghamton, NY: Bilingual Press/Editorial Bilingüe, National Association of Chicano Studies, 1979); Juan Bruce-Novoa, *Chicano Authors: Inquiry by Interview* (Austin, TX: University of Texas Press, 1980); Juan Bruce Novoa, *Chicano Poetry: a Response to Chaos* (Austin, TX: University of Texas Press, 1982); Julio A. Martínez and Francisco Lomelí (eds), *Chicano Literature: a Reference Guide* (Westport, CT: Greenwood Press, 1985); and Héctor Calderon and José David Saldívar (eds), *Criticism in the Borderlands: Studies in Chicano Literature, Culture, and Ideology* (Durham and London: Duke University Press, 1991). For non-Chicano reference, see Nicholas Kanellos, *Biographical Dictionary of Hispanic Literature in the United States: the Literature of Puerto Ricans, Cuban Americans and Other Hispanic Writers* (New York: Greenwood Press, 1989).

27. Guillermo Gómez-Peña: 'Documented/Undocumented', *L.A. Weekly*, 1990. Reprinted in Simonson and Walker (eds), *The Graywolf Annual Five*.

28. For general accounts of recent Native-American history, see: Vine Deloria Jr, *Custer Died for Your Sins* (New York: Macmillan, 1969);

Dee Brown, *Bury My Heart at Wounded Knee: An Indian History of the American West* (New York: Holt, Rinehart and Winston, 1970); Angie Debo, *A History of the Indians in the United States* (Norman, OK: University of Oklahoma Press, 1970; Vine Deloria Jr, *God is Red* (New York: Grosset and Dunlap, 1973); D'Arcy McNickle, *Native American Tribalism* (New York: Delacorte, 1974); F. Berkhover, Jr, *The White Man's Indian, Images of the American Indian from Columbus to the Present* (New York: Knopf, 1978); James L. Axtell, *The European and the Indian* (New York: Oxford University Press, 1981); and Carl Waldman, *Atlas of the North American Indian* (Oxford: Oxford University Press, Facts on File, 1985).

29. Vine Deloria Jr, *Custer Died for Your Sins* (New York: Macmillan, 1969).

30. Dee Brown, *Bury My Heart at Wounded Knee* (New York: Holt, Rinehart and Winston, 1970).

31. Bibliographies and discussions of this achievement are to be found in: Jack W. Marken (ed), *The American Indian Language and Literature* (Illinois: A.M.H. Publishing Corpor-ation, Goldentree Bibliography, 1978); Paula Allen Gunn (ed), *Studies in American Indian Literature* (New York: Modern Language Association of America, 1983); Kenneth Lincoln, *Native American Renaissance* (Berkeley and Los Angeles: University of California Press, 1983); Arnold Krupat, *For Those Who Come After: a Study of Native American Autobiography* (Berkeley and Los Angeles: University of California Press, 1985); Brian Swann and Arnold Krupat (eds), *Recovering the Word: Essays on Native American Literature* (Berkeley and Los Angeles: University of California Press, 1987); and David Murray, *Forked Tongues: Speech, Writing and Representation in North American Indian Texts* (London: Pinter Publishers, 1991).

32. Gerald Vizenor, *Interior Landscapes: Autobiographical Myths and Metaphors* (Minneapolis: University of Minnesota Press, 1990).

33. Full references for these works are as follows: N. Scott Momaday, *House Made of Dawn* (New York: Harper and Row, 1968); Heyemeyohst Storm, *Seven Arrows* (New York: Harper and Row, 1972); Leslie Marmon Silko, *Ceremony* (New York: Viking Press, 1977) and *Storyteller* (New York: Viking Press, 1981); Louise Erdrich, *Love Medicine* (New York: Holt, Rinehart and Winston, 1984), *The Beet Queen* (New York: Henry Holt, 1986), and *Tracks* (Henry Holt, 1988); James Welch, *Winter in the Blood* (New York: Harper and Row, 1974) and *Fools Crow* (New York: Viking, 1986); and Linda Hogan, *Mean Spirit* (New York: Atheneum, 1990).

34. Gerald Vizenor, *Griever: an American Monkey King in China* (Minneapolis: University of Minnesota Press, 1987), *The Heirs of Columbus* (Hanover and London: Wesleyan University Press, 1991) and *Dead Voices* (Norman, OK: University of Oklahoma Press, 1992).

35. Recent general accounts include: Michi Weglyn, *Years of Infamy: the Untold Story of America's Concentration Camps* (New York: Quill, 1976); Hyung-Chan Kim (ed), *Dictionary of Asian American History* (Westport, CT: Greenwood Press, 1986); Roger Daniels, *Asian America: Chinese and Japanese in the United States* (Seattle and London: University of Washington Press, 1988); Ronald Takaki, *Strangers from a Different Shore* (Boston: Little, Brown, 1989); and Sucheng Chan, *Asian Americans: an Interpretive History* (Boston: Twayne Publishers, 1991).

36. Amy Tan, *The Joy Luck Club* (New York: Random House, 1989) and *The Kitchen God's Wife* (New York: Random House, 1991).

37. Maxine Hong Kingston, *The Woman Warrior: Memories of a Girlhood Among Ghosts* (New York: Vintage Books, 1977) and *China Men* (New York: Knopf, 1980); Frank Chin, *The Chickencoop Chinaman and The Year of the Dragon* (reprinted, Seattle, WA: University of Washington Press, 1981); Monica Sone, *Nisei Daughter* (Boston: Little, Brown, 1953, 1979); David Mura, *Turning Japanese: Memories of a Sansei* (New York: Atlantic Monthly Press, 1991); Kim Ronyoung, *Clay Walls* (Sag Harbor, NY: Permanent Press, 1986); May Paik Lee, *Quiet Odyssey: a Pioneer Korean Woman in America* (Seattle, WA: University of Washington Press, 1990); Carlos Bulosan, *America is in the Heart* (New York: Harcourt, Brace and Company, 1946, 1973 and 1981); and Jessica Tarahata Hagedorn, *Dogeaters* (New York: Random House, 1990). Literary-critical accounts of, and bibliographies for, this achievement include: Elaine Kim, *Asian American Literature: an Introduction to the Writings and their Social Context* (Philadelphia: Temple University Press, 1982); and King Kok Cheung and Stan Yogi (eds), *Asian American Literature, an Annotated Bibliography* (New York: Modern Language Association of America, 1988).

38. Jeffery Paul Chan, Frank Chin, Lawson Fusao Inada and Shawn Wong (eds), *Aiiieeeee! An Anthology of Asian American Writers* (Washington DC: Howard University Press, 1974) and *The Big Aiiieeeee! An Anthology of Chinese American and Japanese American Literature* (New York: Meridian, 1991).

39. Denise M. Magnet, 'Faculty Members of Berkeley Offer Courses to Satisfy Controversial "Diversity" Requirement', *Chronicle of Higher Education*, vol. XXXVIII, no. 27 (11 March 1992) pp.A1, A16 and A17.

40. The present essay, accordingly, continues an ongoing series of my own attempts to map this efflorescence. Its predecessors include: 'Making New: Styles of Innovation in the Contemporary Black American Novel' in A. Robert Lee (ed), *Black Fiction: New Studies in the Afro-American Novel Since 1945* (London: Vision Press, 1980) pp.222–50; *Black American Fiction*; 'The Stance of Self-representation: Moderns and Contemporaries in Afro-American Autobiography' in *First Person Singular: Studies in American Autobiography* (London: Vision Press, 1988) pp.151–76; 'Harlem on My Mind: Fictions of a Black Metropolis' in Graham Clarke (ed), *The American City: Literary and Cultural Perspectives* (London: Vision Press, 1988) pp.62–85; 'Ethnic Renaissance: Rudolfo Anaya, Louise Erdich and Maxine Hong Kingston' in Graham Clarke (ed), *The New American Writing: Essays on American Literature Since 1970* (London: Vision Press, 1990) pp.139–64; 'Ethnic America: the Non-European Voice', *The British American*, vol. 3, no. 1, pp.9–10; 'Decolonizing America: the Ethnicity of Ernest Gaines, José Antonio Villarreal, Leslie Marmon Silko and Shawn Wong' in Theo D'haen and Cedric Barfoot (eds), *Shades of Empire: Studies in Colonial and Post-Colonial Literatures* (Amsterdam: Rodopi, 1992) pp.271–84; 'America's Other Japan: the Fiction of Toshio Mori, John Okada, Hisaye Yamamoto, Jessica Saiki and Milton Murayama', *The British American*, vol. 4, no. 1, pp.3–5; 'Acts of Remembrance: America as Multicultural Past in Ralph Ellison, Nicholasa Mohr, James Welch and Monica Sone' in Hans Bak (ed), *Multiculturalism and the Canon of*

American Culture (Amsterdam: University of Amsterdam Press, 1992) pp.81-103; and 'En Busca de Aztlán: Chicano-American Memory in the Novels of Nash Candelaria, Rudolfo Anaya and Ron Arias' in Amritjit Singh and Joseph Skerrett (eds), *Memory and Cultural Politics: New Perspectives on American Ethnic Literatures,* (New York: Oxford University Press, forthcoming).

41. José Antonio Villarreal, *Pocho* (New York: Doubleday, 1959); Raymond Barrio, *The Plum Plum Pickers* (Sunnyvale, CA: Ventura Press, 1969; reprinted: Binghamton, NY: Bilingual Press/Editorial Bilingüe, 1984); Rudolfo Anaya, *Bless Me, Ultima* (Berkeley, CA: Quinto Sol Publications, 1976); Ron Arias, *The Road to Tamazunchale* (Reno: West Coast Poetry Review, 1975; reprinted: Albuquerque, NM: Parajito Publications, 1978); and Rolando Hinojosa, *Klail City y sus alrededores* (Havana, Cuba: Casas de las Américas, 1976), author's English version: *Klail City* (Houston, TX: Arte Publico Press, 1987).

3. The New Feminist Dispensation
Faith Pullin and *Claire Colebrook*

1. Betty Friedan, *The Feminine Mystique* (New York: Dell, 1963).

2. Zillah Eisenstein, *The Radical Future of Liberal Feminism* (New York: Longman, 1981).

3. Betty Friedan, *The Second Stage* (New York: Summit, 1981) p.165.

4. Susan Bassnett, *Feminist Experiences: the Women's Movement in Four Cultures* (London: Allen and Unwin, 1986).

5. C.R. Stimpson, *Where the Meanings are: Feminism and Cultural Studies* (New York: Routledge, Chapman and Hall, 1989).

6. Susan Faludi, *Backlash* (London: Chatto and Windus) p.439.

7. Germaine Greer, 'The Backlash Myth', *New Republic,* 5 October 1992, p.22.

8. Shulamith Firestone, *The Dialectic of Sex: the Case for Feminist Revolution* (New York: Bantam, 1970); Ti-Grace Atkinson, *Amazon Odyssey* (New York: Link, 1974).

9. See, for example, Toril Moi who in *Sexual/Textual Politics* constructs a narrative of three stages of feminism in which Millett's work, as well as the later work of American feminists such as Elaine Showalter, demonstrates a naive confidence in the stability of gender identity. Toril Moi, *Sexual/Textual Politics: Feminist Literary Theory* (London: Methuen, 1985).

10. Andrea Dworkin, *Pornography: Men Possessing Women* (New York: Perigree, 1981).

11. Camille Paglia, *Sex, Art and American Culture: Essays* (London: Viking, 1993) p.5.

12. Paglia, *Sex,* p.53.

13. Nancy Chodorow, *The Reproduction of Mothering: Psycho-analysis and the Sociology of Gender* (Berkeley: University of California Press, 1978).

14. Carol Gilligan, *In a Different Voice: Psychological Theory and Women's Development* (Cambridge, MA: Harvard University Press, 1982).

15. Nina Auerbach, 'Engorging the Patriarchy' in Jerome McGann (ed), *Historical Studies and Literary Criticism* (Madison: University of Wisconsin Press, 1985).

16. Hester Eisenstein, *Contemporary Feminist Thought* (London: Unwin, 1984) p.135.

17. Linda Alcoff, 'Cultural Feminism Versus Post-Structuralism: the Identity Crisis in Feminist Theory', *Signs: Journal of Women in Culture and Society*, no. 13 (1988) pp.405–36.

18. Adrienne Rich, *Of Woman Born: Motherhood as Experience and Institution* (London: Virago, 1977) p.40.

19. Barbara Johnson has persuasively demonstrated that the representation of American deconstruction of the Yale School as primarily a male enterprise fails to take into account the importance both of women theorists in the movement (such as Shoshana Felman, Gayatri Spivak and Margaret Ferguson) as well as the implicit gender-consciousness of the movement. Barbara Johnson, 'Gender Theory and the Yale School' in Elaine Showalter (ed), *Speaking of Gender* (New York: Routledge and Kegan Paul, 1989) p.54.

20. Alcoff, 'Cultural Feminism', p.414.

21. Nancy K. Miller, 'Rereading as a Woman: The Body in Practice', in Susan Rubin Suleiman (ed), *The Female Body in Western Culture: Contemporary Perspectives* (Cambridge MA: Harvard University Press, 1985) pp.354–62.

22. Naomi Wolf, *The Beauty Myth* (London: Chatto and Windus, 1990).

23. Teresa de Lauretis, 'Upping the Anti (sic) in Feminist Theory' in Marianne Hirsch and Evelyn Fox Keller (eds), *Conflicts in Feminism* (New York: Routledge and Kegan Paul, 1990) p.257.

24. Naomi Wolf, 'Father Figures', *New Republic*, 5 October 1992, p.22.

25. Darlene Clark Hine, 'Black Women's History, White Women's History, the Juncture of Race and Class', *Journal of Women's History*, vol. 4, no. 2 (1992) pp.125–33.

4. Partial Factors *Dale Carter*

1. Thomas Pynchon, *V.* (London: Jonathan Cape, 1963) pp.28, 383, 385.

2. Herbert Marcuse, 'Some Social Implications of Modern Technology', in Andrew Arato and Eike Gebhardt (eds), *The Essential Frankfurt School Reader* (Oxford: Basil Blackwell, 1978) p.303.

3. Marshall McLuhan, *The Mechanical Bride: Folklore of Industrial Man* (1951; reprinted Boston: Beacon Press, 1967) pp.97, 98, 141; Marshall McLuhan, Quentin Fiore and Jerome Agel, *War and Peace in the Global Village* (New York: Bantam, 1968) p.18.

4. McLuhan, *The Mechanical Bride*, pp.93–7.

5. Karl Marx, *Early Writings*, ed. Quentin Hoare (Harmondsworth: Penguin/New Left Books, 1977) pp.323–31.

6. Ralph Waldo Emerson, 'Works and Days' in *Society and Solitude* (1870); reprinted in *Complete Prose Works* (London: Ward Lock, 1889) p.442; Thorstein Veblen, *The Instinct of Workmanship* (1914; reprinted New York: B.W. Huebsch, 1922) p.306; Lewis Mumford, *Technics and Civilization* (1934; reprinted New York: Harcourt, Brace and World, 1963) pp.361–2.

7. Harry Braverman, *Labor and Monopoly Capital: the Degradation of Work in the Twentieth Century* (New York: Monthly Review Press, 1974); Siegfried Giedion, *Mechanization Takes Command* (New York: W.W. Norton, 1948) pp.77–8.

8. John Kouwenhoven, *Made in America: the Arts in Modern Civilization* (1948; reprinted Newton Centre, MA: Charles Bronford, 1957) pp.221–2. There is a considerable literature on Taylorism. In addition to Braverman's *Labor and Monopoly Capital*, Sudhir Kakar, *Frederick Taylor: a Study in Personality and Innovation* (Cambridge, MA: MIT Press, 1970) is of particular interest.

9. Shoshana Zuboff, *In the Age of the Smart Machine: the Future of Work and Power* (London: Basic Books, 1988) pp.45–6; Larry Hirschhorn, *Beyond Mechanization: Work and Technology in the Post-industrial Age* (Cambridge, MA: MIT Press, 1984) pp.13–14; Kostas Axelos, *Alienation, Praxis and Techne in the Thought of Karl Marx* (Austin: University of Texas Press, 1976) pp.77–9; Braverman, *Labor and Monopoly Capital*, pp.185–6; Giedion, *Mechanization Takes Command*, p.115; John Dos Passos, *U.S.A.* (1938; reprinted Harmondsworth: Penguin, 1966) p.774.

10. Kouwenhoven, *Made in America*, pp.222–4; Antonio Gramsci, 'Americanism and Fordism' in *Selections from the Prison Notebooks*, ed. and trans. Quentin Hoare and Geoffrey Nowell Smith (London: Lawrence and Wishart, 1978) p.302; Hirschhorn, *Beyond Mechanization*, p.13.

11. Zuboff, *Age of the Smart Machine*, pp.230–1; Hirschhorn, *Beyond Mechanization*, p.13; Braverman, *Labor and Monopoly Capital*, pp.141–3; Clive Bush, *Halfway to Revolution* (New Haven and London: Yale University Press, 1991) pp.277–8; Peter Ling, *America and the Automobile* (Manchester University Press, 1990) pp.141, 152, 154–8; Gramsci, 'Americanism', p.304; James J. Flink, *The Car Culture* (Cambridge, MA: MIT Press, 1975) pp.80, 88–9.

12. Counter Information Service, *Ford: Anti-Report* (London: CIS, 1978) pp.13–21; Gramsci, 'Americanism', pp.297, 300, 302.

13. Marcuse, 'Some Social Implications', p.145; Hirschhorn, *Beyond Mechanization*, p.13; Gramsci, 'Americanism', p.303; Mumford, *Technics and Civilization*, pp.361–2; Jacques Ellul, *The Technological Society*, trans. John Wilkinson (New York: Random House, 1964) p.411; Herbert Marcuse, *One Dimensional Man* (1964; reprinted London: Abacus, 1974) p.23.

14. Daniel Nelson, *Managers and Workers: Origins of the New Factory System in the US, 1880–1920* (Madison: University of Wisconsin Press, 1975) p.74; James Bright, *Automation and Management* (Boston: Harvard Business School Press, 1958) pp.199–200, 211; Robert Blauner, *Alienation and Freedom* (University of Chicago Press, 1964); Zuboff, *Age of the Smart Machine*, pp.45, 48, 51–4, 98–119; Marcuse, 'Some Social Implications', pp.34–5; Braverman, *Labor and Monopoly Capital*, pp.147, 149, 293–358; Anne Jardim, *The First Henry Ford* (Cambridge, MA: MIT Press, 1970) pp.118–19; Flink, *The Car Culture*, pp.84, 89–90.

15. Hirschhorn, *Beyond Mechanization*, pp.13, 62–5; Zuboff, *Age of the Smart Machine*, pp.117–21; Braverman, *Labor and Monopoly Capital*, pp.144–50.

16. Marcuse, 'Some Special Implications', p.23; Lewis Mumford, *The Pentagon of Power* (London: Secker and Warburg, 1971) pp.164–96, 321–45; Stanley Aronowitz, *False Promises: the Shaping of American Working Class Consciousness* (1973); reprinted New York: McGraw Hill, 1974); Ellul, *Technological Society*, pp.397–8, 408–9.

17. Norbert Wiener, *The Human Use of Human Beings: Cybernetics and Society* (1950; reprinted London: Sphere, 1974) pp.140–1; Brian

Ash (ed), *The Visual Encyclopedia of Science Fiction* (London: Pan, 1977) p.182.

18. McLuhan, *Mechanical Bride*, pp.102-3, 141; Ash, *Visual Encyclopedia*, pp.189, 301.

19. Samuel Butler, *Erewhon* (1872; reprinted London: Jonathan Cape, 1927) p.235; Ash, *Visual Encyclopedia*, pp.173, 189. On the theory and practice of the cyborg, see David Rorvik, *As Man Becomes Machine: the Evolution of the Cyborg* (London: Souvenir Press, 1973; Sphere, 1975), a study which, while journalistic and now rather outdated, is still of use.

20. Ash, *Visual Encyclopedia*, pp.182-3.

21. It is impossible in a paper of this size to give anything more than the briefest survey of major developments in computing. A useful non-technical history, upon which this paragraph is largely based, is Dirk Hanson, *The New Alchemists: Silicon Valley and the Microelectronics Revolution* (Boston: Little, Brown, 1982).

22. Again, space constraints preclude further discussion. Two informative histories of artificial intelligence are Pamela McCorduck, *Machines Who Think* (San Francisco: W.H. Freeman, 1979) and John Haugeland, *Artificial Intelligence: the Very Idea* (Cambridge, MA: MIT Press, 1985). The current, vast, debate over the meaning, significance and prospects of artificial intelligence may be followed through Stephen R. Graubard (ed), *The Artificial Intelligence Debate* (Cambridge, MA: MIT Press, 1988); and Margaret A. Boden (ed), *The Philosophy of Artificial Intelligence* (Oxford: Oxford University Press, 1990).

23. Jasia Reichart, *Robots: Fact, Fiction and Prediction* (London: Thames and Hudson, 1978) p.157; Hanson, *New Alchemists*, pp.57-9, 102, 139, 174; Zuboff, *Age of the Smart Machine*, pp.415-6.

24. David Waltz, 'The Prospects for Building Truly Intelligent Machines' in Graubard (ed), *Artificial Intelligence Debate*, pp.203-4; Sherry Turkle, *The Second Self: Computers and the Human Spirit* (New York: Simon and Schuster, 1984) pp.240-1, 260; Reichart, *Robots*, pp.28-30.

25. Critiques of the theoretical bases of artificial intelligence include Hubert Dreyfus, *What Computers Can't Do: a Critique of Artificial Reason*, 2nd edn (New York: Harper and Row, 1979); Hubert and Stuart Dreyfus, 'Making a Mind versus Modelling the Brain: Artificial Intelligence Back at a Branch Point' in Boden (ed), *Philosophy of Artificial Intelligence*, pp.309-33; and John Searle, 'Minds, Brains and Programs' in Boden (ed), *Philosophy of Artificial Intelligence*, pp.67-88.

26. Alan Turing, 'Computing Machinery and Intelligence' (1950), reprinted in Boden (ed), *Philosophy of Artificial Intelligence*, p.49; Norbert Wiener, *God and Golem, Inc.* (London: Chapman and Hall, 1964) p.15; Butler, *Erewhon*, p.235; McCorduck, *Machines Who Think*, pp.346, 353.

27. Kouwenhoven, *Made in America*, p.221.

28. McCorduck, *Machines Who Think*, p.346; Robert Jastrow, 'Toward an Intelligence Beyond Man's', *Time*, 20 February 1978, p.59; Aronowitz, *False Promises*, p.115.

29. Jeremy Bernstein, *Science Observed* (New York: Basic Books, 1982) pp.30-1, 37; B.F. Skinner, *Beyond Freedom and Dignity* (Harmondsworth: Penguin, 1974) pp.17-30, 200-1; Michael Crichton, *The Ter-*

minal Man (1972; reprinted New York: Bantam, 1973) p.89; Wiener, *Human Use of Human Beings*, pp.25–6, 57–62.

30. William Burroughs, *The Naked Lunch* (1959; reprinted London: Corgi, 1976) pp.185–6.

31. Zuboff, *Age of the Smart Machine*, p.416; Hanson, *New Alchemists*, pp.208–9.

32. Marcuse, 'Some Social Implications', p.43.

33. Turkle, *Second Self*, pp.55, 165, 170–4.

34. Hirschhorn, *Beyond Mechanization*, pp.1–2, 62–4, 67–73, 89, 114–23.

35. Zuboff, *Age of the Smart Machine*, pp.4, 9–11, 62–3, 75–6, 92, 94, 181, 185, 195, 303–4, 349.

36. Turkle, *Second Self*, pp.175–85; Hanson, *New Alchemists*, p.208.

37. Turkle, *Second Self*, pp.167, 170, 175, 186–9, 199, 201, 205–23.

38. Zuboff, *Age of the Smart Machine*, pp.182, 207, 242.

39. Zuboff, *Age of the Smart Machine*, pp.249–54, 258–61, 268, 278–83; Turkle, *Second Self*, pp.216–18. The difference between informating and automation discussed here may be compared to that between flexibility and integration in Hirschhorn, *Beyond Mechanization*, pp.57–8.

40. Zuboff, *Age of the Smart Machine*, pp.248–50, 277, 283, 315–24. On Jeremy Bentham and his Panopticon designs, see Michel Foucault, *Discipline and Punish: the Birth of the Prison* (New York: Vintage, 1979) pp.201–8.

41. Zuboff, *Age of the Smart Machine*, pp.67–9, 132–3, 136–41, 151, 268–73, 303–4, 401–4; Hirschhorn, *Beyond Mechanization*, pp.59, 70, 72, 89, 96. A number of other studies come to similar conclusions. See David Noble, *Forces of Production: a Social History of Industrial Automation* (New York: Oxford University Press, 1986) pp.144–92; Harley Shaiken, *Work Transformed: Automation and Labor in the Computer Age* (New York: Holt, Rinehart and Winston, 1985), p.264; Robert Howard, *Brave New Workplace* (New York: Viking, 1985), pp.15–35.

42. Zuboff, *Age of the Smart Machine*, pp.268–73; Hirschhorn, *Beyond Mechanization*, p.57.

43. Robert Boguslaw, *The New Utopians: a Study of System Design and Social Change* (New York: Prentice-Hall, 1965).

44. Hirschhorn, *Beyond Mechanization*, p.117; Zuboff, *Age of the Smart Machine*, pp.241–2; Richard Edwards, *Contested Terrain: the Transformation of the Workplace in the Twentieth Century* (New York: Basic Books, 1979) pp.132–52.

45. Hanson, *New Alchemists*, pp.265–6; Zuboff, *Age of the Smart Machine*, p.399; Mike Davis, *Prisoners of the American Dream* (London: Verso, 1986) pp.216–21; Robert Kuttner, *The Economic Illusion: False Choices Between Prosperity and Social Justice* (Boston: Houghton Mifflin, 1984).

46. Marcuse, 'Some Social Implications', p.138.

5. 'Lost Connections' *Graham Clarke*

1. Robert Lowell, *Life Studies* (London: Faber and Faber, 1959) p.99.
2. Ibid., p.100.

3. *The Fifties* (New York: Museum of Modern Art, 1985) Introduction.

4. Ibid., unpaginated. The photograph, originally published in *Life* magazine, was taken by Capa in Michigan City, Indiana, in 1954.

5. Roland Barthes, *Camera Lucida* (New York: Hill and Wang, 1981) pp.26–7.

6. *Mirrors and Windows: American Photography since 1960* (New York: Museum of Modern Art, 1978) p.13.

7. See Peter Turner (ed), *American Images: Photography 1945–1980* (Harmondsworth: Penguin, 1985) pp.11–22.

8. Susan Sontag, *On Photography* (Harmondsworth: Penguin, 1977) p.47.

9. See my essay 'Investing the Glimpse: Raymond Carver and the Syntax of Silence' in Graham Clarke (ed), *The New American Writing* (London and New York: Vision Press, 1990) pp.99–122.

10. See *Mirrors and Windows*, pp.40 and 75.

11. Richard Avedon, *In the American West* (London: Thames and Hudson, 1985).

12. Ibid., Foreword, unpaginated.

13. Ibid.

14. I am thinking, of course, of the 'vision' of America as seen in Michael Lesey's *Wisconsin Death Trip* which, in a nineteenth-century context, not only reverses the surface appeal of Whitman's America, but offers a nineteenth-century parallel to Avedon's images. The text is full of images at once disturbing, menacing, violent and, in their own way, surreal.

15. For a gloss on this see William Stott, *Documentary Expression and Thirties America* (London: Oxford University Press, 1973).

16. Avedon, *American West*, unpaginated.

17. Robert Frank, *Les Américains* (New York: Pantheon, 1958); published in 1959 as *The Americans*, with an introduction by Jack Kerouac.

18. Ibid., pp.5–8.

19. Walker Evans, *American Photographs* (New York: Museum of Modern Art, 1938). The essay by Lincoln Kirstein might be fruitfully compared with Kerouac's introduction to *The Americans*.

20. Frank, *The Americans*, p.80, but see also pp.78, 86 and 92.

21. Patricia Bosworth, *Diane Arbus: a Biography* (New York: Avon, 1984) pp.189–90.

22. See Weegee, *Naked City* (New York: Da Capo, 1945).

23. Diane Arbus, *Aperture Monograph* (New York, 1972) unpaginated. All the Arbus images referred to here are in this volume.

24. See *American Images*, p.136.

25. Brief biographies and biographical information on all these figures may be found in Mike Weaver (ed), *The Art of Photography 1839–1989* (London: Royal Academy of Art, 1989); and Cecil Beaton and Gail Buckland, *The Magic Image* (London: Pantheon, 1989).

26. See Susan D. Moeller, *Shooting War* (New York: Basic Books, 1989) pp.366–7.

6. Paradigm Regain'd *Robert Giddings*

1. See Daniel J. Boorstin, *The Americans: the National Experience* (New York: Vintage, 1958) pp.362–3.

2. Sharon Churcher, 'The Uncut Alistair Cooke', *New York Magazine*, 17 December 1979, p.85.

3. Anthony Burgess, 'Is America Falling Apart?' *New York Times* magazine, 7 November 1971, p.23.

4. Alistair Cooke, *Alistair Cooke's America* (New York: Knopf, 1974) p.93.

5. Ibid., p.388.

6. Maldwyn Jones's volume in the Short Oxford History of the Modern World, *The Limits of Liberty: American History 1607–1980* (1983) does not refer to Cooke at all. Nor does Hugh Brogan's *History of the United States of America* (1985). In David Dimbleby and David Reynolds's *An Ocean Apart: the Relationship between Britain and America in the Twentieth Century* (1988) Alistair Cooke is mentioned in passing as having fronted American television broadcasts of British costume dramas such as 'The Forsyte Saga' and is interestingly described as 'the transplanted English journalist'. In this respect Alistair Cooke seems to be unique.

7. *New York Magazine*, 17 December 1979, pp.85–6.

8. Cooke, *America*, p.385.

9. Ibid., p.389.

10. Ibid., p.395.

11. Ibid., p.30.

12. Ibid., pp.93ff.

13. See especially John Upton Terrell, *Land Grab: the Truth About 'The Winning of the West'* (New York: Dial Press, 1972); and Dee Brown, *Bury My Heart at Wounded Knee: an Indian History of the American West* (London: Barrie and Jenkins, 1971).

14. Cooke, *America*, p.274.

15. Ibid., p.278.

16. Alistair Cooke, 'Preface to the British Reader', *Letters From America* (London: Rupert Hart-Davies, 1951) pp.9–10.

17. Ibid., p.10.

18. Cooke, *America*, p.351.

19. Gar Alperovitz, 'Why We Dropped the Bomb' in Barton J. Bernstein and Allen J. Matusow (eds), *Twentieth Century America: Recent Interpretations* (New York: Harcourt, Brace, Jovanovich, 1969) p.402.

20. Ibid., p.403.

21. Norman Cousins and Thomas Finletter, 'A Beginning of Sanity', *Saturday Review of Literature*, vol. 29 (5 June 1946). See also Louis Morton, 'The Decision to Use the Atomic Bomb', *Foreign Affairs*, vol. 35 (January 1957); and Rudolph Winnacker, 'The Debate About Hiroshima' in *Military Affairs*, vol. II (Spring 1947). See also Herbert Feis *The Atomic Bomb and the End of the Second World War* (Princeton, NJ: Princeton University Press, 1966).

22. Alistair Cooke, *A Generation on Trial: USA v. Alger Hiss* (London: Rupert Hart-Davies, 1950) p.39.

23. Ibid., p.vi.

24. Frank Mankiewicz, *Nixon's Road to Watergate* (London: Hutchinson, 1973) p.57.

25. Ibid., p.59.

26. This is superb Nixonianism. Ms Douglas had had nothing to do with the Hiss case at all, and Hiss had actually left government service before Nixon had even heard of him.

27. Among the contributors was the father of H.R. Haldeman.

28. Bruce Mazlish, *In Search of Nixon: a Psychobistorical Inquiry* (Baltimore: Penguin, 1972) p.72. Also Richard Nixon, *Six Crises* (New York: Doubleday, 1962) pp.73–129; and David Wise, *The Politics of Lying–Government Deception, Secrecy and Power* (New York: Vintage/Random House, 1973) pp.326ff. Checkers, the dog for whom this speech is named, soon passed into national mythology. In *The Last Hurrah* (1958), the film version of the novel by Edwin O'Conor, Spencer Tracy's political rival wins the election after appearing on television, parading his wife, children and an appropriately ludicrous hound. The film of the Checkers speech is now a rarity. The Nixon entourage took every step to remove the recording from circulation. See Arthur Woodstone, *Nixon's Head* (London: Olympia Press, 1972) pp.28–9.

29. Woodstone, *Nixon's Head*, pp.30–1 and cf. Nixon, *Six Crises*, pp.73ff.

30. Wise, *Politics of Lying*, pp.328–9.

31. Alistair Cooke, 'Letter From America' 26 January 1969, in *The Americans – Fifty Letters from America on our Life and Times* (London: Bodley Head, 1979) p.20.

32. Ibid., pp.24–5.

33. Ibid., 7 August 1974, p.164.

34. Ibid., 16 September 1972, p.108.

35. Ibid., 12 May 1972, pp.129–30.

36. Cooke's coverage does eventually turn sour. See ibid., 19 October 1973, pp.138–42.

37. Alistair Cooke, *America Observed – The Newspaper Years of Alistair Cooke* (London: Reinhardt, 1988) pp.123–6.

38. The original broadcast talk is reprinted in the *Listener*, 26 August 1965, p.292. The edited version appears in *Talk About America 1951–1968* (Harmondsworth: Penguin, 1968) pp.226–7.

39. Cooke, *Talk About America*, p.268.

40. 'Letter From America', *Listener*, 4 March 1965, p.322.

41. Ibid.

42. George Scott, 'Postscript', *Listener*, 1 December 1977, p.707.

43. 'We Are the Party of Main Street, the Small Town', *Listener*, 24 July 1980, p.100.

44. Michael Hudson, *Super Imperialism* (New York: Holt, Reinhart and Winston, 1972) pp.228ff.

45. Ibid., p.229 and cf. Gore Vidal, 'The Day the American Empire Ran Out of Gas', *Nation*, 11 January 1986, reprinted in *At Home – Essays 1982–1988* (New York: Random House, 1988) pp.105ff.

46. Alistair Cooke, 'No Doubt About It, We are About to Live in Interesting Times', *Listener*, 13 November 1980, p.639.

47. I am greatly indebted for this analysis of the 1980 presidential election to Steve Riley of Keynes College, the University of Kent at Canterbury. See also Gerald Pomper, *The Election of 1980* (Chatham, NJ; Chatham House, 1981) pp.65ff.

7. Michael Cimino's America *Brian Lee*

1. Steven Bach, *Final Cut: Dreams and Disaster in the Making of Heaven's Gate* (New York: Morrow, 1985).
2. In order to make the film more commercially viable, it was cut by more than a quarter of its length. This shorter version is unintelligible and does not represent Cimino's intentions.
3. Richard Combs, 'Heaven's Gate', *Monthly Film Bulletin*, vol. 48, no. 573 (October 1981).
4. Michael Ryan and Douglas Kelner, *Camera Politica: the Politics and Ideology of Contemporary Hollywood Film* (Bloomington and Indianapolis: Indiana University Press, 1990) p.236.
5. Jeanine Basinger, *The World War II Combat Film: Anatomy of a Genre* (New York: Columbia University Press, 1986) p.176.
6. Gilbert Adair, *Hollywood's Vietnam: from The Green Berets to Full Metal Jacket* (London: Heinemann, 1989) pp.92–3.
7. Robin Wood, *Hollywood from Vietnam to Reagan* (New York: Columbia University Press, 1986) p.273.
8. Antony Easthope, 'Realism and its Subversion: Hollywood and Vietnam' in Alf Louvre and Jeffrey Walsh (eds), *Tell Me Lies About Vietnam: Cultural Battles for the Meaning of the War* (Milton Keynes: Open University Press, 1988) p.35.
9. Mike Westlake, 'The Deer Hunter 1', *North by Northwest*, no. 8 (Autumn 1979).
10. Adair, *Hollywood's Vietnam*, p.91.
11. Norman Mailer, *Why are We in Vietnam?* (London: Fontana) p.140.
12. Richard Poirier, *Mailer* (London: Collins, 1972) p.150.
13. Robert B. Ray, *A Certain Tendency of the Hollywood Cinema, 1930–1980* (Princeton, Princeton University Press, 1985) chapter 1.
14. Wood, *Hollywood*, p.317.

8. The Politics of Formalism in Post-war American Poetry

David Murray

1. Barrett Watten, *L=A=N=G=U=A=G=E*, vol. 4, no date, p.129; Jerome Rothenberg, *Pre-faces & Other Writings* (New York: New Directions, 1981) p.65; George Oppen, quoted in Robert von Hallberg (ed), *Poetics and Poetic Value* (Chicago and London: Chicago University Press, 1987) p.315.
2. Generalising about, or labelling, any group of writers is always dangerous, but those poets involved with *L=A=N=G=U=A=G=E*, *Hills* and *Poetics Journal* and represented in Douglas Messerli's *'Language' Poetries: an Anthology* (New York: New Directions, 1987) clearly have enough shared concerns and views to make it reasonable to make their published views and discussions usable as a reference point. George Hartley's *Textual Politics and the Language Poets* (Bloomington: Indi-

ana University Press, 1989) gives a good account of their differences, as well as what unites them.

3. See particularly Betsy Erkkila, *Whitman the Political Poet* (New York: Oxford University Press, 1989).

4. See Joseph Riddell, 'Decentering the Image: The "Project" of "American" Poetics', *Boundary 2*, vol. 8, no. 1 (1979).

5. Jerome Rothenberg, *Revolution of the Word: a New Gathering of American Avantgarde Poetry, 1914–1945* (New York: Seabury Press, 1974).

6. See William Van O'Connor and Edward Stone (eds), *A Casebook on Ezra Pound* (New York: Crowell, 1959).

7. Bob Perelman, 'The First Person', *Hills*, no. 6/7 (Spring 1980) p.161.

8. Ibid., p.162.

9. Frank O'Hara, *Selected Poems* (New York: Vintage, 1974) p.138.

10. Barrett Watten, 'Method and Surrealism: the Politics of Poetry', *L=A=N=G=U=A=G=E*, vol. 4, no date, p.133.

11. Barrett Watten, *Poetics Journal*, no. 1, p.56.

12. David Bromige, 'Intention and Poetry' *Hills*, no. 6/7 (Spring 1980) p.38.

13. Watten, quoted in Hartley, *Textual Politics*, p.39.

14. See *Hills* no. 6/7 (Spring 1980) p.72.

15. Ibid., p.56.

16. George Oppen, quoted in Michael Heller, *Conviction's Net of Branches: Essays on the Objectivist Poets and Poetry* (Carbondale: Southern Illinois University Press, 1985) p.4.

17. Louis Zuhofsky, *Prepositions: the Collected Critical Essays of Louis Zukofsky* (Berkeley: California University Press, 1981) p.12.

18. Ibid., p.99.

19. James Sherry, 'Limits of Grammar', *L=A=N=G=U=A=G=E*, vol. 4, no date, p.112.

20. Peter Burger, *Theory of the Avant-garde* (Minneapolis: Minnesota University Press, 1984). See also Walter Kalaidjian, 'Transpersonal Poetics: Language Writing and the Historical Avant-gardes in Postmodern Culture', *American Literary History*, vol. 3, no. 2 (1991).

21. Ron Silliman, 'The Political Economy of Poetry', *L=A=N=G=U=A=G=E*, vol. 4, no date, p.60.

22. Ibid., p.65.

23. Charles Altieri, 'Without Consequences is No Politics: a Response to Jerome McGann' in Robert von Hallberg (ed), *Politics and Poetic Value* (Chicago University Press, 1987).

24. Ibid., p.312.

25. Silliman, 'Political Economy of Poetry', p.65.

26. Rothenberg, *Pre-faces*, p.221.

27. Ibid., p.41.

28. Charles Olson, 'A Bibliography on America for Ed Dorn' reprinted in *Additional Prose* (Bolinas: Four Seasons Foundation, 1974) p.7.

29. Charles Olson, *Maximus Poems* (Berkeley and London: California University Press, 1983) p.184.

30. Ibid., p.185.

9. Entre Americanos *Jacqueline Kaye*

1. Edna Buchanan, *The Corpse Had a Familiar Face* (New York: 1988) p.9.
2. Benedict Anderson, *Imagined Communities: Reflections on the Origins and Spread of Nationalism* (London: Verso, 1983).
3. Robert Kennedy, *13 Days: the Cuban Missile Crisis, October, 1962* (London: Macmillan, 1968) pp.121–2.
4. Haynes Johnson, *The Bay of Pigs* (London: Hutchinson, 1964).
5. Ibid., p.343.
6. John Clytus, *Black Man in Red Cuba* (University of Miami, 1970).
7. Jacqueline Kaye, 'Martí and the Great Uprising of Labour', *Ibero-Amerikanisches Archiv*, N.F. Jg. 13. H2, 1987 pp.207–28; 'Martí in the United States: the Flight from Disorder' in C. Abel and N. Torrents (eds), *José Martí Revolutionary Democrat* (London: Athlone Press, 1986) pp.65–82.
8. José Martí, *Obras Completas* (Havana, 1961) vol. 24, pp.189, 200.
9. Fernando Ortiz, *Entre Cubanos* (Paris, 1914).
10. Edmundo Desnoes, *Memorias del Subdesarrollo* (Havana: Instituto del Libro, 1965).
11. Norberto Fuentes, *Hemingway in Cuba* (Secaucus, NJ: Carol Publishing, 1984).
12. Edmundo Desnoes, *Punto de Vista* (Havana: Instituto del Libro, 1967).
13. Fuentes, *Hemingway*, p.13.
14. Desnoes, *Punto de Vista*, p.42.
15. Fuentes, *Hemingway*, p.283.
16. Ibid., p.238.
17. Ibid., p.174.
18. Eduardo Heras León, *Los pasos en la hierba* (Havana: Casa de las Américas, 1970); Norberto Fuentes, *Los condenados de Condado* (Havana: Instituto del Libro, 1968).
19. Miguel Barnet, *Biografía de un Cimarrón* (Havana: Editorial Letras Cubanas, 1966); Enrique Cirules, *Conversación con el último norteamericano* (Havana: Instituto del Libro, 1973); Moreno Fraginals, *El ingenio* (Havana: Editorial de Ciencias Sociales, 1978).
20. Oscar Hijuelos, *The Mambo Kings Play Songs of Love* (New York: Farrar, Strauss and Giroux, 1989).
21. *Guardian*, 27 July 1991.
22. Jacobo Timerman, *Cuba: a Journey* (New York: Knopf, 1990).

With many thanks to Mary Turner.

10 'This Uncertain Content of an Obscure Enterprise of Form' *Clive Bush*

1. In the sixteenth and seventeenth centuries music and poetry were always closely connected. For a short introductory piece on contemporary interactions, see Eric Mottram, 'Transformations of Music and Poetry', *Spanner* 19, vol. 2, no. 9 (November 1980) pp.220–32.

2. Eric Mottram, 'Beware of Imitations', *P.S.* [Poetry Student] no. 1 (February 1975) p.7.

3. Christopher Hill, *Milton and the English Revolution* (1977; reprinted London and Boston: Faber and Faber, 1979) p.7.

4. Richard Ellman, *Oscar Wilde* (London: Hamish Hamilton, 1987) p.159.

5. Jean Paul Sartre, 'A Plea for Intellectuals', in *Jean Paul Sartre: Between Existentialism and Marxism*, trans John Mathews (New York: Pantheon, 1974) pp.226–85.

6. Paul N. Siegel (ed), *Leon Trotsky on Literature and Art* (New York: Pathfinder, 1970) p.69.

7. Patrick Brantlinger, *Crusoe's Footsteps: Cultural Studies in Britain and America* (New York and London: Routledge, 1990) p.156.

8. See Wolf Lepenies, *Between Literature and Science: the Rise of Sociology* (*Die Drei Kulturen*, 1985), trans R.J. Hollingdale (Cambridge University Press, 1988).

9. Muriel Rukeyser, *The Life of Poetry* (New York: Current Books, 1949). The whole of the first part, 'Resistances', is relevant, pp.3–58.

10. With the possible exception of the State University of New York at Buffalo.

11. Eric Mottram, 'A Preface to *Visions of Cody*', *Review of Contemporary Fiction*, vol. II, no. 2 (Summer 1983) pp.50–61.

12. Eric Mottram, *Entrances to the Americas: Poetry, Ecology, Translation* (London: Polytechnic of Central London booklet, 1975).

13. Eric Mottram, 'Sir George Cayley, a Nineteenth-century Scientific Pioneer: 1773–1857'. Unpublished lecture. With thanks to Professor Mottram for loaning me the typescript.

14. Eric Mottram, 'American Studies in Europe' (Gröningen, Djakarta: J.B. Wolters, 1955) p.3.

15. Ibid., p.9.

16. Ibid.

17. Ibid., p.11.

18. Eric Mottram, *Homage to Braque* (London: Blacksuede Boot Press, 1976).

19. Eric Mottram, 'No Centre to Hold: a Commentary on Derrida', in Paul Buck (ed), *Curtains* nos 14–17, pp.38–57.

20. Mottram has written more on Olson than on any other writer: see 'Charles Olson's Appollonius of Tyana', *Sixpack*, no. 3/4 (March 1973); '"Chaos is not our condition": Charles Olson in his Time–an introductory note', *Akros*, no. 49 (April 1982), pp.52–73; 'Performance: Charles Olson's Rebirth between Power and Love', *Sixpack*, no. 6 (Winter 1973–4) pp.95–114.

21. Eric Mottram, 'The Romantic Politics of the Body in Michael McClure', *Margins*, no. 18 (1975), pp.6–16.

22. Greta Jones, *Social Darwinism and English Thought: the Interaction between Biological and Social Theory* (Sussex: Harvester; Atlantic Highlands, NJ: Humanities Press, 1980). See especially Chapter 4, 'Individualism and Collectivism'.

23. Lewis Mumford, *The Myth of the Machine/The Pentagon of Power* (London: Secker and Warburg, 1971) p.115.

24. Eric Mottram, 'Where the Real Song Begins: the Poetry of Jerome Rothenberg', *Vort* 7, vol. 1, no. 1 (1975), p.177.

25. Eric Mottram, '"Eleusions Truths": Harry Mathews's Strategies and Games', *Review of Contemporary Fiction* vol. 7, no. 3 (Fall 1987) p.159.

26. Eric Mottram, 'Henry Adams: Index of the Twentieth Century' in Y. Hakutani and L. Fried (eds), *American Literary Naturalism* (Heidelberg: Carl Winter Universitätsverlag, 1975) pp.90–105.

27. Eric Mottram, *Paul Bowles: Staticity and Terror* (London: Aloes Books, 1976) p.23.

28. In this respect one of his most interesting essays is 'Pound, Olson and the Secret of the Golden Flower', *Chapman*, vol. II, no. 2 (Summer 1972) pp.20–31, 55–64. The essay looks at parallels with (and influences from) Chinese and Tantric thought – the I Ching, for example – and yoga in the poetry of Pound and Olson.

29. Eric Mottram, *William Faulkner* (Profiles in Literature) (London: Routledge and Kegan Paul, 1971) p.13.

30. Eric Mottram, 'A Raft against Washington: Mark Twain's Criticism of America' in Robert Giddings (ed), *Mark Twain: a Sumptuous Variety* (London: Vision and Barnes & Noble, 1985) p.245.

31. Eric Mottram, '"The Infected Air" and "The Guilt of Interference": Henry James's Short Stories' in A. Robert Lee (ed), *The Nineteenth-Century American Short Story* (London: Vision and Barnes & Noble, 1985) p.188.

32. See Eric Mottram, *William Burroughs: the Algebra of Need* (London: Boyars, 1977).

33. Eric Mottram, 'William Burroughs: Survivalist in a Manichean World' in William Burroughs, *The Final Academy: Statements of a Kind* (London: Final Academy, 1982) p.33.

34. '"The Persuasive Lips": Men and Guns in America' (1976) reprinted in Eric Mottram, *Blood on the Nash Ambassador* (London: Hutchinson Radius, 1989) p.2.

35. Eric Mottram, 'Ross Macdonald and the Past of a Formula' in Bernard Benstock (ed), *Essays on Detective Fiction* (London: Macmillan, 1983) p.103.

36. Eric Mottram, 'Don DeLillo's Novels' in Graham Clarke (ed), *The New American Writing: Essays on American Literture Since 1970* (London: Vision Press; and New York: St Martin's Press, 1990) p.52.

37. Eric Mottram, 'Poe's Pym, and the American Social Imagination' in Robert J. DeMott and Sanford E. Marovitz (eds), *Artful Thunder: Versions of the Romantic Tradition in American Literature in honour of Howard P. Vincent* (Ohio: Kent State University Press, 1975) p.30.

38. 'Existential and Political Controls in the Fiction of Gabriel Marquéz', author's typescript.

39. Eric Mottram, 'The Limits of Survival with the Weapons of Humour: William Eastlake', *Review of Contemporary Fiction* (Spring 1983) p.69.

40. Eric Mottram, 'The Hostile Environment and the Survival Artist' in Malcolm Bradbury and D. Palmer (eds), *The American Novel in the Nineteen Twenties* (London: Edward Arnold, 1967) p.241.

41. Eric Mottram, 'The Poetics of Rebirth and Confidence: an Introduction to Clayton Eshleman's *Coils*', *Poetry Information*, no. 11 (Autumn 1974) p.41.

42. There are, happily, increasing signs of a change, with a rash of anthologies of varying competencies and claims. But as late as 1988 in vol. 9 of *The Cambridge Guide to the Arts in Britain* (Cambridge University Press, 1988) edited by Boris Ford, Gilbert Phelps writes mainly about Larkin, Hughes, Betjeman and Heaney, and all information about the real revival of British poetry in the 1970s is censored.

43. Eric Mottram, *Elegies* (London: Galloping Dog Press, 1981), epigraph.

Notes on Contributors

Clive Bush is Director of American Studies at King's College, London. In addition to his many articles on American themes, he has written *The Dream of Reason: American Consciousness and Cultural Achievement from Independence to the Civil War* (1977) and *Halfway to Revolution: Investigation and Crisis in Henry Adams, William James and Gertrude Stein* (1991). He has also published three books on poetry, *clearing the distance* (1978), *the range taken* (1983) and *shifts in undreamt time* (1989).

Dale Carter took degrees at Warwick University, the Institute of United Studies and King's College, London. Currently he is Lecturer in American Studies at the University of Århus, Denmark. His *The Final Frontier: the Rise and Fall of the American Rocket State* was published in 1988. He also edited Eric Mottram's *Blood on the Nash Ambassador: Investigations in American Culture* (1989). His teaching and research interests include American foreign relations and post-war culture and technology.

Graham Clarke teaches literary and visual arts at the University of Kent at Canterbury. He is the author of *Walt Whitman: the Poem as Private History* (1991) and editor of *The American City: Literary and Cultural Perspectives* (1988) and *The New American Writing* (1990). His other recent articles have dealt with T.S. Eliot, Alfred Stieglitz, William Faulkner and American landscape painting.

Claire Colebrook is Lecturer in English at the University of Edinburgh, where she recently completed a doctoral thesis on John Milton and William Blake. She has published several articles on Blake and is currently writing a book on feminism and post-colonialism.

Robert Giddings is Senior Lecturer at Bournemouth University and has been a regular contributor to the *Listener*, the *Guardian*, the *Sunday Times*, *Music and Musicians* and other periodicals. He is author of *The War Poets 1914–1918* (1990) and co-author (with Keith Wensley) of *Screening the Novel* (1990), and editor of critical volumes on Dickens, Tolkien, Mark Twain and Matthew Arnold. His autobiography, *You Should See Me in Pyjamas*, was published in 1981.

Jacqueline Kaye is Lecturer in the Department of Literature, the University of Essex. She is interested in intercultural studies and has recently published *The Ambiguous Compromise*, a study of language and national identity in Algeria and Morocco. She is currently editing a collection of essays on Ezra Pound and an anthology of North African writing.

A. Robert Lee teaches American Studies at the University of Kent at Canterbury. His publications include Everyman editions of *Moby-Dick* (1973, 1992). *Typee* (1993) and *Billy Budd and Other Stories* (1993); *Black American Fiction Since Richard Wright* (1983); eleven collections in the Vision Critical Studies Series, among them *Black Fiction: New Studies in the Afro-American Novel Since 1945* (1980), *Herman Melville: Reassessments* (1984), *Scott Fitzgerald: the Promises of Life* (1989) and *William Faulkner: the Yoknapatawpha Fiction* (1990); and a wide range of journal articles. He has written especially on American multiculturalism.

Brian Lee is Professor of American Studies in the University of Nottingham. Among his publications are *The Novels of Henry James: a Study of Culture and Consciousness* (1978) and *American Fiction, 1865–1940* (1987), together with the BAAS pamphlet *Hollywood*. He is now working on a longer study of American film and society.

David Murray, Reader in American Studies at the University of Nottingham, includes in his research interests American poetry, critical theory and North American Indians. Among his publications are (ed) *Literary Theory and Poetry: Extending the Canon* (1989) and *Forked Tongues: Speech, Writing and Representation in North American Indian Texts* (1991).

Faith Pullin teaches English and American Literature at the University of Edinburgh, where she directs a postgraduate course in 'Modernism, Gender and Writing' and an undergraduate course 'Writing by Women'. She has written extensively on American literature of the nineteenth and twentieth centuries and her book *Women Modernist Writers* is forthcoming. She has a new critical study of Eudora Welty currently in progress.

Ralph Willett studied at the University of Nottingham and, under the tutelage of Eric Mottram, at King's College, London. He is Senior Lecturer in American Studies at the University of Hull and author of *The Americanization of Germany, 1945–1949* (1989). His current interests include a study of hard-boiled detective fiction.

Index